# Images of OLD LLANELLI & DISTRICT

Vernon Morgan

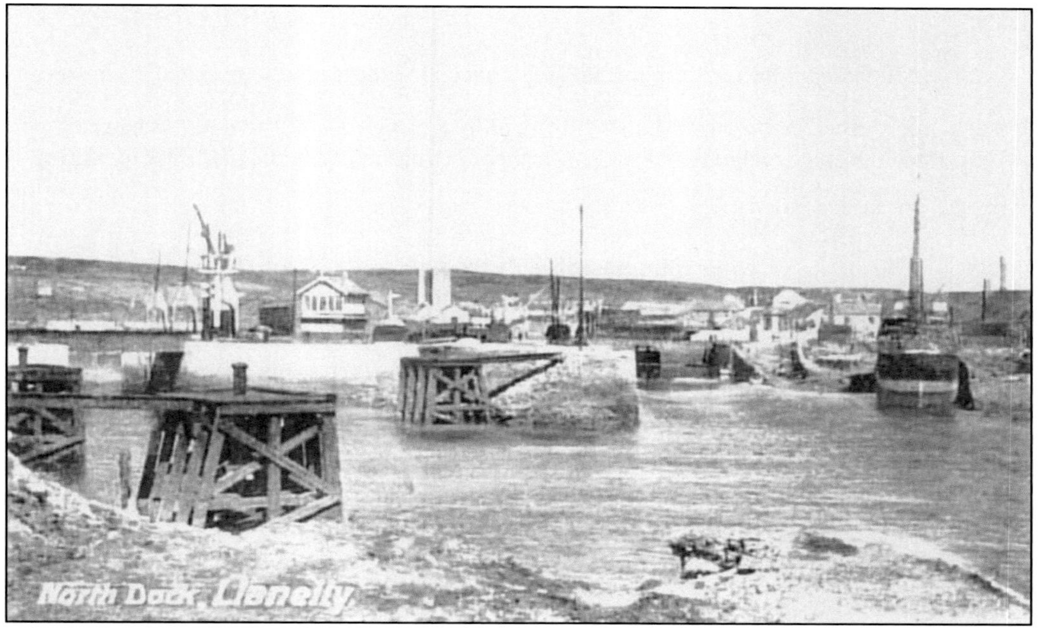

# Images of Old Llanelli & District

Published by Vernon Morgan.

September 2014

Designed by Proprint, Carmarthen.

Printed in Wales by Proprint, Carmarthen.

ISBN No: 978-0-9574045-2-6



All photographs are from the author's collection unless otherwise stated.



Other titles published by the same author,

**James of Ammanford** (A History of J. James & Sons Ltd. Ammanford)

**SWT100** (The South Wales Transport Co Ltd. 100th Anniversary)

**Front cover picture:** (Centre) A view taken from The Graig in Pwll. All the works visible in the background have since disappeared. The area now forms part of Llanelli's Festival fields and Millennium Coastal Path. (Lower left) Stepney Street, Llanelli, taken during World War 1 in 1917. (Top left) A postcard dated 1949 shows the Town Hall Square, Llanelli, viewed from the Town Hall clock tower. (Top right) Lower Stepney Street, Llanelli, with Beestons Bakery shop - part of the group of shops beneath Lucania Billiard Hall, with the Llanelly Cinema next door (nowadays a Weatherspoon's bar), and the YMCA building. (Lower right) The Mansion House at Park Howard, Llanelli. (All part of the V. Morgan collection.)

**Rear cover picture:** This splendid postcard view of Colby Road, Burry Port, was taken circa 1900 by Ernest T. Bush of Burry Port. The view was taken from the top of Achddu looking eastward down Colby Road, and takes in the junction of Dandorlan Road, just visible to the left, and the Pemberton Arms is also in view at the bottom of the hill. The house on the right stands on the junction of Colby Road and Pencoed Road. (Mrs. C. Ridgeway collection.)

**ACKNOWLEDGEMENTS**

I would like to take this opportunity to thank numerous people for their sincere help and assistance in compiling this book.

First of all I would like to thank my daughter Katie for her contribution in the production of this book – correcting grammatical errors, and assisting in scanning, editing, and embedding the photographs. Also to Kath, my wife for her co-operation and understanding, and proof reading my notes.

Special thanks are due to Mrs. Cheryl Ridgeway of Burry Port, for allowing me to use several photographs from her collection, Peter Evans of John Evans & Sons (Llanelly) Ltd, Wayne Harris, Chris Carter, Jane Evans, T. S. Powell, M. J. Haywood, John Jones, John Phillips, my brother Malcolm and to the late Ernie Sage and George West, for kindly allowing me to use their photographs to illustrate this book. Other photographs were taken by myself, or from my own collection, some being the copyright of persons unknown as the photographs are not back stamped. No discourtesy to the photographer is intended through lack of acknowledgement, in lieu of which I trust they will accept my sincere thanks.

Thanks also to Albie Smosarski of Cofion Books, Tenby, for supplying me with a large amount of excellent postcard views from his stock, which are also published in this book.

## INTRODUCTION

The postcard views, photographs and memorabilia contained in this book are *mostly* from my own private collection, a collection which had been gathered over a period of some forty years. Some of the views published were taken by myself during my schooldays, living in the village of Pwll, near Llanelli. Many of the photographs were taken at Duport Steelworks, Llanelli, formerly known as Llanelly Steel (1907) Ltd, where I worked as a foreman fitter, responsible for the maintenance and repair of all locomotives and internal transport. My fascination with transport is also reflected in this publication, with many historical transport views included.

It must be pointed out that prior to 1965, Llanelli was spelt 'Llanelly' and this spelling is used where appropriate.

For the reader not familiar with the district, and for completeness, I have produced a map of the area on page 5.

This publication also contains numerous photographs which have never been published before, giving a magnificent view of the town's historical and industrial past.

However, it must be noted that although I have provided the dates of most of photographs in this book, some photographs were not stamped with a date. In those few cases, I was unable to provide an exact date.

Some of these views bring back pleasant memories to me, and I sincerely hope that this publication will give you the reader as much pleasure reading it as I've had in compiling it.

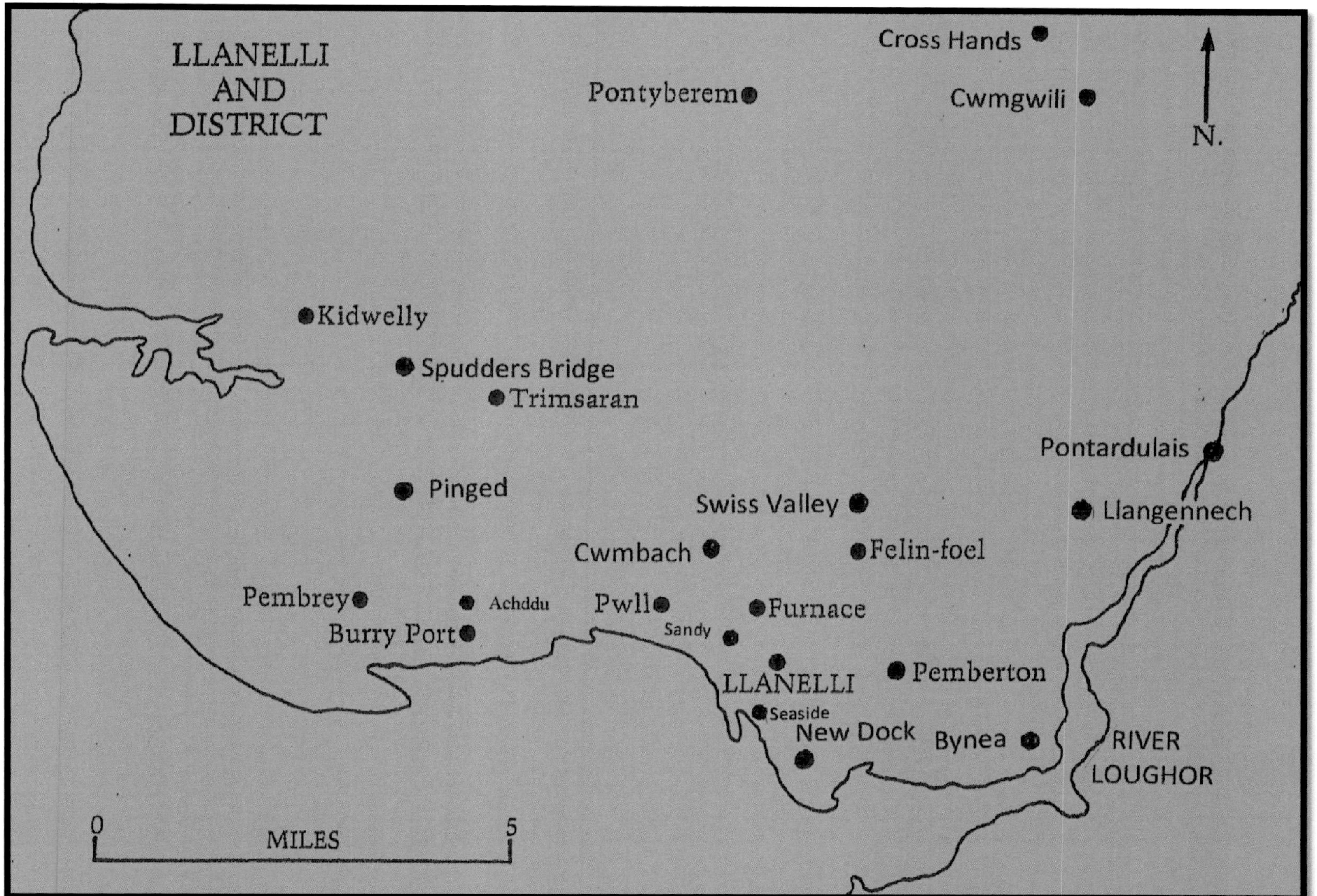
LLANELLI
AND
DISTRICT
Cross Hands
Pontyberem
Cwmgwili
N.
Kidwelly
Spudders Bridge
Trimsaran
Pontardulais
Pinged
Swiss Valley
Llangennech
Cwmbach
Felin-foel
Pembrey
Achddu
Pwll
Furnace
Burry Port
Sandy
LLANELLI
Pemberton
Seaside
New Dock
Bynea
RIVER
LOUGHOR
0
MILES
5

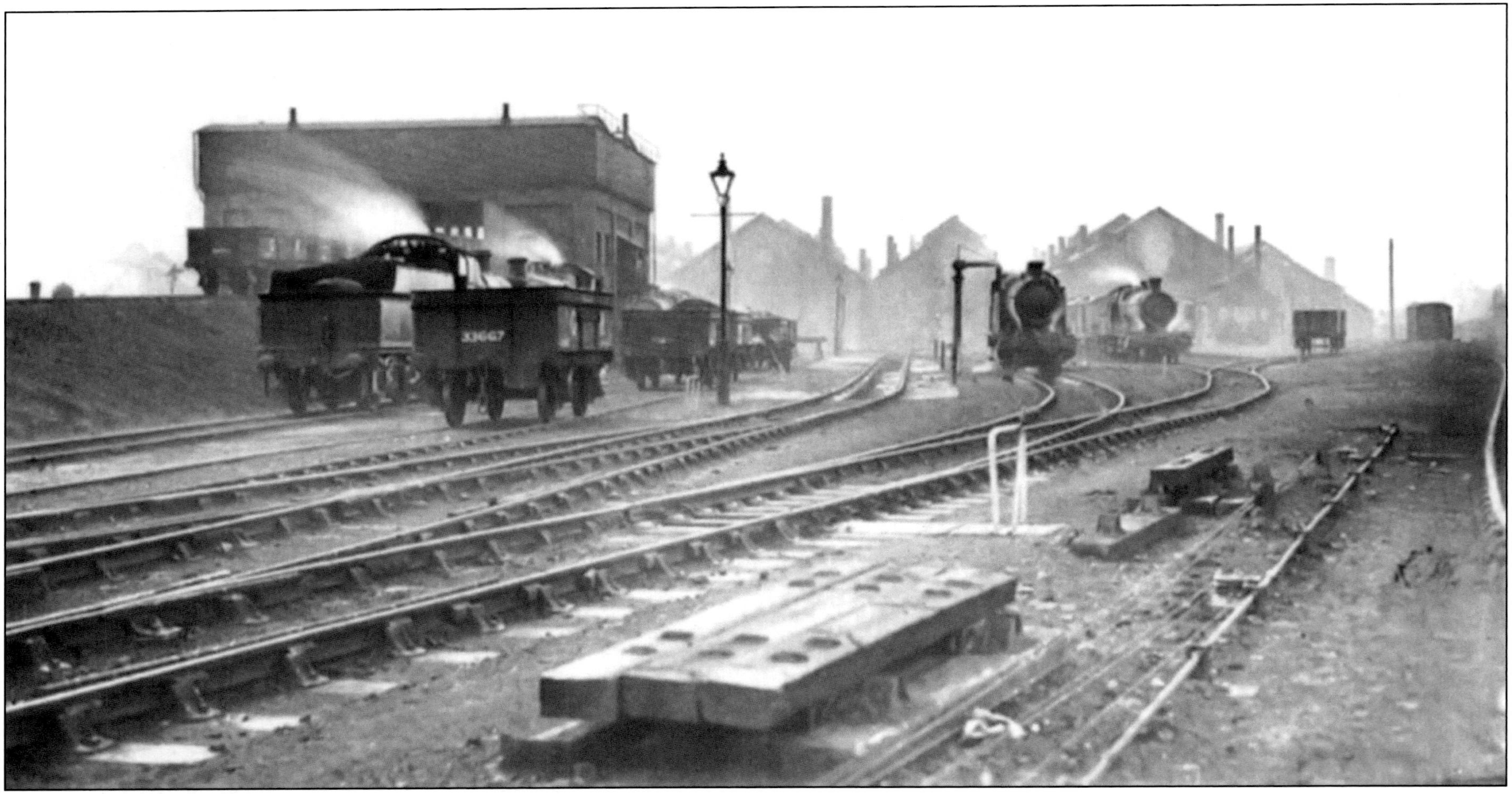

The Great Western Railway Co Ltd, built this railway engine shed at Morfa, (New Dock) Llanelli, in 1925. This engine shed had replaced an earlier depot built on the site in 1840 by The Llanelly Railway & Dock Co, and acquired by GWR in 1875. In its heyday, 62 locomotives were housed at this depot, which finally closed its doors in 1965.

(T. S. Powell collection).

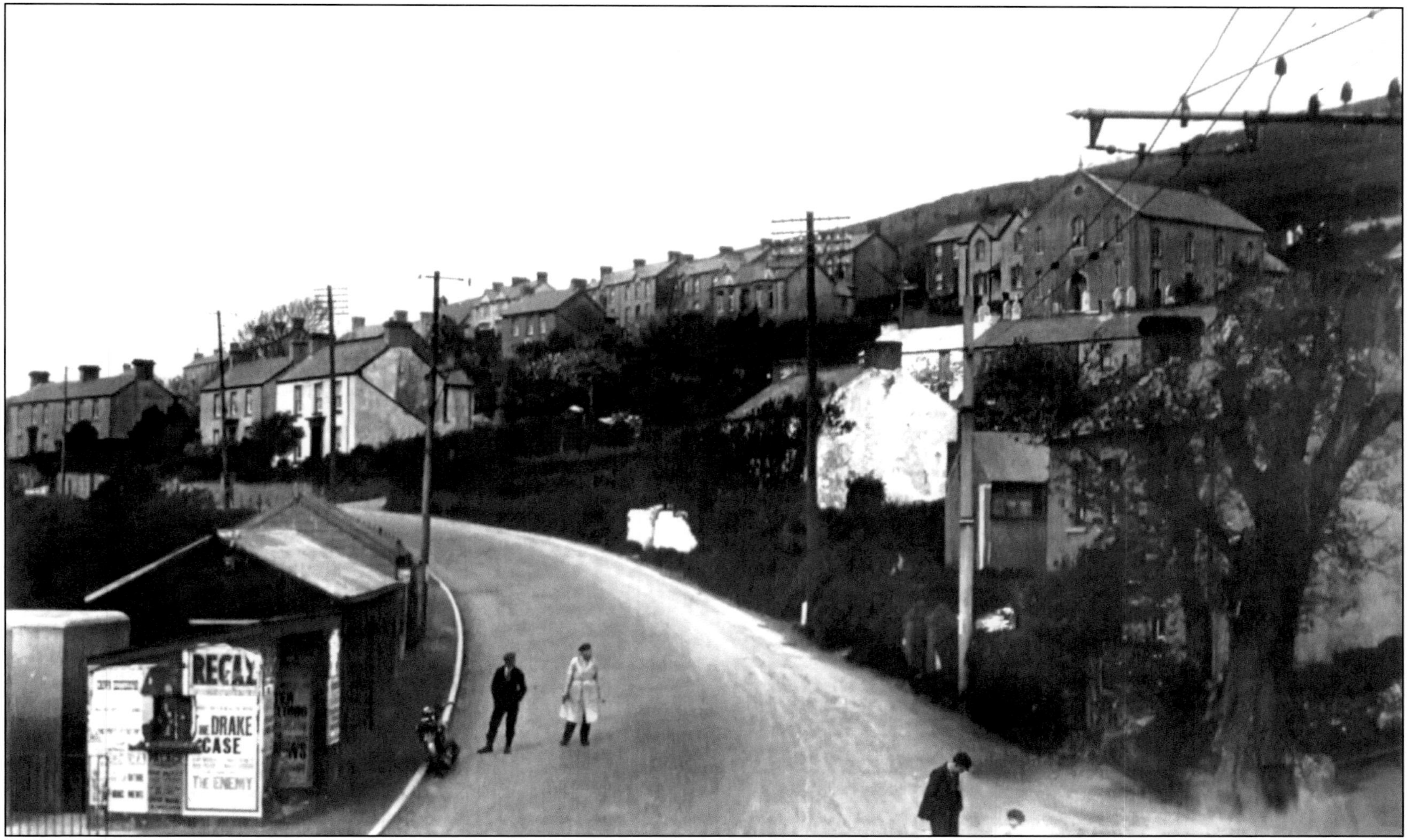


A view of the tram terminus in Pwll, circa 1920, with the overhead electric wiring that powered the trams just visible on the top right hand side. Libanus Chapel is the large building visible behind the tramways overhead wiring, and the first house on the right hand side is No 1 Pwll Road. The structure on the left of the picture, with all the cinema advertisements, is a wooden 'tram waiting room' with a shoe repairer's shop 'Tom the cobbler' next door. The shop was also built from timber. Note the absence of street lighting. This part of Pwll was known as 'Erw Fach', in those far gone days.

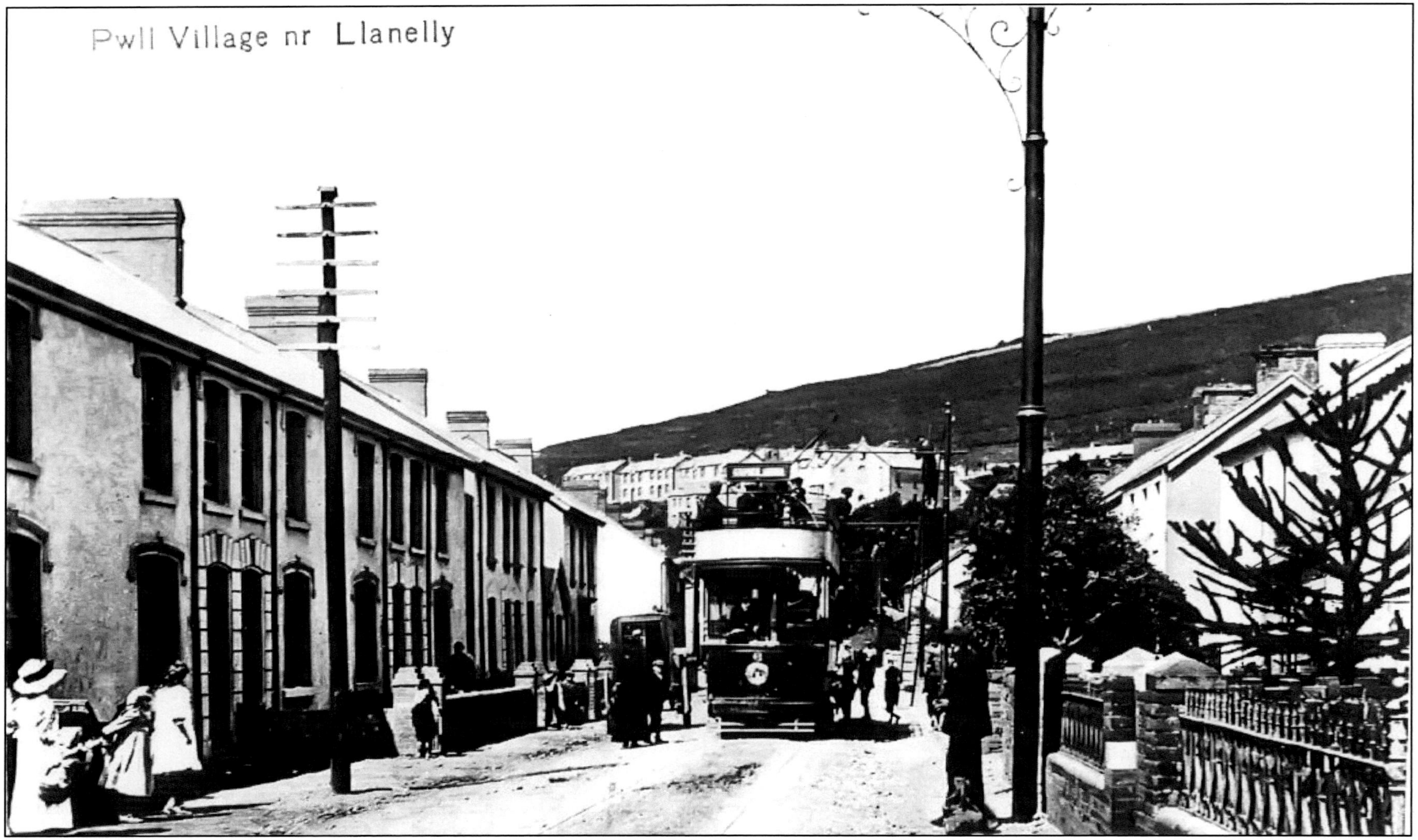


This view of Bassett Terrace, Pwll was taken during Edwardian times, when the houses had front gardens, no pavements and a 'dirt track' road. The electric tram (No 6) on route to Llanelli Railway Station, was owned by The Llanelly & District Electric Lighting and Transport Co, (later LLANESCO – Llanelly Electric Supply Company). The electric trams which started in March 1908 were powered by electricity, generated at the company's own power station at North Dock, Llanelli, (pictured on page 55). The privately owned power station also provided electricity to every household in Llanelli.

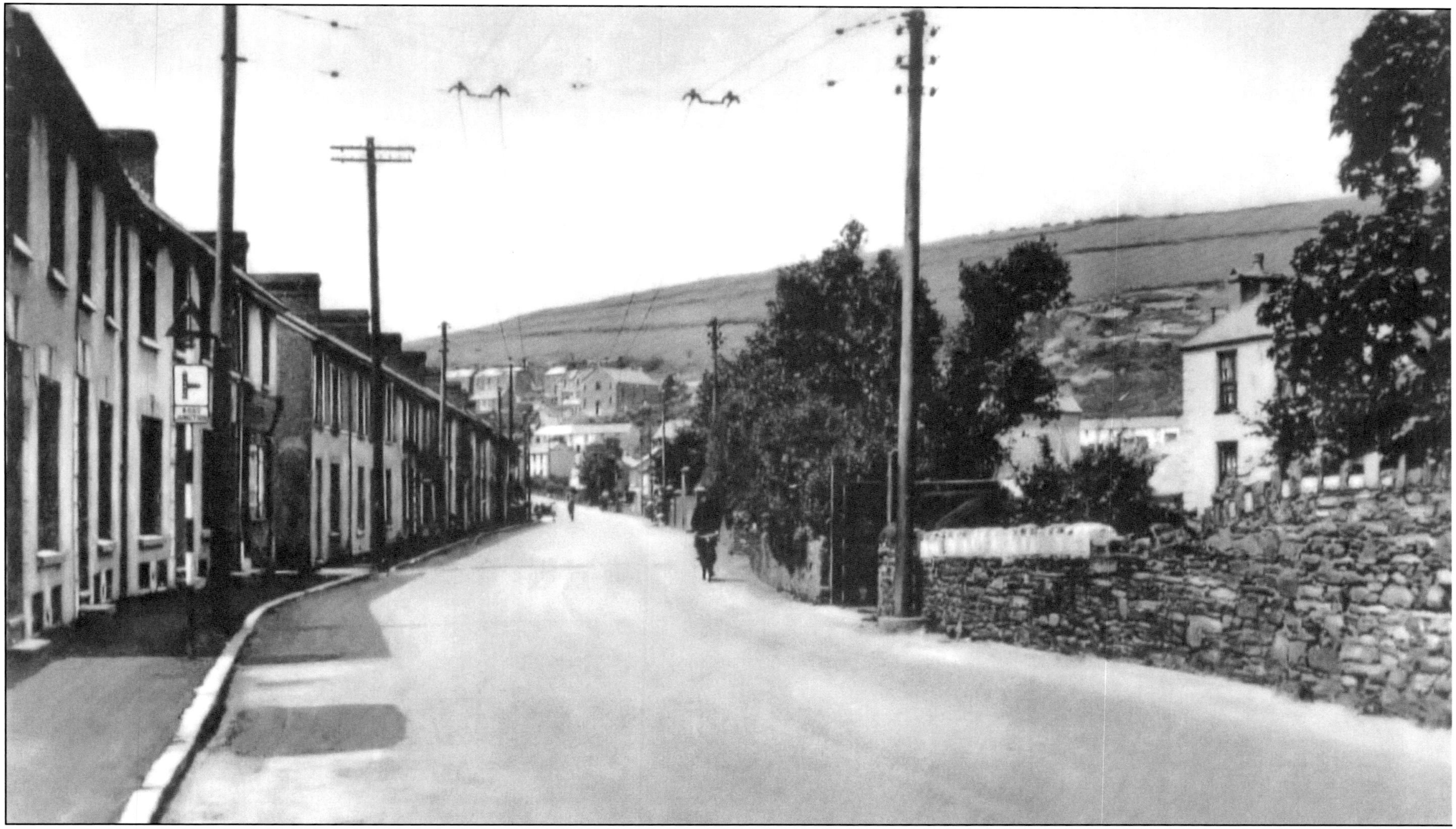

This view of Bassett Terrace, Pwll, was taken in the late 1930's, after the tramlines in the roadway had been removed and the tramways overhead wiring modified to suit the electric trolley-buses. Libanus Chapel is just visible on the hill in the background. Note also the quarry on the hill to the right of the picture, and the absence of traffic – today it's an extremely busy highway.

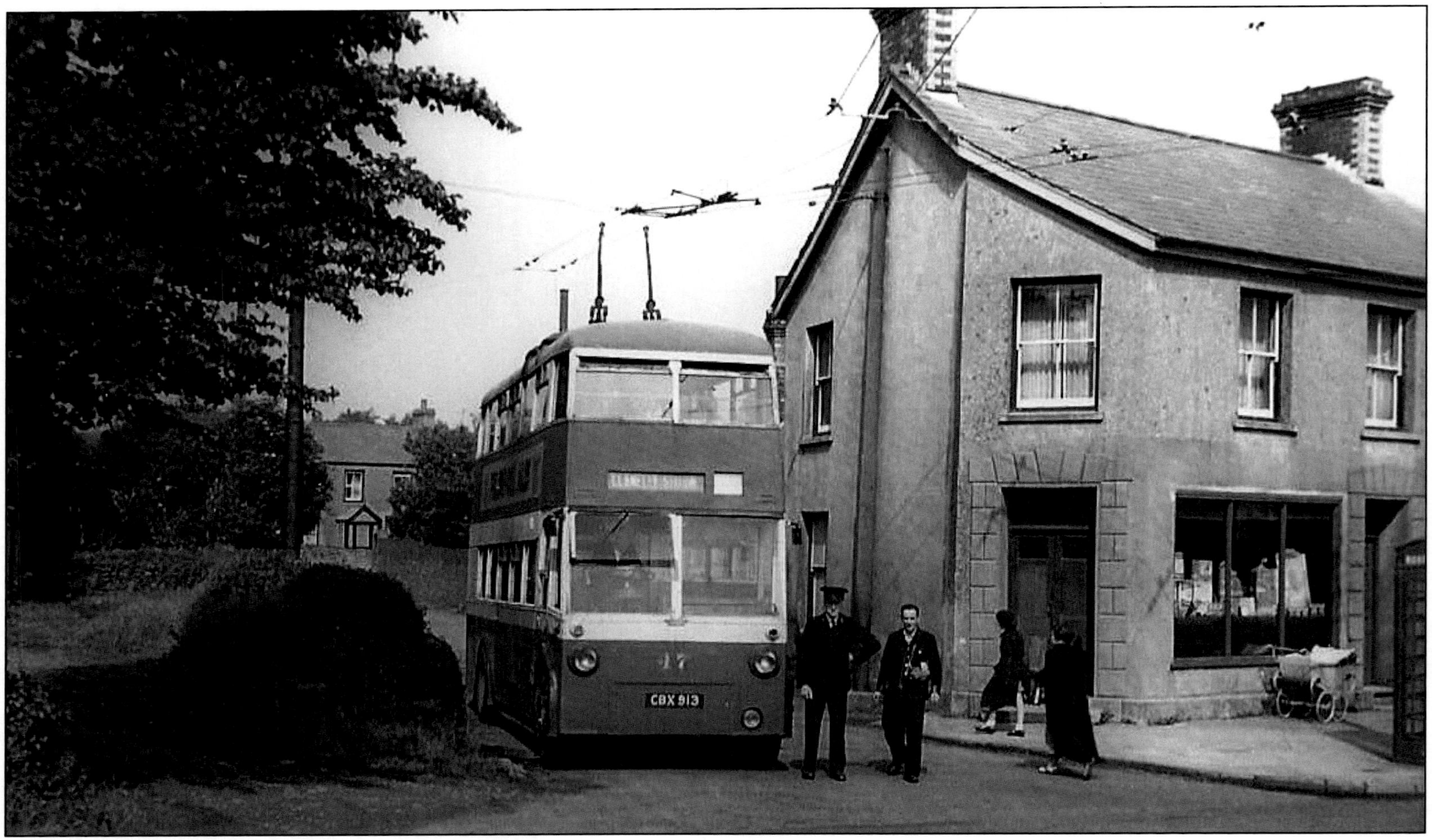


The trolleybus terminus at the junction of Basset Terrace and Waeneos, Pwll, is captured, here, in June 1952, by Chris Carter of London, who came to Llanelli to photograph the trolleybus system, shortly before its demise in 1952. The trolleybuses made their reversing manoeuvre into this cul-de-sac called Waeneos, before making their return journey to Llanelli railway station. The overhead trolley booms were always removed for the reversing manoeuvre, and the bus would reverse using battery power. The ticket inspector, Bryn Rees, and conductor, Rufus Thomas (right), pose for the camera in this historic view. The grocers shop, on the right, later became a butchers shop for villager Henry Warner. Note the vintage 'Silver Cross' pram outside the shop – a collector's item today.

(Chris Carter).

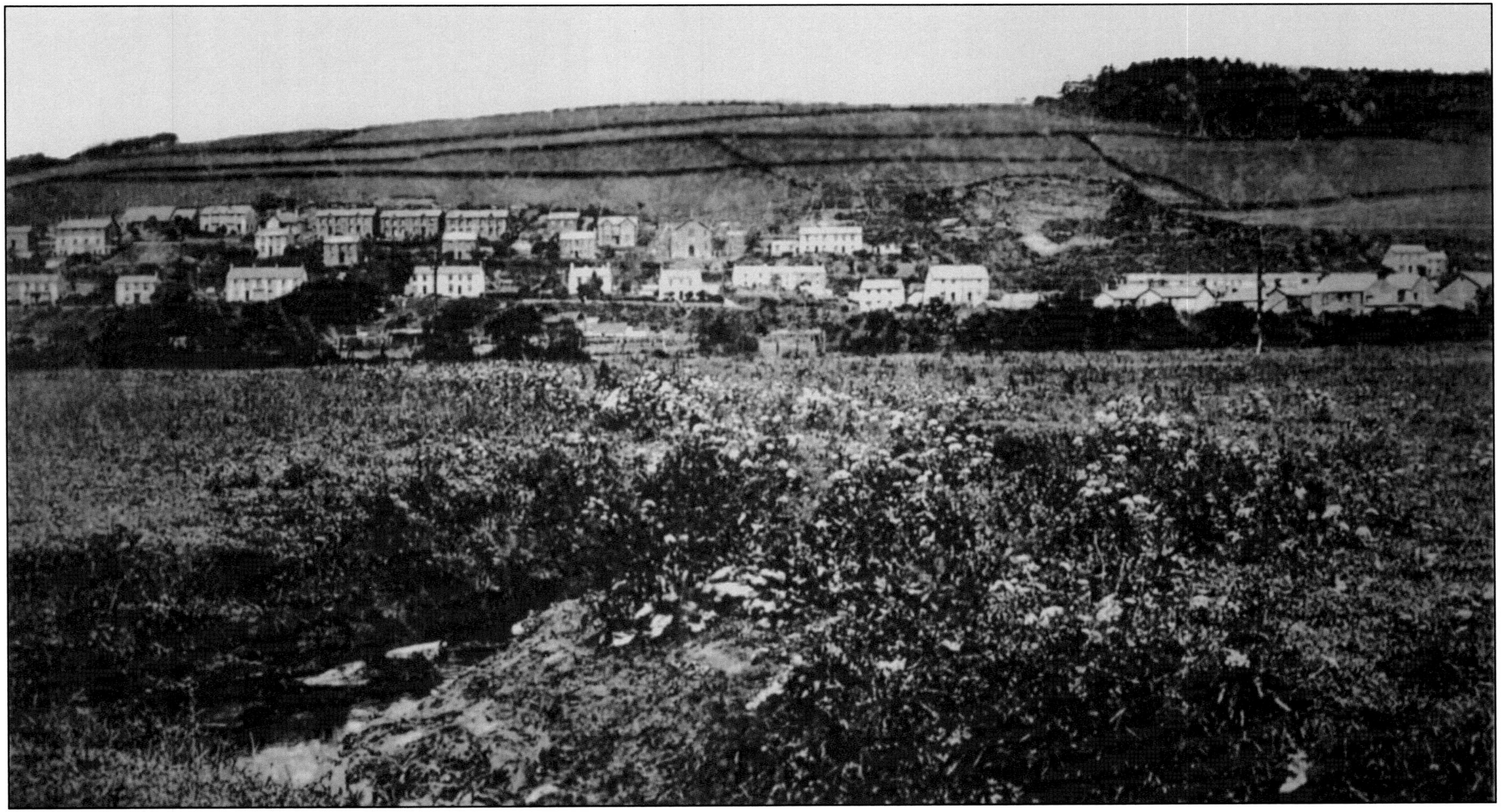

Viewed from the London – Fishguard railway line in the 1930's is the eastern half of Pwll village. Bassett Terrace is to the right hand side of the view, with Stradey Hill visible just behind. New Road (now renamed Elgin Road) is the top level of houses to the left of picture with Pwll Road being the lower level. Libanus Chapel is prominent in the centre of the picture, and the quarry behind Stradey Hill can be seen to the right of Libanus Chapel. Coal and clay was mined from beneath the Graig (the hill in the background), to supply Pwll brickworks. The drift mine entrance was located on the marsh (immediately below Libanus Chapel), where the group of sheds can be seen. That area was known as Pwll-y-Cwar; a quarry, which was filled in with landfill after WW2 had ended.

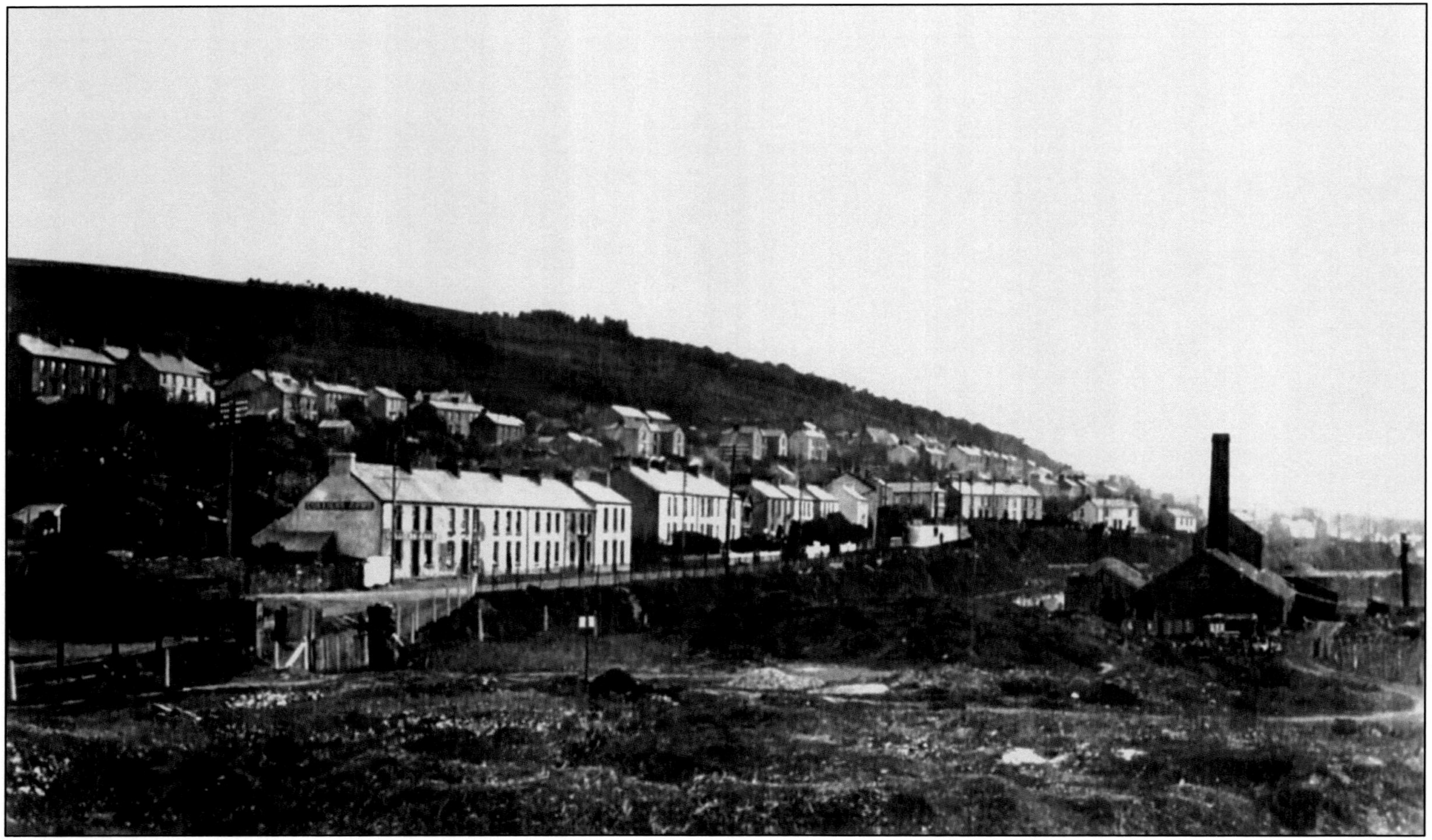

The village of Pwll is just a little over 1 mile in length, and this view taken around 1930, shows the middle part of Pwll Road; nearest the camera is No. 99, and the house furthest away is No. 45. The original Colliers Arms (No. 99 Pwll Road) is the house nearest the camera, which was demolished in 1948, along with the next two houses in order to widen the road. The Colliers Arms was afterwards relocated to a double-fronted house, 11 houses away at No 77, where it is today. New Road (nowadays Elgin Road), is the upper level of houses where Holy Trinity Church is situated. The works on the right hand side was a brickworks owned by Pwll Coal & Brick Co. They specialised in making fire-bricks, fire clay and a by-product of building mortar, made from the kiln's ashes. The mounds in front of the brickworks is waste material brought out from the company's own mine, which was a level tunnelled, here, under Pwll Road, between No's 87/89, and another level tunnelled under Pwll Road, between No's 5 and 7, which worked beneath Libanus Chapel. The brickworks with a rail link to the Burry Port & Gwendraeth Valley Railway closed in 1964, and was subsequently demolished after a 100 year working life.

(V Morgan Collection)

**Right:** This view of Pwll brickworks, built in 1865 was taken sometime after its closure in 1964. The view takes in the track-bed of the former Burry Port & Gwendraeth Valley Railway Company's railway line, which had previously been a tram-road, built to carry coal in horse drawn trams from Pwll (Pool) Colliery to the Llanelli docks. The tram-road had been built on top of the original sea-wall. Consequently, the brickworks had been built on re-claimed land from the sea, after a new sea-wall carrying the 'South Wales Railway' had been built on the causeway some 100 yards away, in 1852. The high wall, visible on the left, is the retaining wall for the A484 trunk road running through the village (Pwll Road), built between 1948-1959.

(V. Morgan collection).

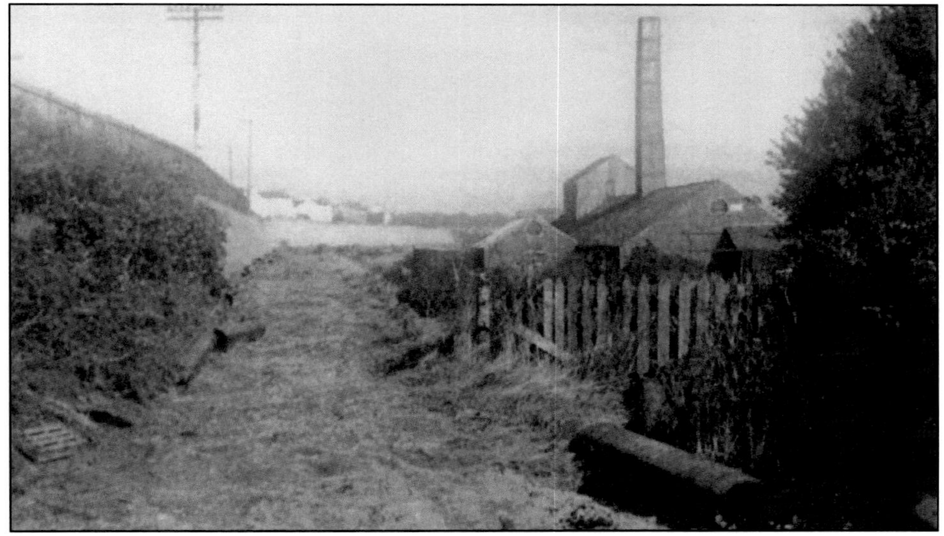

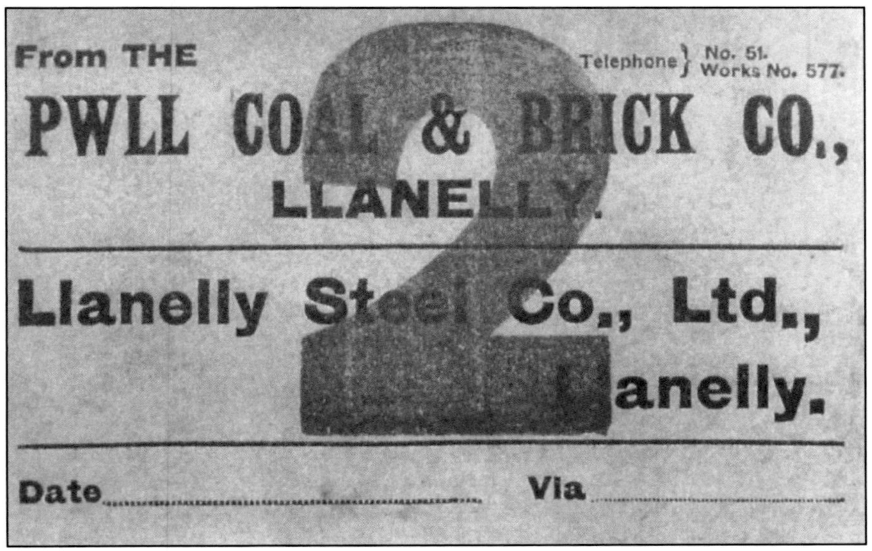


**Left:** This carriage label would have been attached to railway trucks leaving the brickworks, giving the railway company's delivery details. Llanelly Steel Co. Ltd, would have been receiving a consignment of fire-bricks, used in the re-building and repair of the furnaces, and ingot 'soaking pits'.

(V. Morgan collection).

**Right:** This is Pwll Road, Pwll, looking eastward from a point opposite the Colliers Arms. It was taken in 1958, shortly before work commenced to widen the road and remove the gradient by Tyle Catherine, in the background. Number 71 Pwll Road (Hendy House), is nearest the camera.

(V. Morgan).

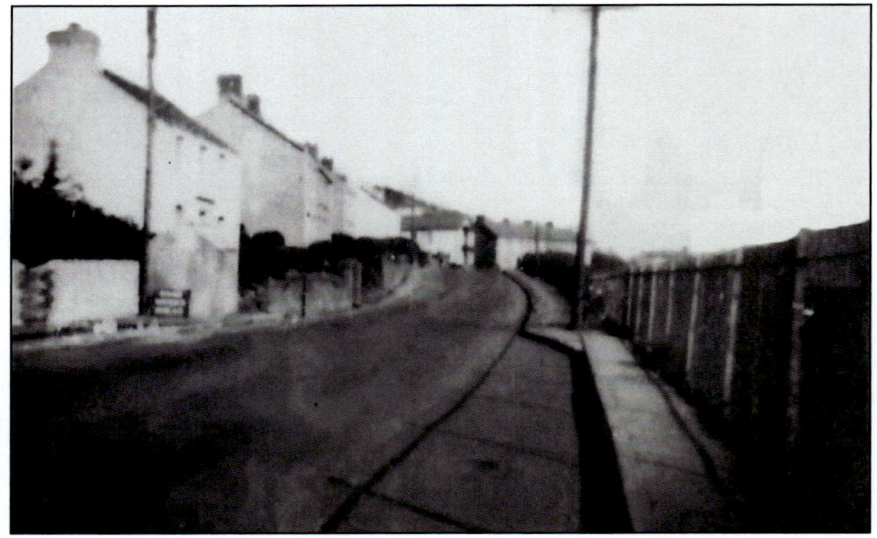

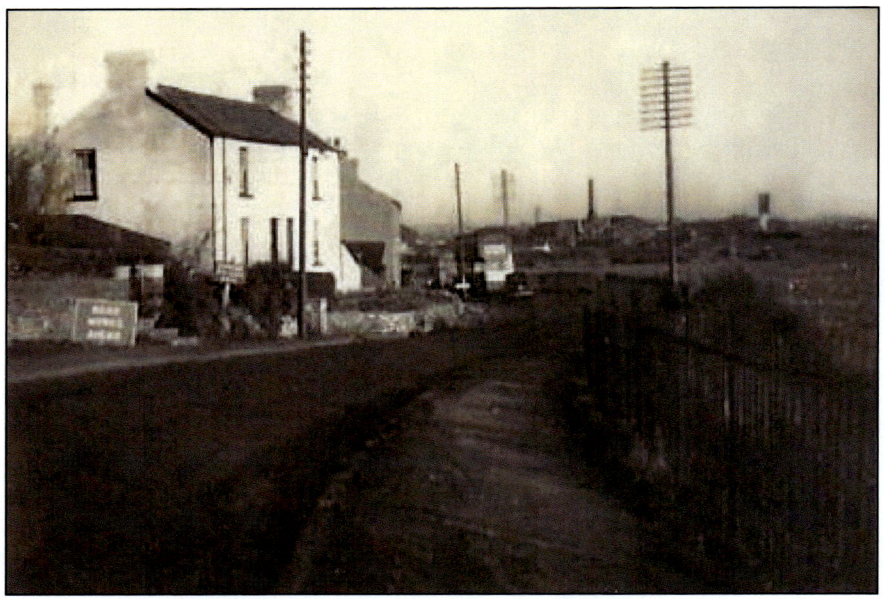

**Left:** This view of Pwll Road, near Tyle Catherine junction was taken in February 1958, shortly before the road widening work started. Note the front gardens outside numbers 49 and 47 (nearest the camera), which were completely removed during the road improvement scheme. Sandy sheet-works is just visible in the background, with its 160 feet high chimney stack.

(V. Morgan).

**Right:** The road widening work outside Nos. 41 and 43 Pwll Road, Pwll, had just began when this photograph was taken in February 1958. The front gardens and boundary walls had already been removed to accommodate a pavement, with new boundary walls built 8 feet closer to the houses. Additionally, the road to the left of the picture was substantially widened after a 2 feet wide stone faced wall, reinforced with 8 feet width of concrete, was built to support the roadway. The road outside No. 43 had previously been so narrow, two commercial vehicles could barely pass. In March 1943, a double decker bus crashed through the railings at this point, landing on its roof, 20 feet down the embankment. Three people were killed and forty injured – mostly workers from the Pembrey munitions factory.

(V. Morgan).

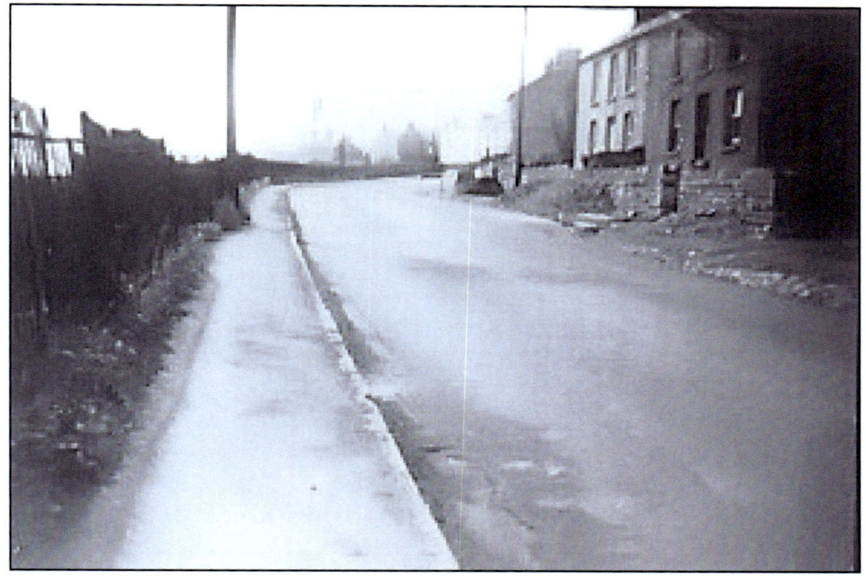

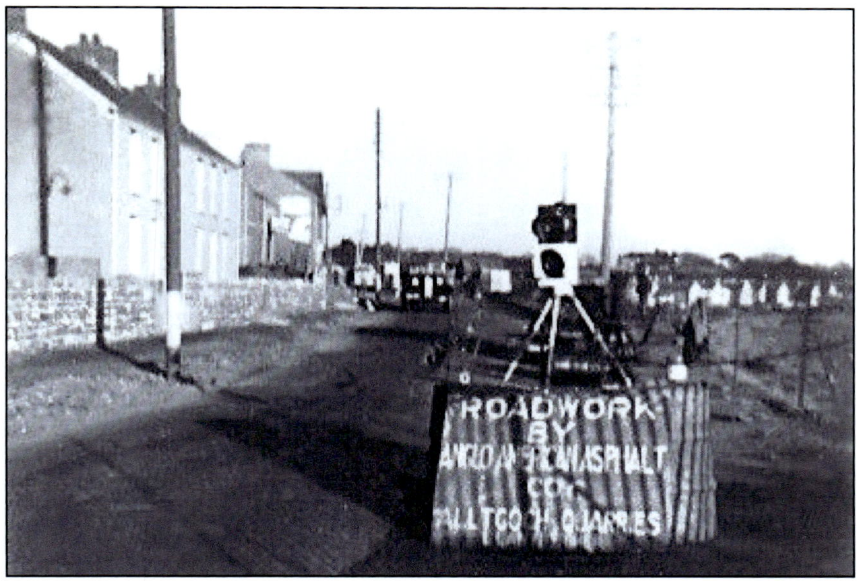


**Left:** The contractor engaged to carry out the road improvement, from a point outside Pwll Community Centre, to a point outside 49 Pwll Road, was the Anglo-American Asphalt Co, of Alltgoch Quarries, Cwrtnewydd, Cardiganshire. A 20 feet high stone faced wall, reinforced with 8 feet of concrete was built to support the road along this section of highway. In this view, dated February 1958, Nos. 37 and 35 Pwll Road are nearest the camera. The traffic lights were very unusual, having red and green lights only. The Austin lorry travelling along the highway was owned by B.C. Lloyd of Sandy Road, Llanelli, and is featured on the next page.

(V. Morgan).

**Right:** Cliff Lloyd was a renowned local coal merchant in the area of west Llanelli and Pwll. Operating his business from 90 Sandy Road, Llanelli, he bought this Austin lorry brand new in February 1948 for his door to door coal deliveries. The lorry, capable of carrying 3 tons, had an unladen weight of 2 ton 2 cwt, and normally worked as a platform lorry carrying 1cwt. bags of coal, operating on a 'B' licence. In those far gone days, every household had open fires as their means of heating. It must have been a lucrative business in the winter time!

(V. Morgan collection).

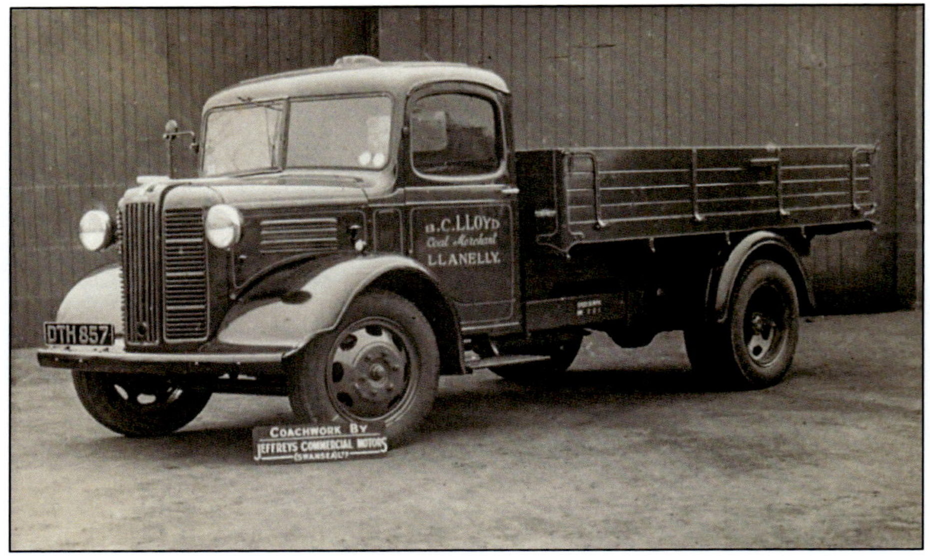


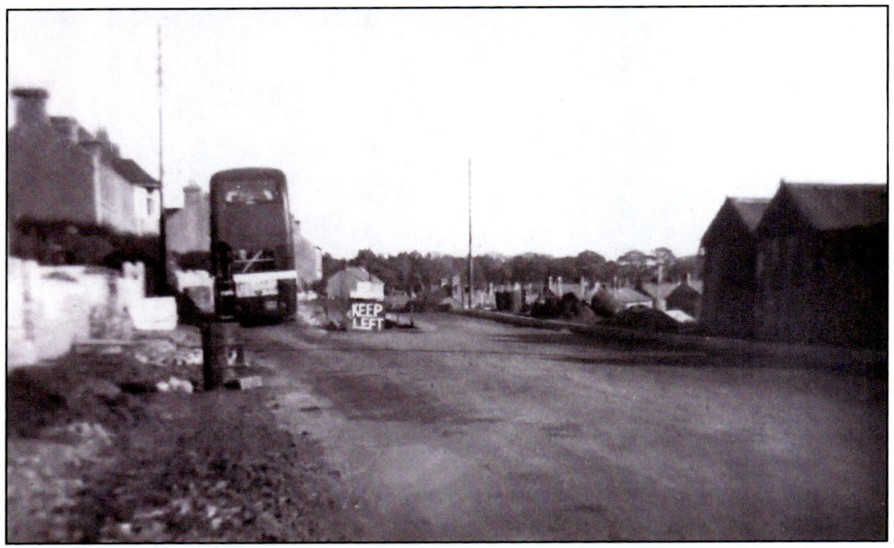


**Left:** Carmarthenshire C.C. undertook the road improvement work themselves on the section of Pwll Road from the old tram terminus (junction of Wauneos) to the Community Centre. This picture was taken in July 1957, and Nos. 11 and 9 Pwll Road are just visible on the left hand side.

(V. Morgan).

**Right:** 'Siop Fach' (111A Pwll Road) was purchased by Edwin and Phyllis Jones in 1952, and could be regarded as a typical village store, selling everything. It competed well against the Co-operative store, next door, and gave an excellent service to the community until its closure in 1991. After its closure, the land was sold for development, and now houses a new house. This picture, owned by Jane 'Siop Fach', was taken in 1965.

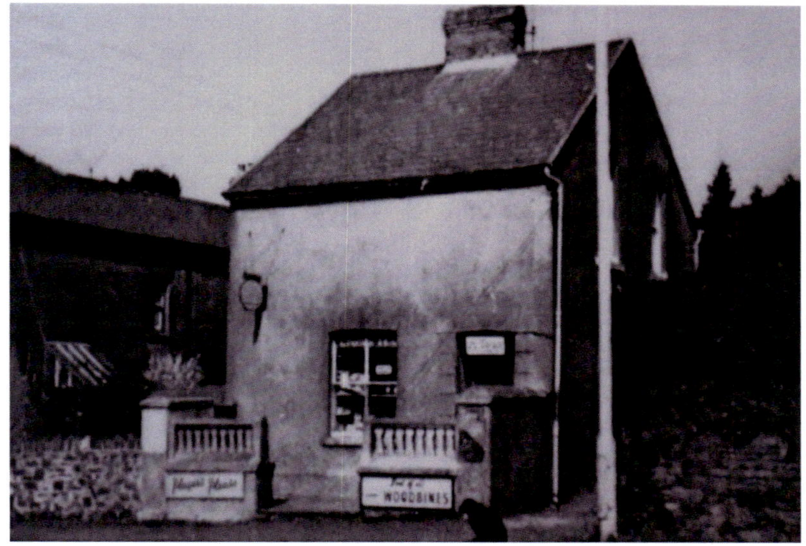


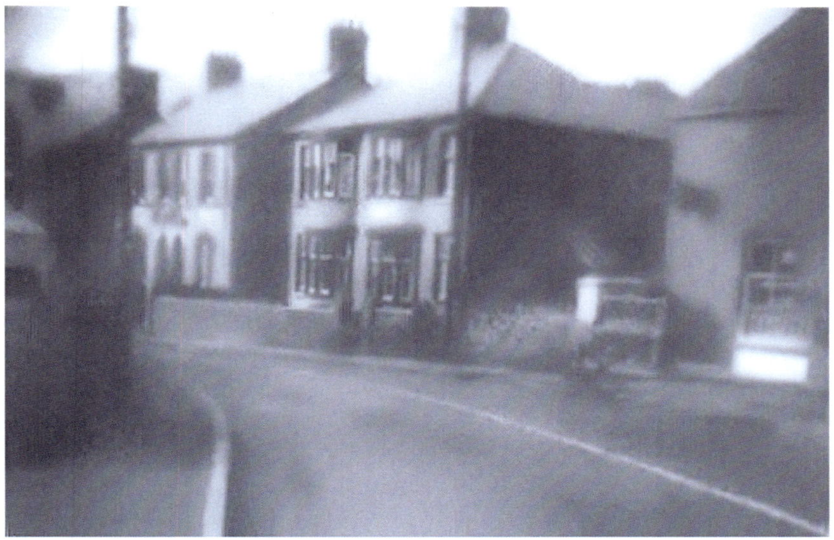

**Left:** This view of 'siop fach' was taken around 1955, looking westward towards Burry Port. It also captures the neighbouring houses of 113 – 119 Pwll Road, long before the road was straightened out and widened.

(Malcolm Morgan).

**Two views at the same location in Pwll, taken in 1958.**

**Right:** In this view looking westward towards Burry Port, the three houses on the left are Nos 2, 4, and 6 Pwll Road, respectively, which were demolished in 1965 to widen the road and straighten out the corner. 'Siop Fach' is tucked away in the right-hand corner, and the lady walking along the pavement is Mrs. Nancy John.

(V. Morgan).

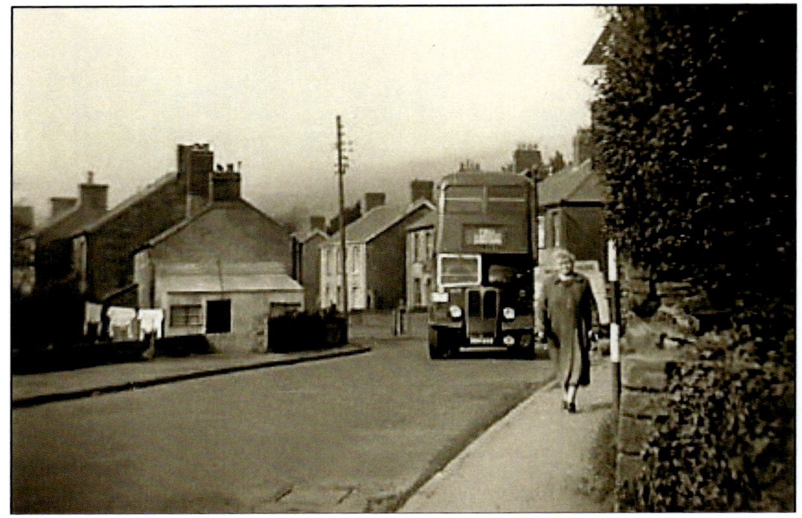

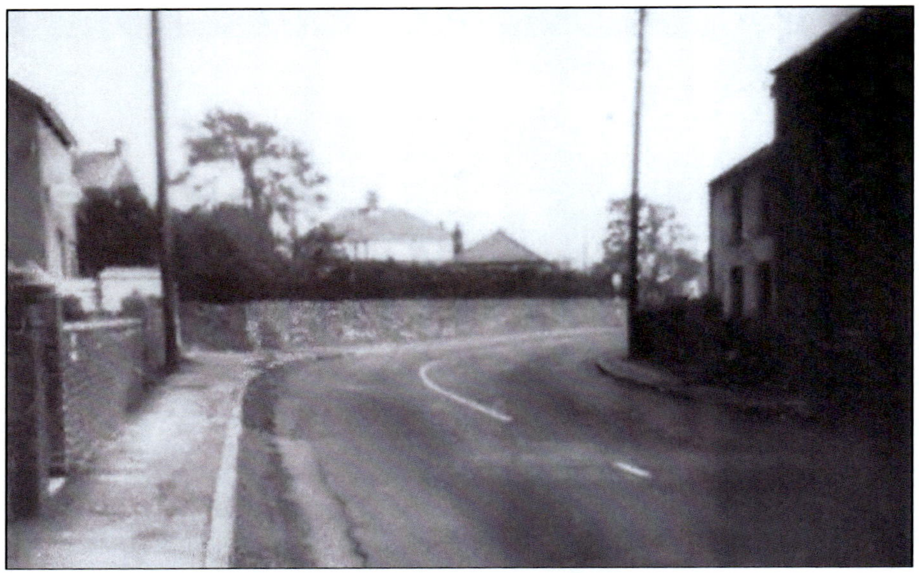

**Left:** In this view, looking eastward along Pwll Road, towards Llanelli, 'Siop Fach' is tucked away in the left hand corner, and the front garden walls of Nos. 115 and 113 Pwll Road are prominent on the left. Opposite side of the roadway are Nos. 4 and 2 Pwll Road, respectively.

(Malcolm Morgan).

**Right:** The street of Isfryn, in Pwll, pictured here, forms part of Pwll Road, the main thoroughfare through the village. The buildings visible in the background (right hand side), were garages of the Llanelly Rural District Council, which stood on land originally occupied by the Pwll (Pool) Colliery. The tall building with the chimney, was previously the colliery engine house, and was used by the L.R.D.C. as a stores and office. Pwll Colliery closed in 1879, and after a sale of valuable equipment in 1880, the 'Harvey' beam engine, of Cornish manufacture, found its way to the Severn Tunnel, where it was used to pump out the flooded tunnel during its construction. The colliery engine house was finally demolished in 1986, and the site was levelled off.

(V. Morgan).

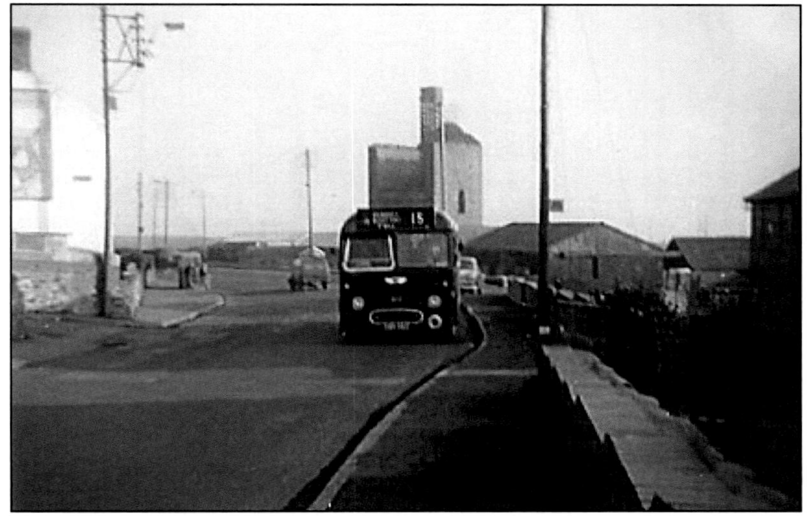

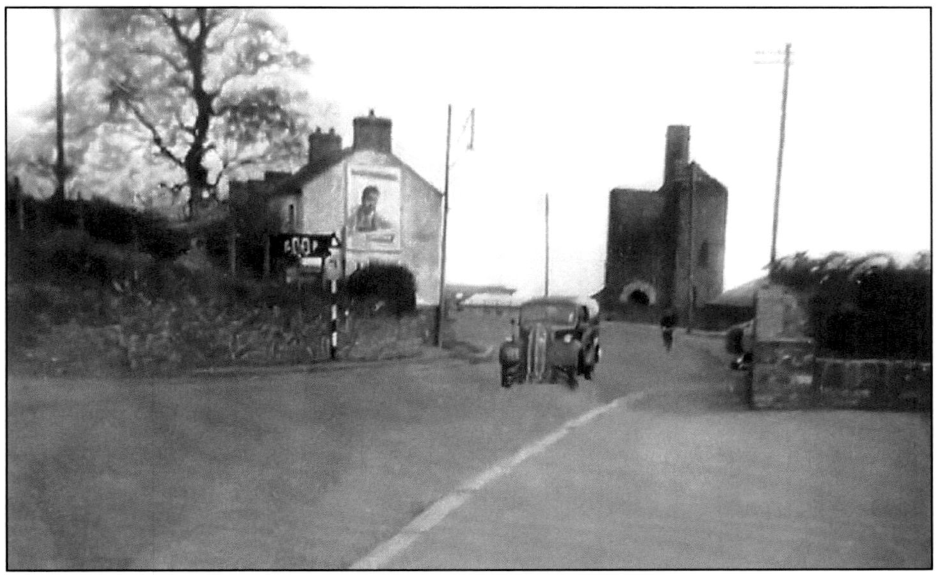

**Left:** Another view of Isfryn (Pwll Road), taken from a different point along the road, shows 'Rock House', along with the remains of Pwll (Pool) Colliery engine house. This was, again, before the road was widened at Isfryn. Pwll (Pool) Colliery, was first worked by Edward Rees of Cilymaenllwyd, around 1765, but closed later due to flooding. Re-opening in 1865, with a huge engine to pump out the flood water, it was abandoned again in 1879, never to re-open.

(Malcolm Morgan).

**Right:** Pwll C. P. School year 6, 1955.

Left to right standing: Miss Jones form-teacher, Ronald Elliott, David Slack, Jeffrey Collins, Iorwerth Thomas, Raymond Thomas, Vernon Morgan, Clive Richards, Philip Evans, Alan Hopkins, Keith Williams, Dai Shapley, Mr Aubrey - headmaster.
Seated Carol Rogers, Gwyneth Jones, Arleen -?- , Pat Samuel, Christine Wheeler, Nigel Henley.
Front row, Susan Richards, Pamela Evans, Edith Seedhouse, Gaynor Bonnell, Ann Rees, Jane Jones, Sian Powell, Valerie Davies, Barbara Thomas, Lavinia Howells.

(V. Morgan collection).

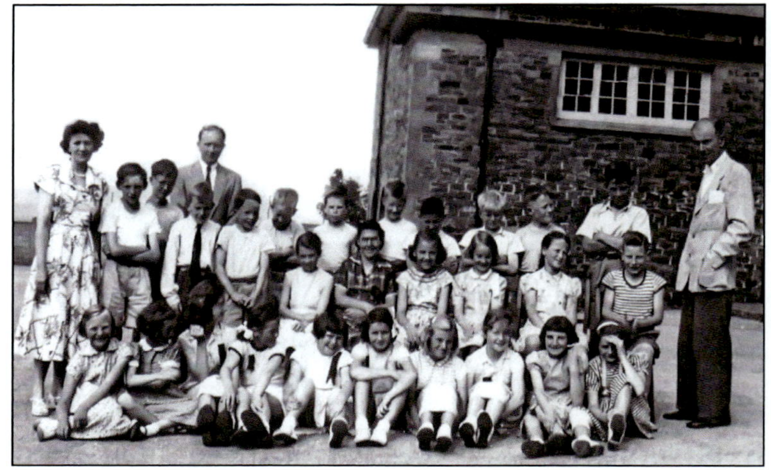

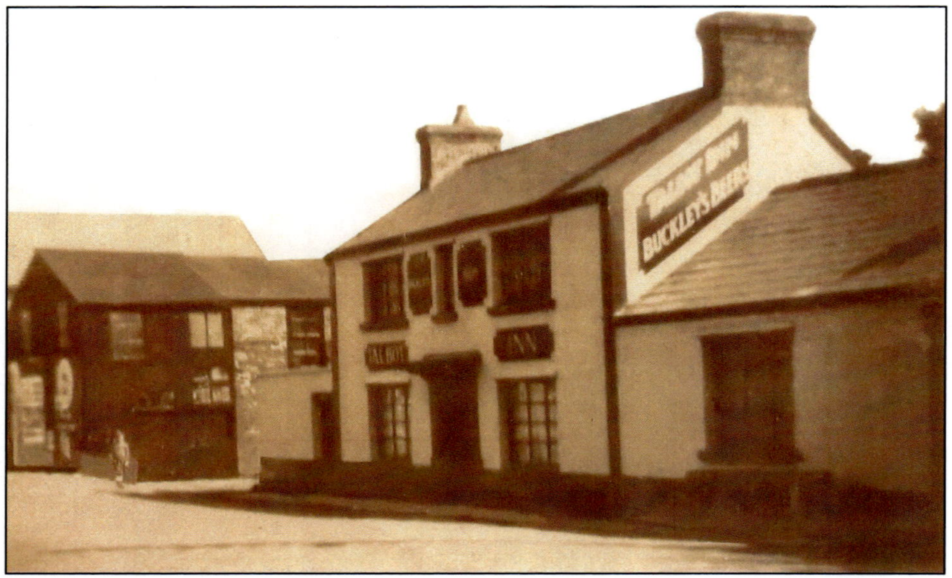


**Left:** This view of the Talbot Inn at Pwll, was taken in 1956; twenty-five years before its renovation and extension. This famous watering hole finally closed its doors in 2010, and was sold off by Brains Brewery as a private residence – which is, at the moment, undergoing a major rebuild. The building to the left of the picture, was a woollen mill making blankets. It closed down circa 1962, and was demolished in 1970 after a mysterious fire.

(Malcolm Morgan).

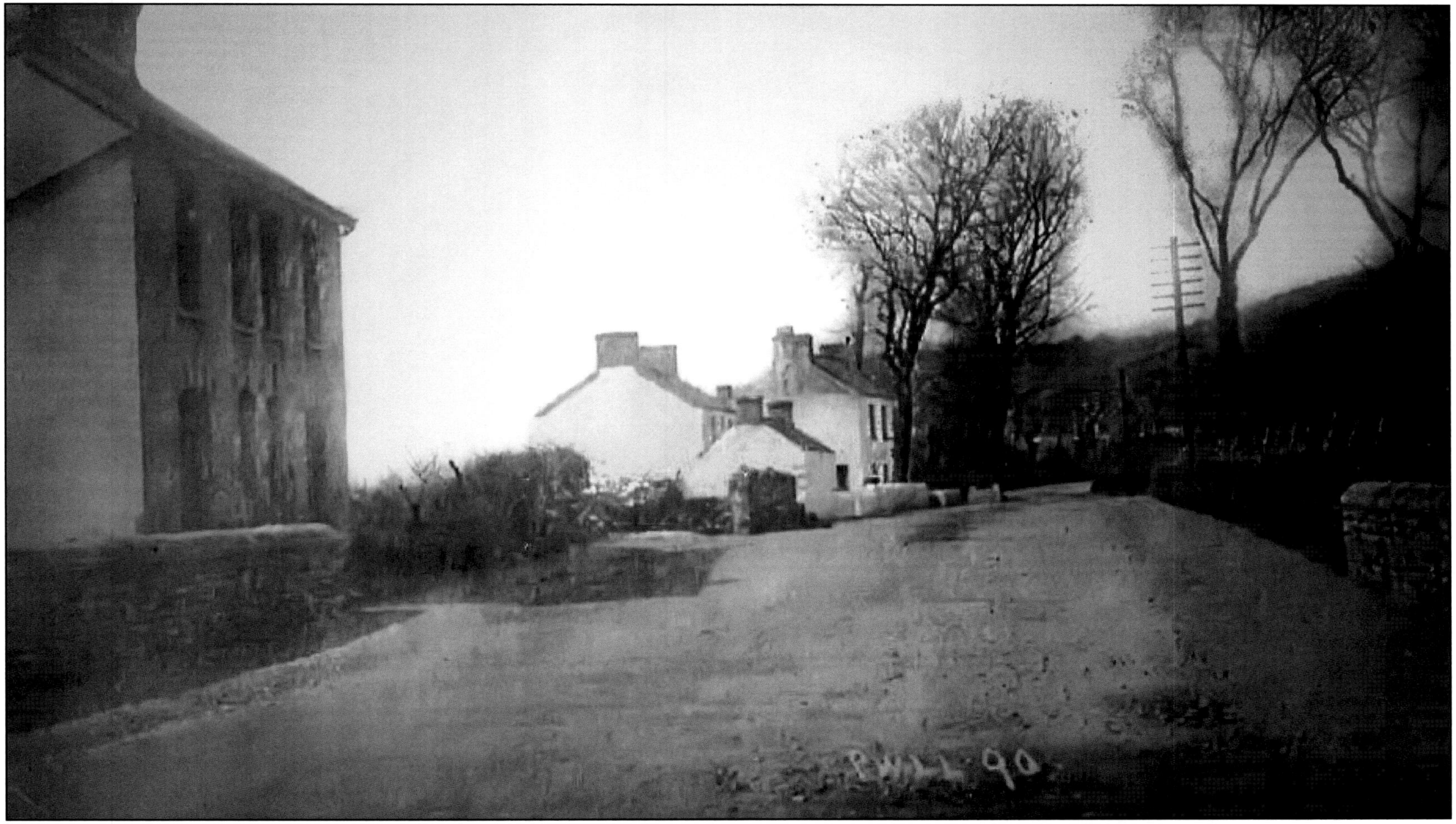


Although not a good quality picture, we have another view of Pwll village taken around 1910. The houses on the extreme left are Nos. 12 and 14 Pwll Road, with Almond Cottage at No. 20, and its wash-house the next building along the roadway. Tyrwaun is on the bend in the background, before the houses and Wheeler's Garage were built. The parapet of Cilymaenllwyd river bridge can be seen in the foreground.

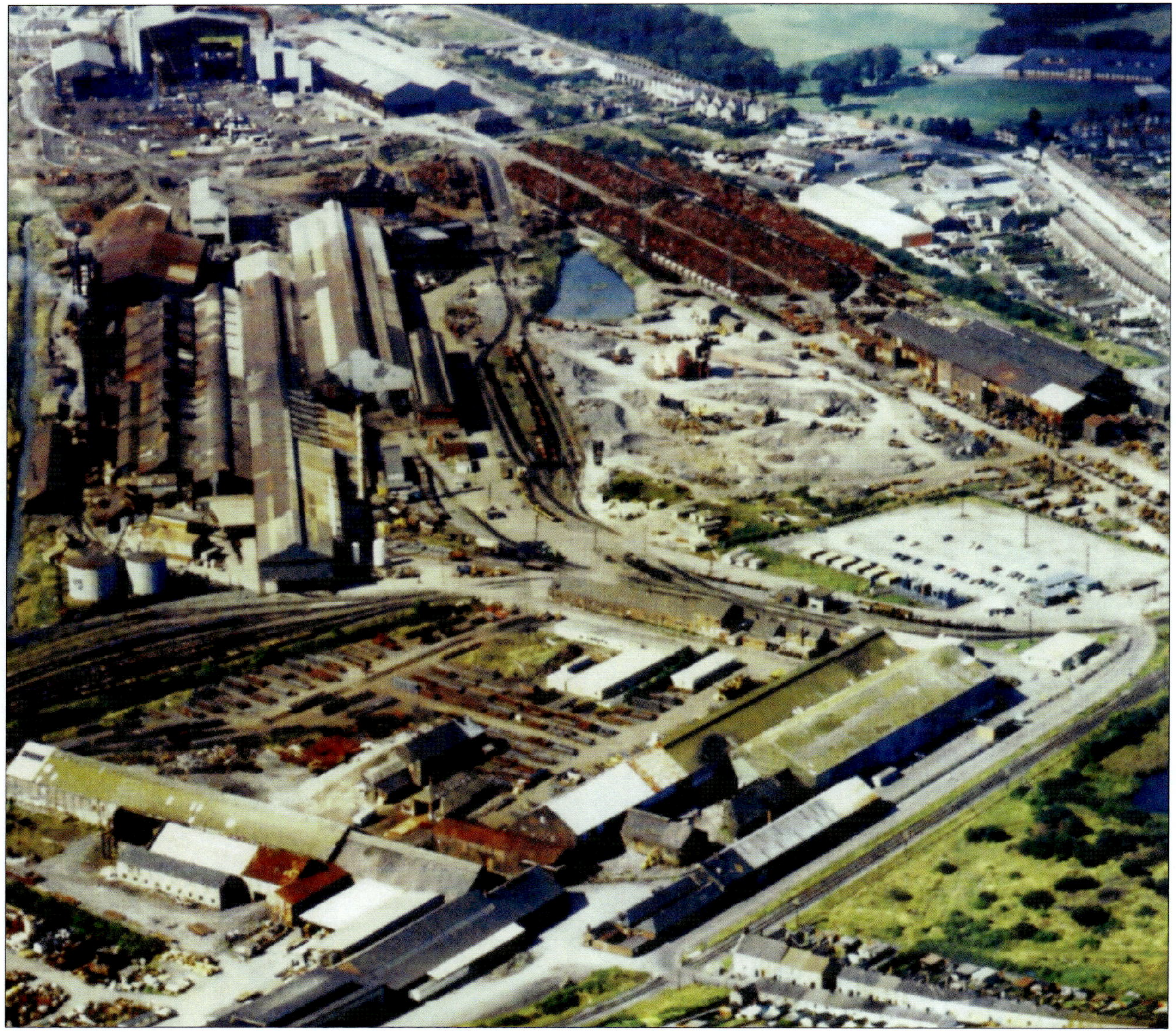

This aerial view of Duport Steelworks, Llanelli; (formerly Llanelly Steel Co. Ltd.) was taken in 1976, when the new electric arc furnaces were being constructed on the former Sandy Sheet-works site. All the buildings nearest the camera, were formerly the Old Castle Tinplate works, by then occupied by Thyssen G. B. Ltd, and also by Duport Steelworks. The buildings centre right were formerly Llanelly Foundry & Engineering Co. Ltd, by then, occupied by Duport as a loco shed and engineering workshop, and was additionally used as a steel ingot storage area. Stradey School is just visible in the top right hand corner, and Sandy Road, the Llanelli to Burry Port main road, is also visible. The bottom end of Old Castle Road can be seen in the right hand fore-ground.

The new electric arc furnaces were commissioned in 1977, closing down the out-dated open hearth furnaces which were located to the extreme left of this view. The arc furnaces, however, had a very short life, closing down in March 1981 when Duport Steelworks, employing 1200 people, went into liquidation.

(John Phillips collection).

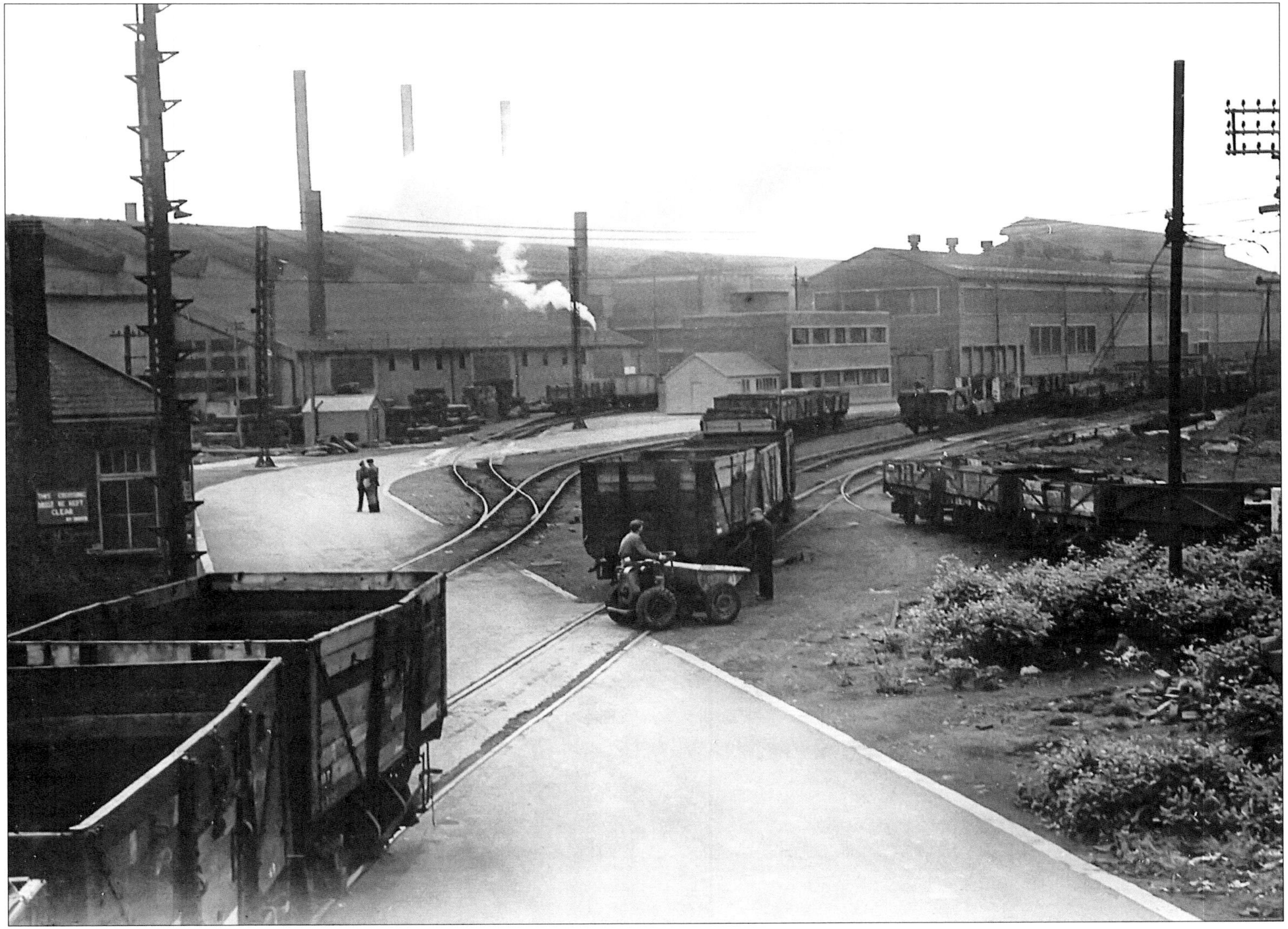

The Llanelly Steel Company (1907) Ltd, locally known as the 'KLONDIKE', was taken over by the Duport Group in 1960. This view of the steelworks was taken from the eastern end of the site soon after the Duport take-over. The rolling mill, and oil fired ingot 'soaking pits', are seen in the background; the electric power house / workshop is the large building on the right hand side, with CSO/Despatch Office in centre of photo. This roadway was the main thoroughfare through the works, with the laboratory and road weighbridge, to the left of this photo.

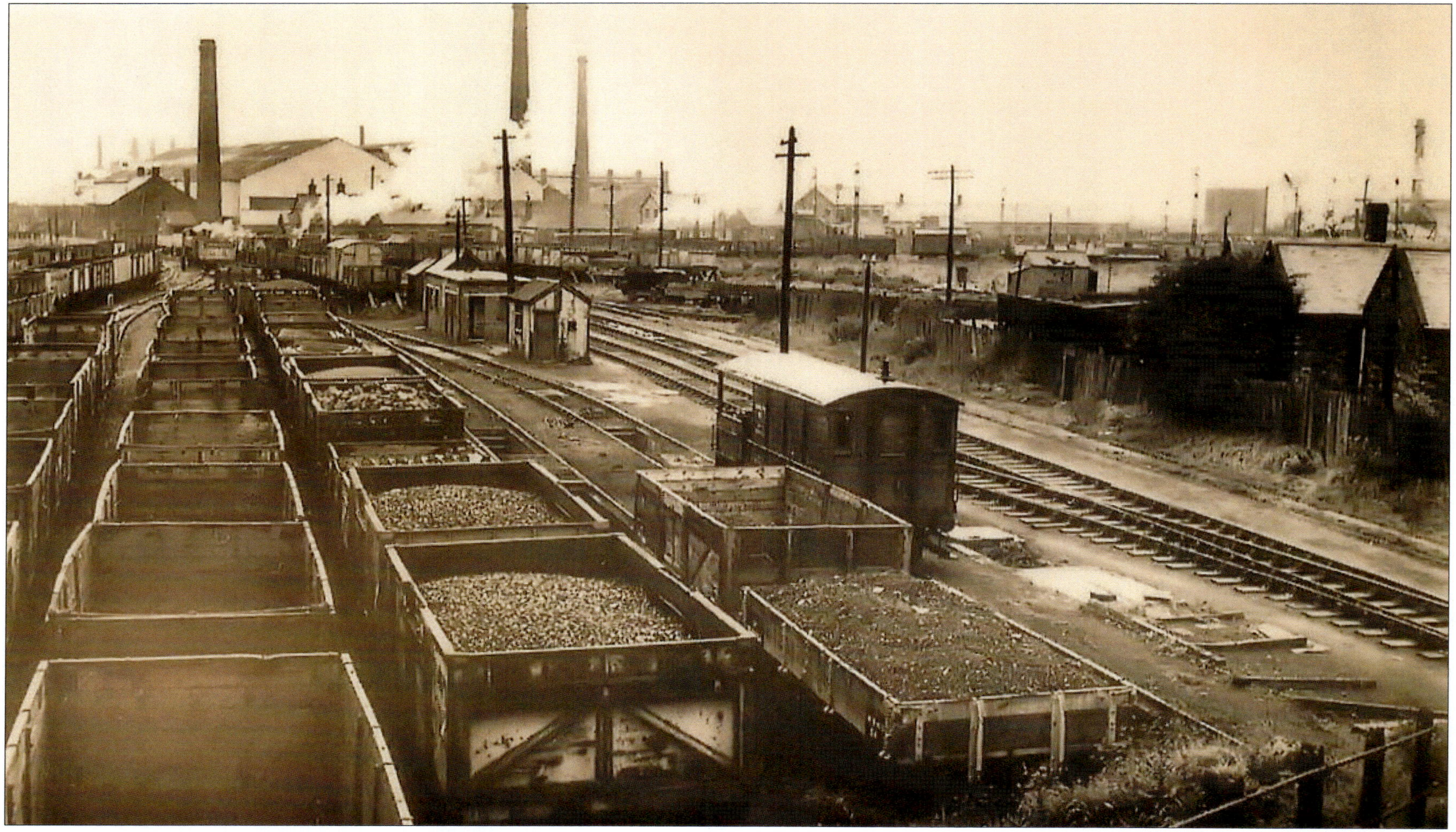

It is difficult to imagine how much change has taken place at this location; every building and railway line has disappeared! This view looking southwards from Sandy Bridge, in the mid 1950's, takes in the Old Castle tinplate works, and the eastern end of the Llanelly Steel works, along with the British Railway's gangers sheds adjacent to the Mynydd Mawr railway line, and all the railway sidings on the left hand side of the view. These days, this area forms part of Llanelli's Millenium Coast and Sandy Water Park, with a cycle path to Cross Hands (which passes under Sandy Bridge), built along the course of the Mynydd Mawr railway line on the extreme right. Additionally, the town's southern by-pass (or relief road) crosses the area to the centre of the picture.

(V. Morgan collection).

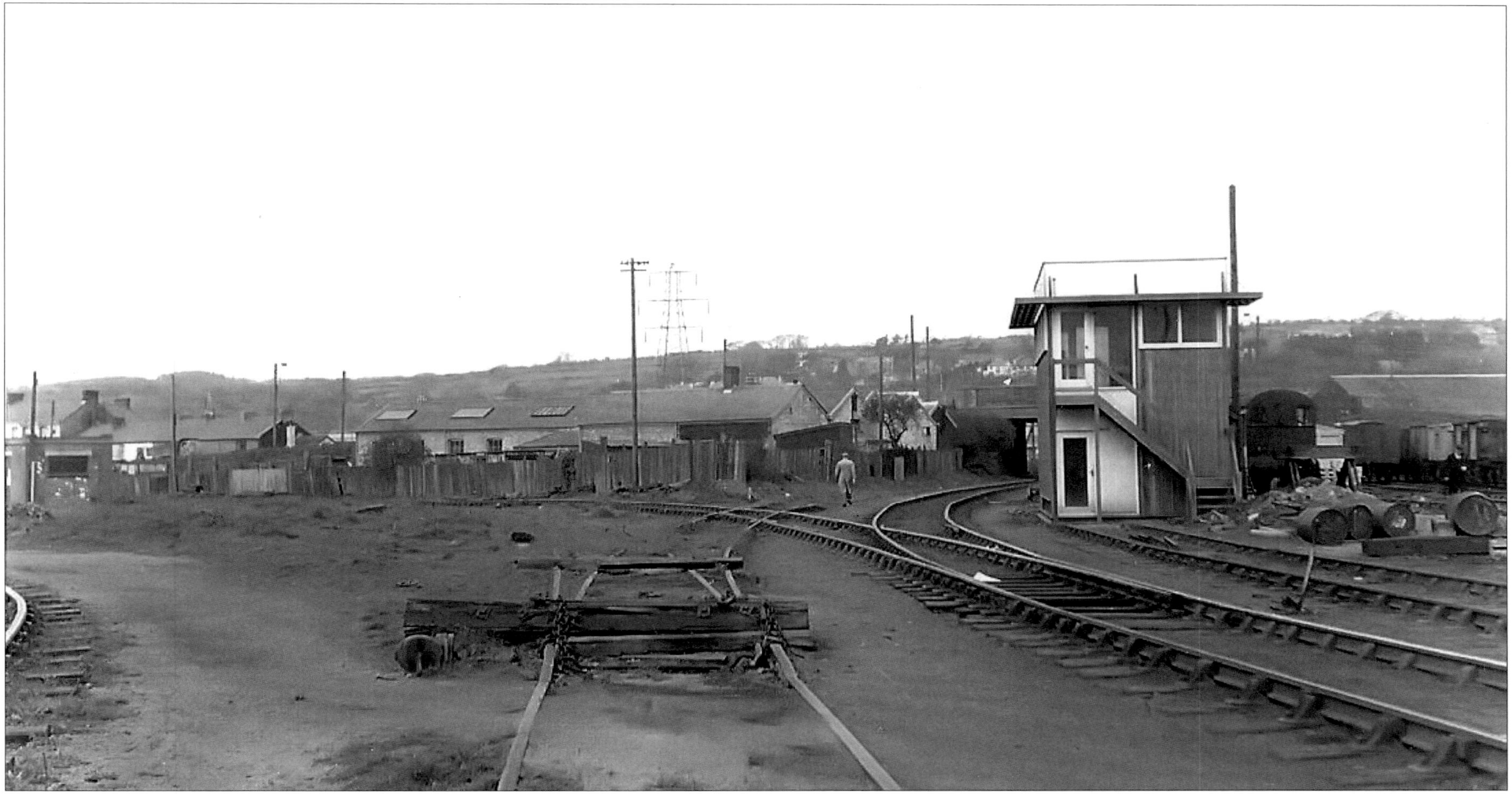

This photograph taken in 1961, is the same location as the previous page but viewed from the opposite direction (looking northward). Sandy Bridge is just visible behind the signal box, and the wagon repair shops owned by Hall Lewis & Co, are on the left, latterly an electrical showroom for Weslec Ltd. The 'new' signal box had been built alongside the Mynydd Mawr railway line to cope with increased traffic to the newly built Cynheidre Colliery. The disused railway line (centre) was privately owned by Mansell-Lewis (Stradey Estate), and originally carried coal from Cille Colliery (Castle Colliery) Furnace, to the North Dock for shipment. Today, the new Llanelli southern by-pass passes over land to the extreme left of this picture, and a cycle path runs along the track-bed of the railway line under Sandy Bridge.

(V. Morgan collection).

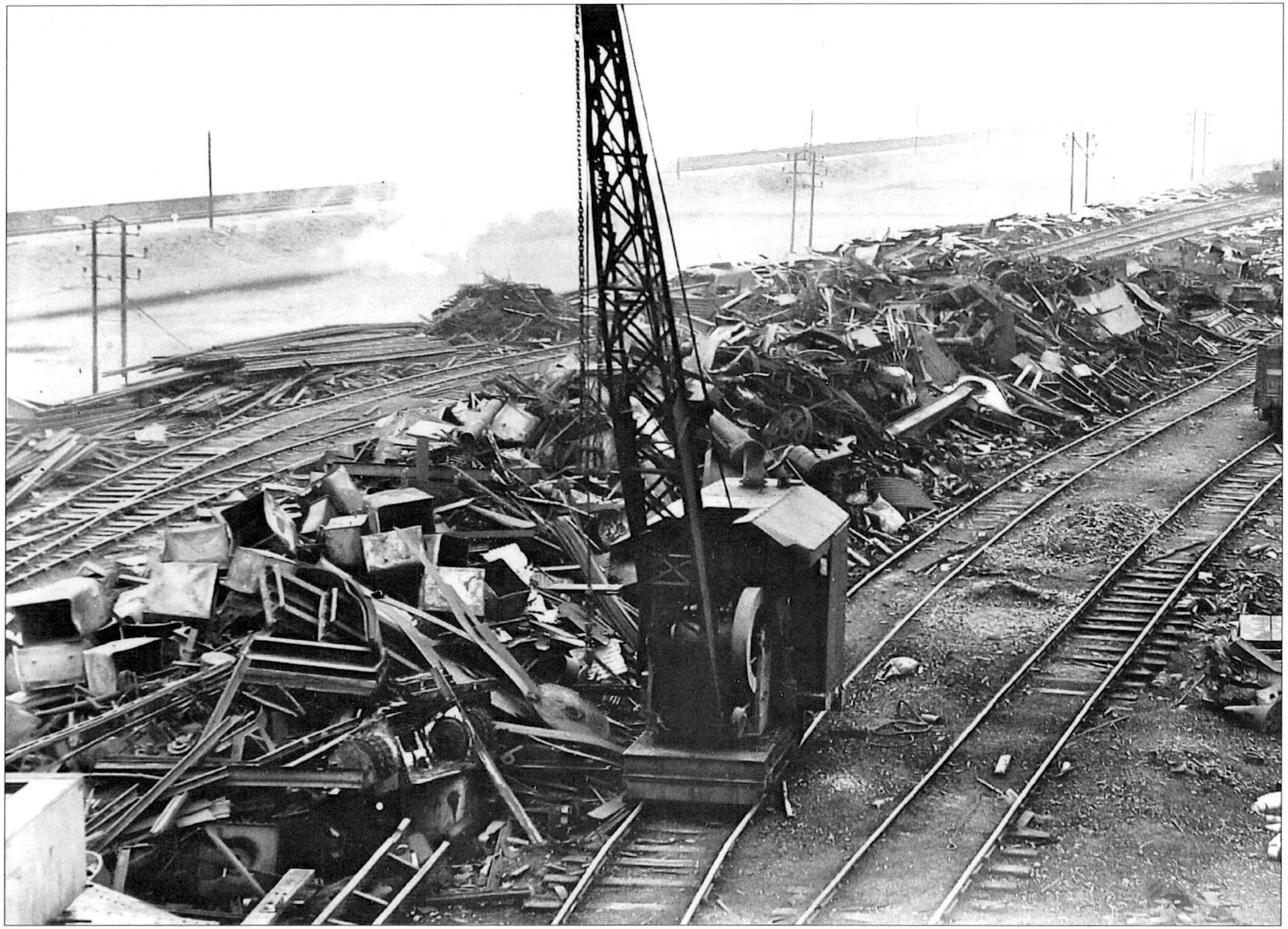

**Metal recycling.**

This unusual type of view, dated 1st. April, 1958, was taken from a lighting tower on the western end of Llanelly Steelworks, and shows the stock of scrap metal on the 'tip'. The 'Thos. Smith' steam crane was used to load scrap metal into railway wagons feeding the open hearth furnaces. The main London to Fishguard railway line built in 1852 is just visible on the embankment in the background, complete with sea wall. This land, all re-claimed from the sea, now forms part of the Festival Fields. The crane named 'Bessie' worked at the steelworks until the works' closure in 1981. It was then donated to the Kidwelly Heritage Centre & Museum Trust.

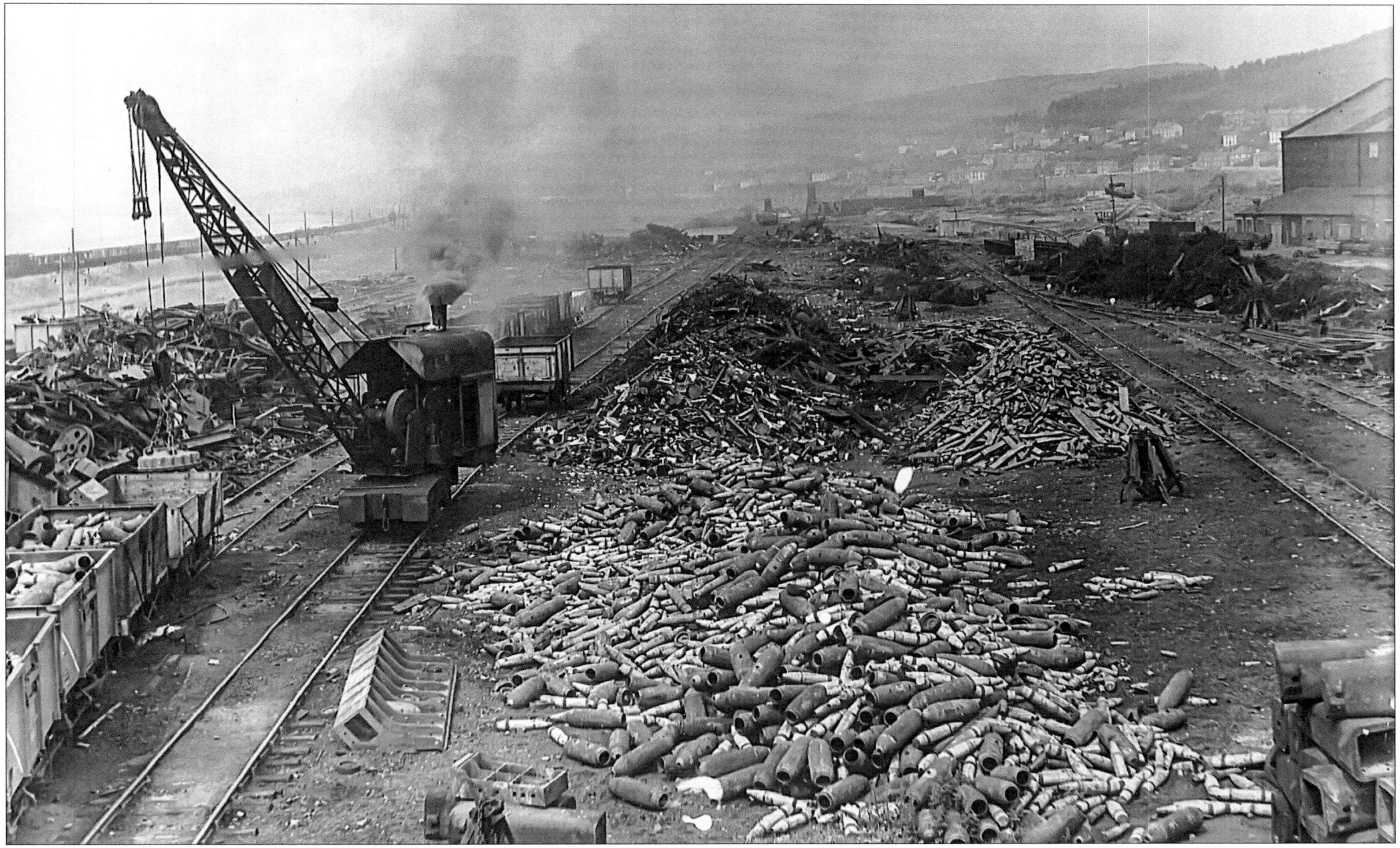

**<u>Steam in action.</u>** A different view of the Llanelly Steelworks 'tip' taken on 1[st]. July, 1958. The coal fired steam crane is working hard loading railway trucks with scrap metal, which includes an estimated 400 tons of empty bombs and shells visible in the foreground. Pwll village is just visible in the background, and the main Fishguard to London railway line is running along the sea wall to the left of this picture, with a freight train heading west.

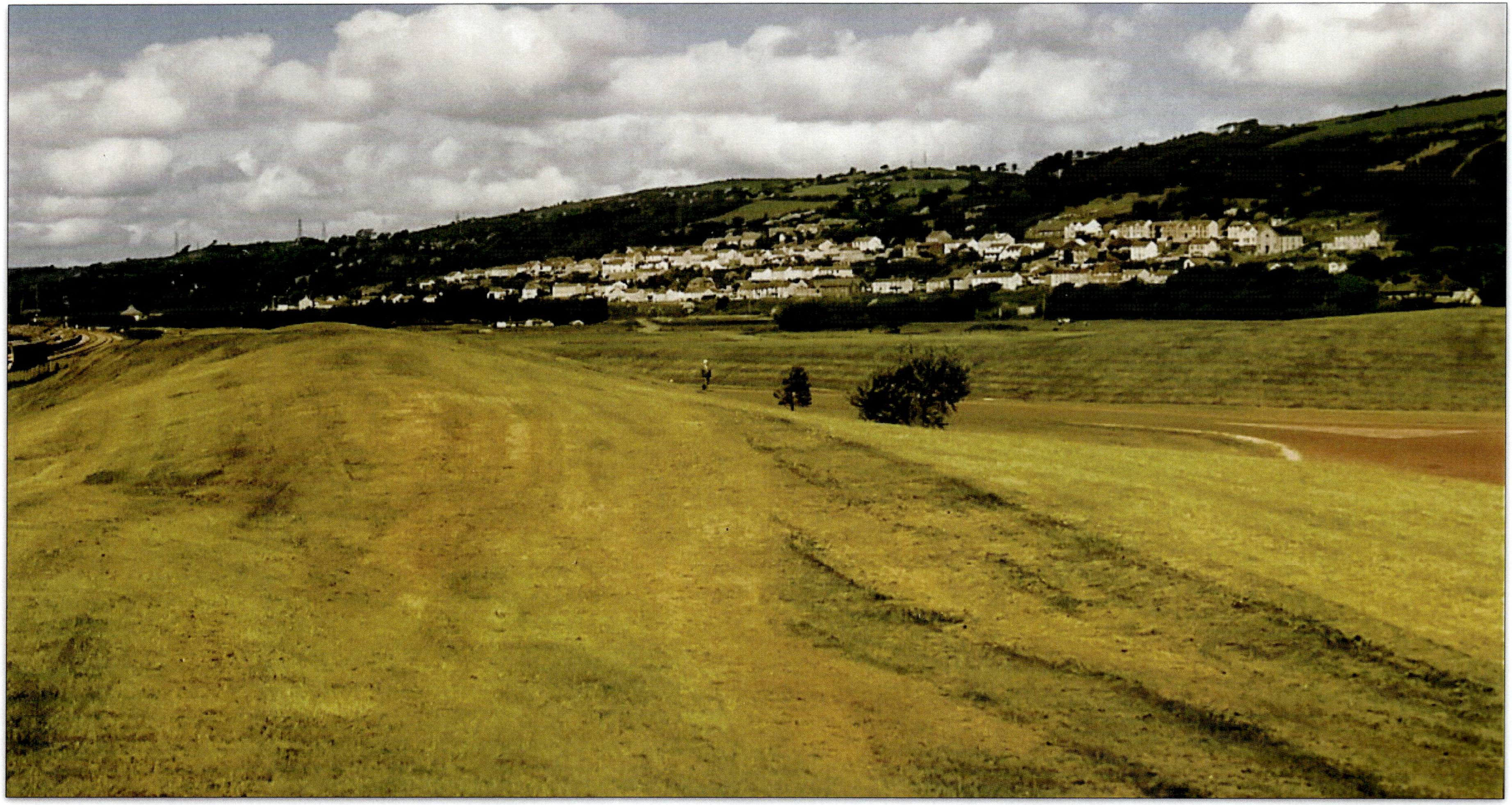

It is hard to imagine how much this area has changed over the last 30 years. This view of the Festival Fields and Millennium coastal path, with Pwll village in the background was taken from the same position as the view on the previous page, some 45 years later in 2003. It is seen, here, complete with a passenger train on the Fishguard - London railway line (left hand side of picture).

(V. Morgan).

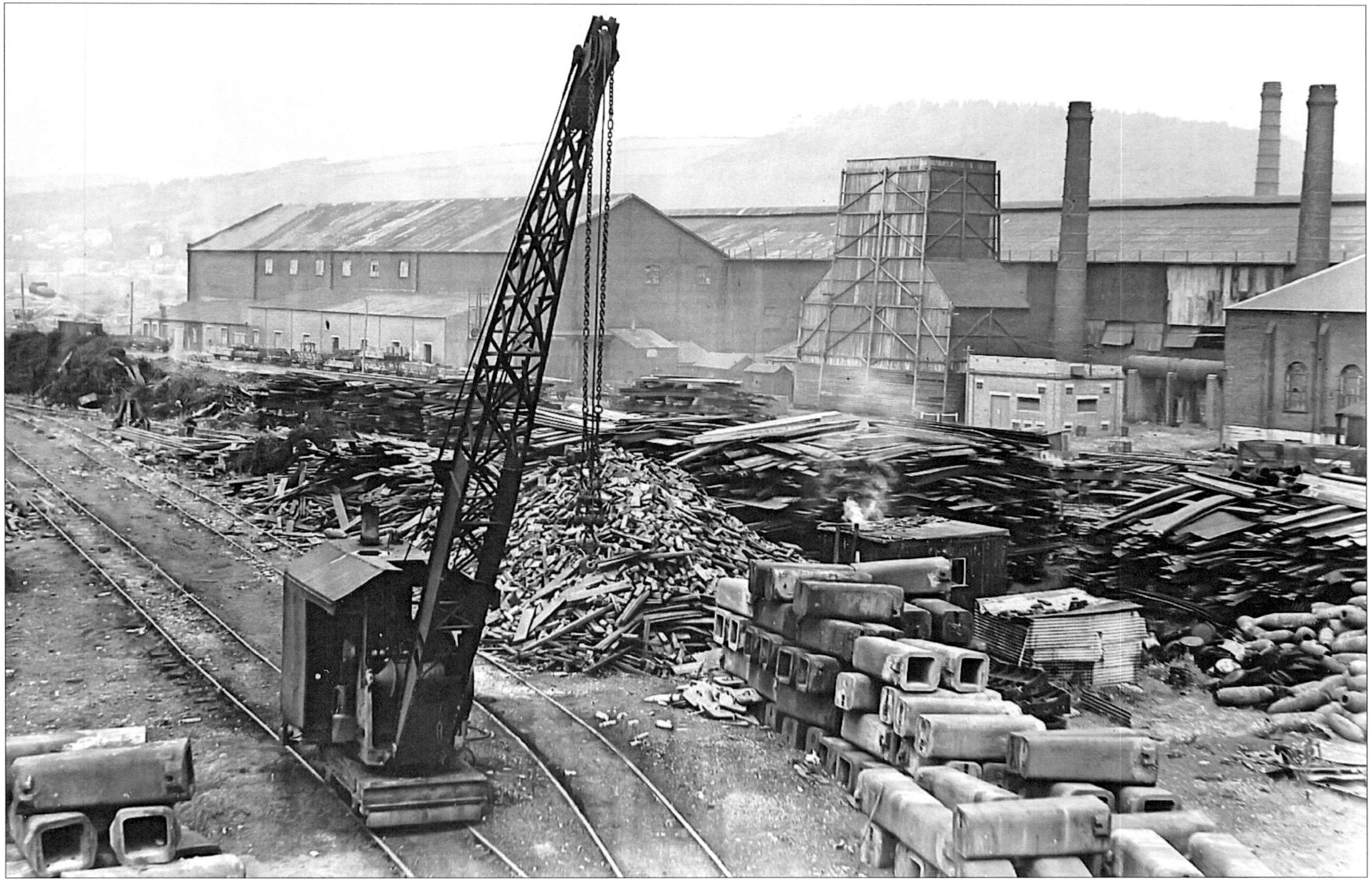

Another view of the steelworks 'tip' taken from a different angle on 1st. July, 1958, shows more bombs and scrap metal, with a stock of ingot moulds in the foreground. The steam crane appears to be idle – the crane men were probably 'brewing up' in their rat infested shanty visible behind the ingot moulds. The buildings in the background built in 1928-32, was Llanelly Sheetworks, known as Sandy sheet works because of its location – Sandy Road. Stradey woods, Pwll village and the Graig are just visible behind the sheet works.

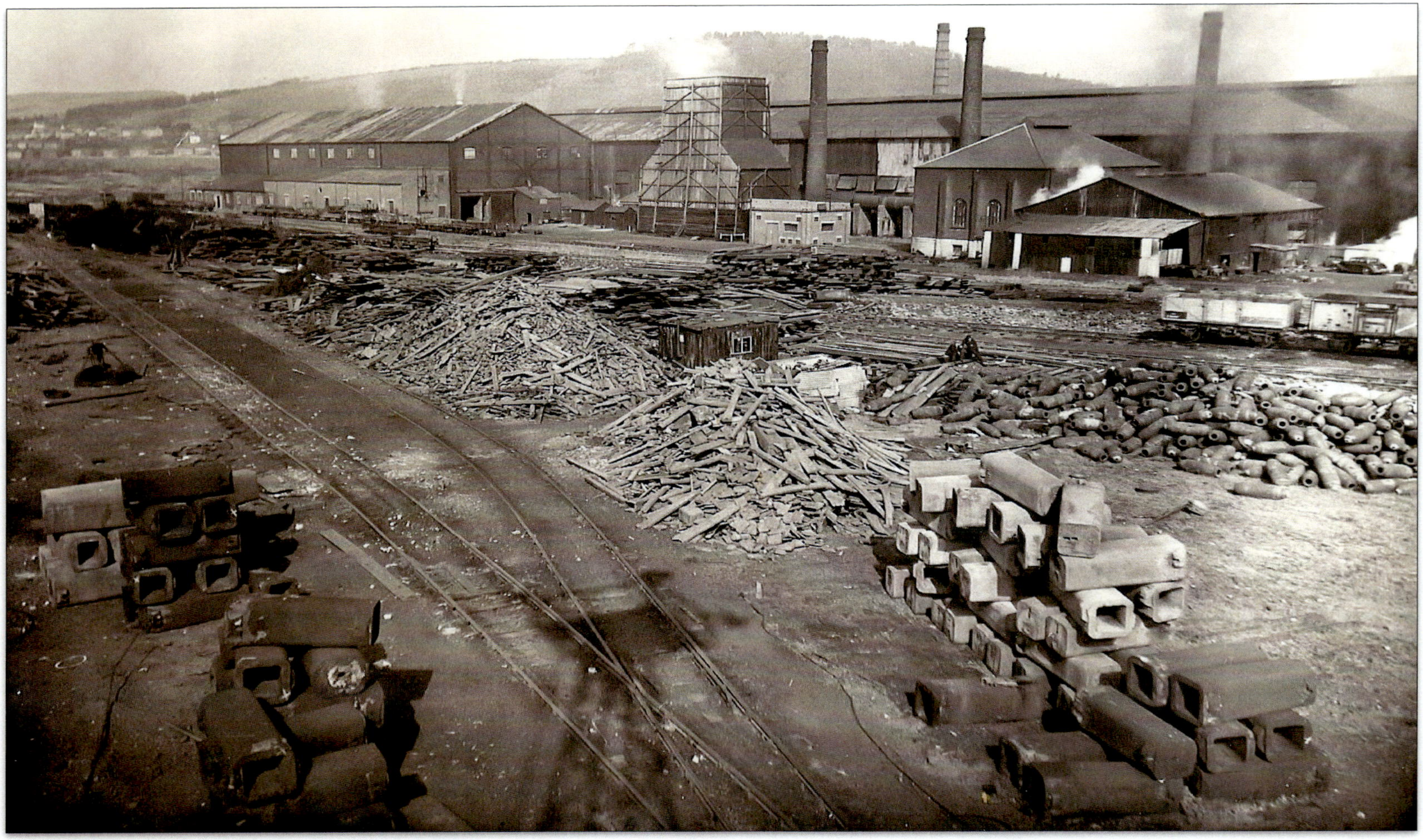

An almost identical view to the previous page, this one was dated 1st April, 1959, and taken from the same lighting tower. The sheet works, in the background, closed down in 1962, and remained partially empty until the mid-1970s when it was renovated and became a mould preparation bay for the new electric arc furnace plant built on this site 1976/7.

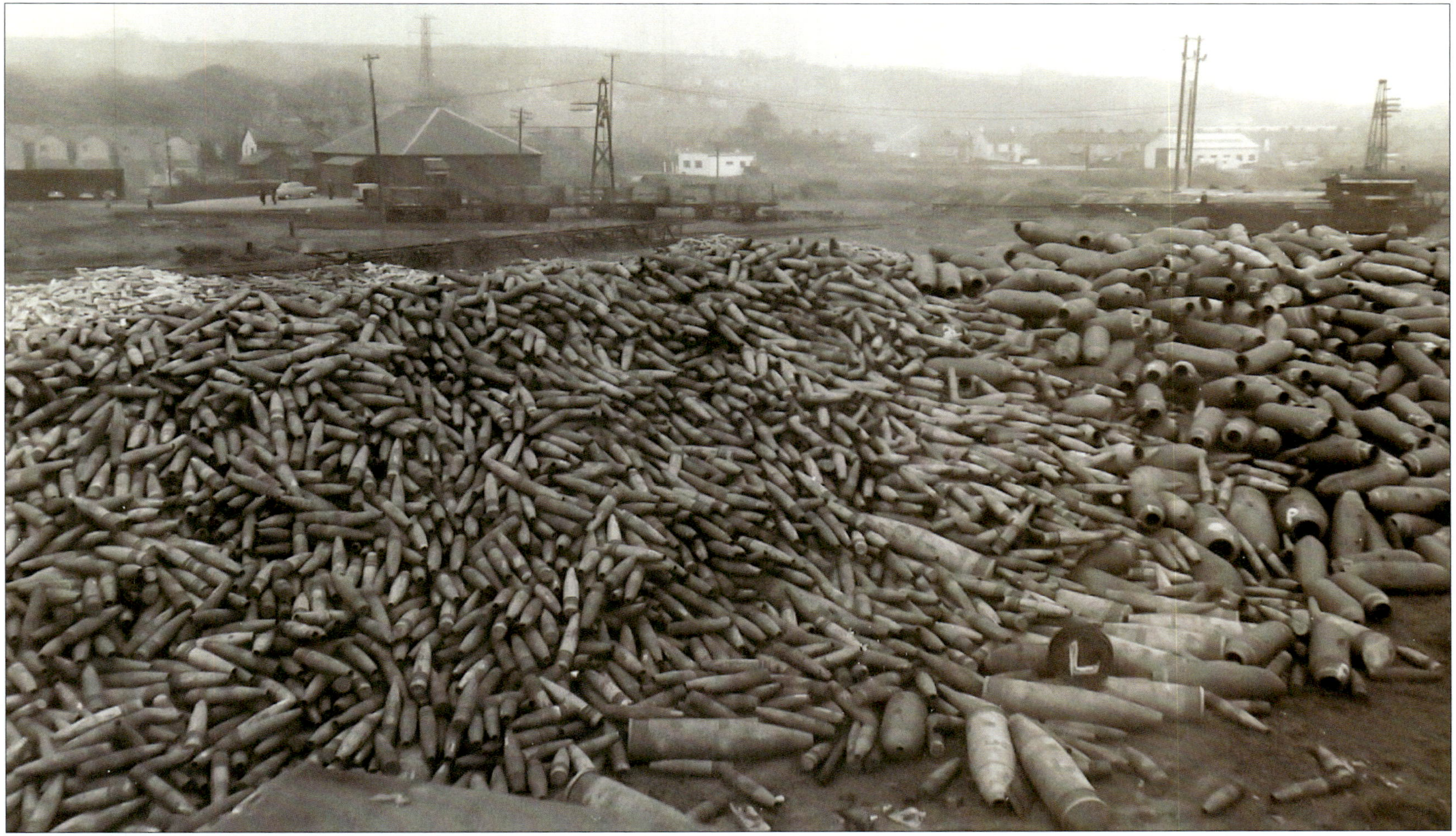

There were an estimated 1,600 tons of empty bombs and shells visible in this picture, taken on the steelworks 'tip' in 1958. The square building, in the centre of this view, was the Sheet-works weighbridge and office. The small white building (centre background) was the ESSO petrol filling station on Sandy Road, occupied by J. E. De-Schoolmeester, and on the right hand side of this view is Denham Garage, then owned by John Evans & Son (Llanelly) Ltd. A photograph of this garage appears on page 76.

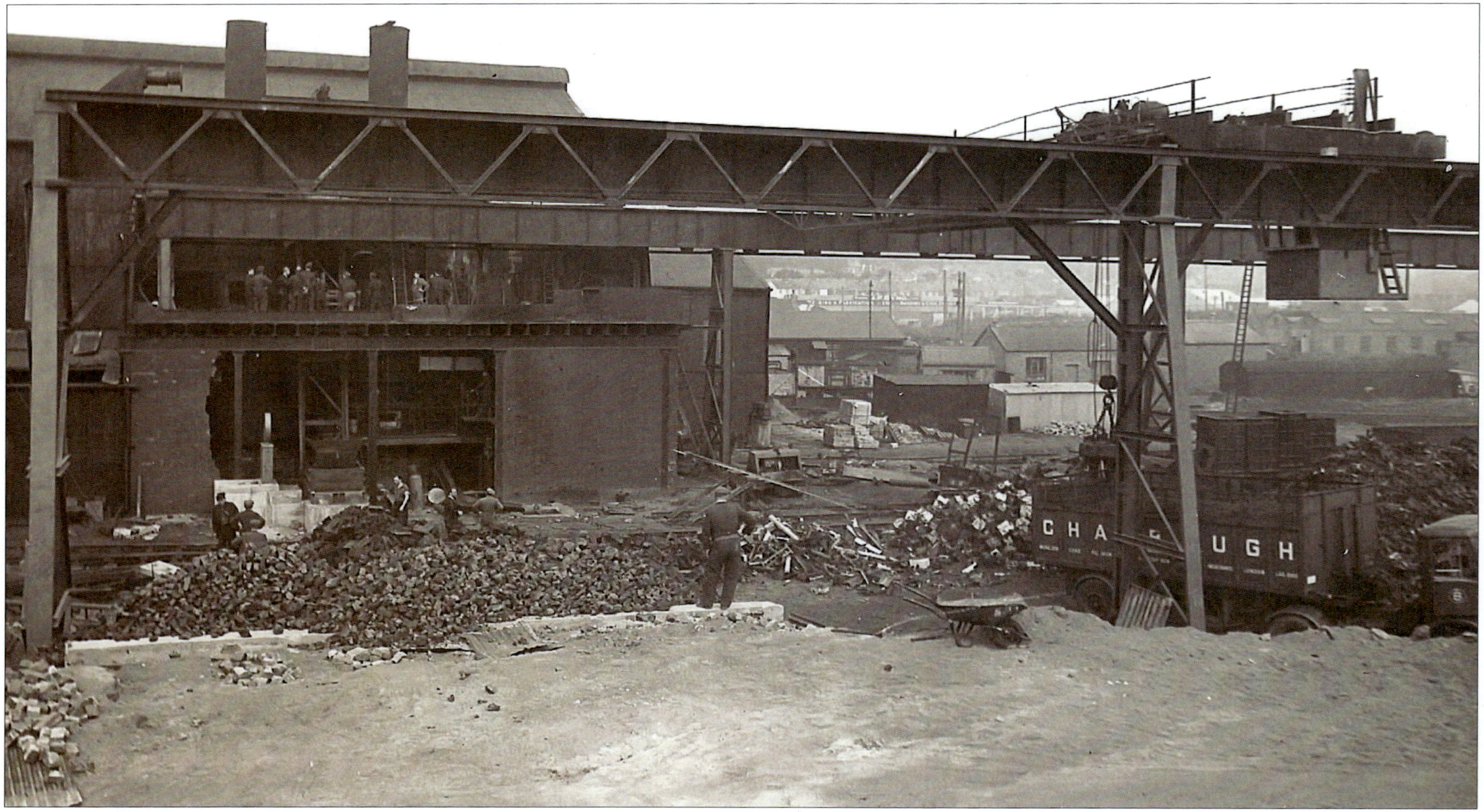


A lorry load of scrap iron is being unloaded here at the Llanelly Foundry, with an overhead 'Gantry' crane. The Llanelly Foundry & Engineering Co. Ltd, a subsidiary of The Llanelly Steel Co (1907) Ltd, was built on steelworks land near Sandy Bridge. They made ingot moulds for the steelworks and produced 'pig iron' from the furnace. The foundry closed down in 1965 after regular complaints about air pollution; and was afterwards used by the steelworks for ingot storage, with the loco shed and transport maintenance workshop moving in to the former machine shop in 1967. Sandy Bridge is located in the right hand background, behind the ladder. To the right of the ladder is the wagon repair works, then owned by Hall-Lewis (nowadays, a skate-board park). After redevelopment of this land in more recent years, the Sandpiper Restaurant has been built here, on the site previously occupied by the overhead crane.

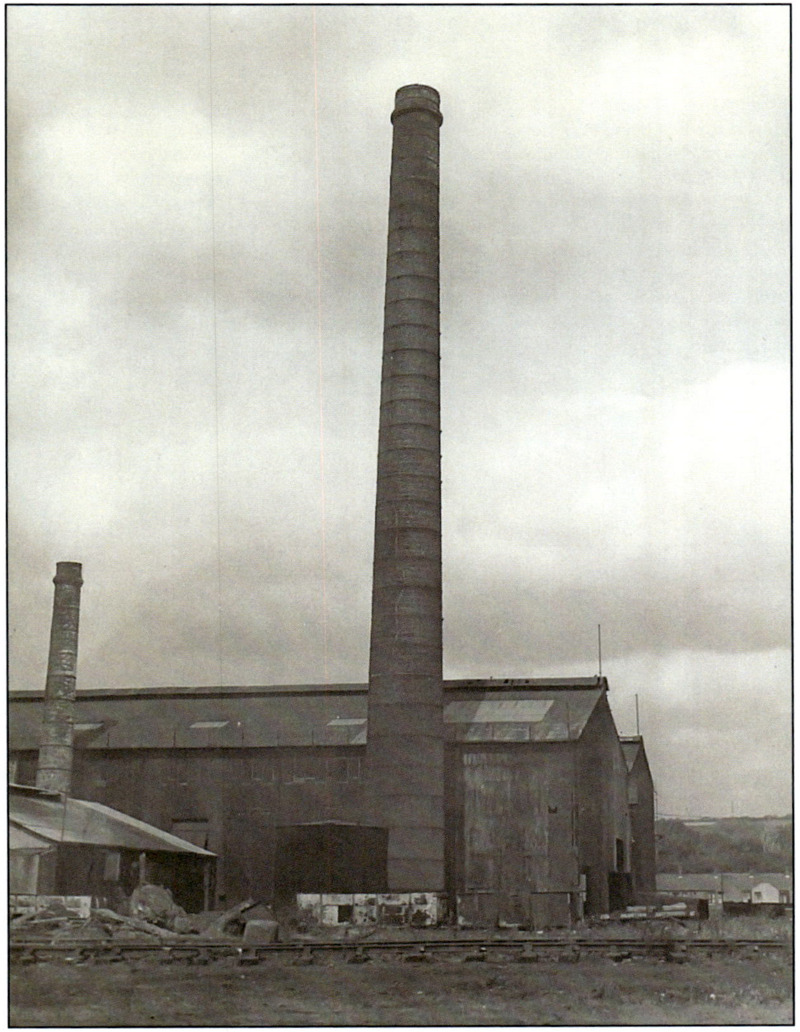

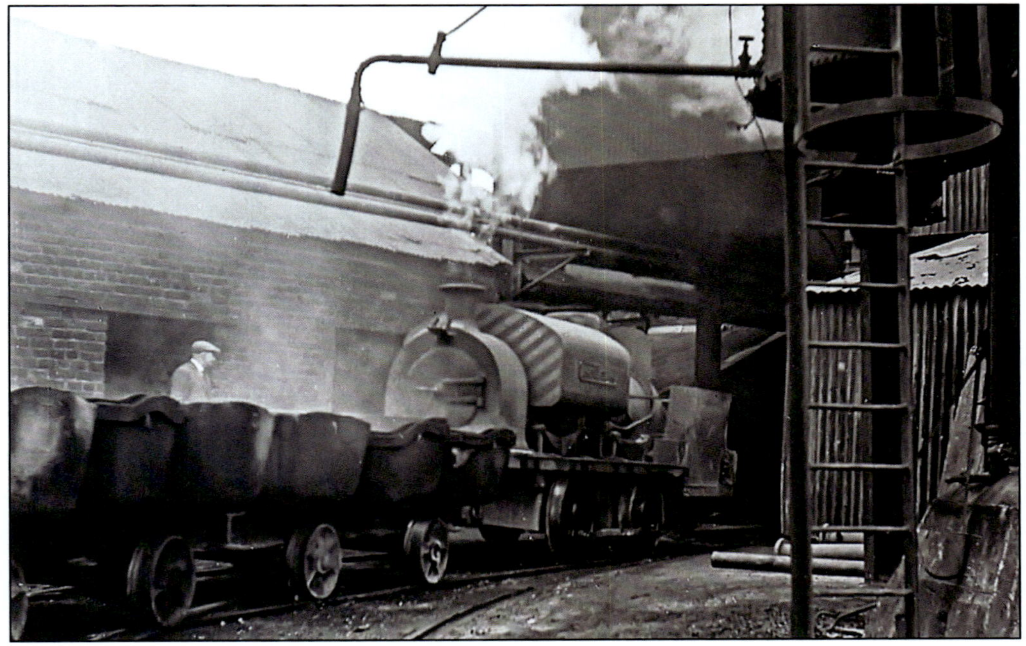

**Above:** Llanelly Steelworks operated numerous steam locomotives throughout the years before modernising to diesel locos in later days. In 1912, a pair of Andrew Barclay 0-4-0 locos were specially built to the steelworks' specification – built to a low overall height with no drivers cab, just an open footplate. They worked in restricted headroom hauling these trolleys loaded with boxes full of scrap metal into the melting shop (furnaces). The locos passed within inches of the furnace doors, where each box of scrap would be emptied in turn into the furnace by means of a mechanically operated machine called a charger. This loco 'Lindsey' is pictured here, outside the melting shop bringing out a load of empty boxes ready for refilling with scrap metal.

**Left:** The tallest chimney stack of Sandy sheet-works was brick built to a height of 160 feet. Note that part of Sandy road is visible in the background of this view taken in 1964.

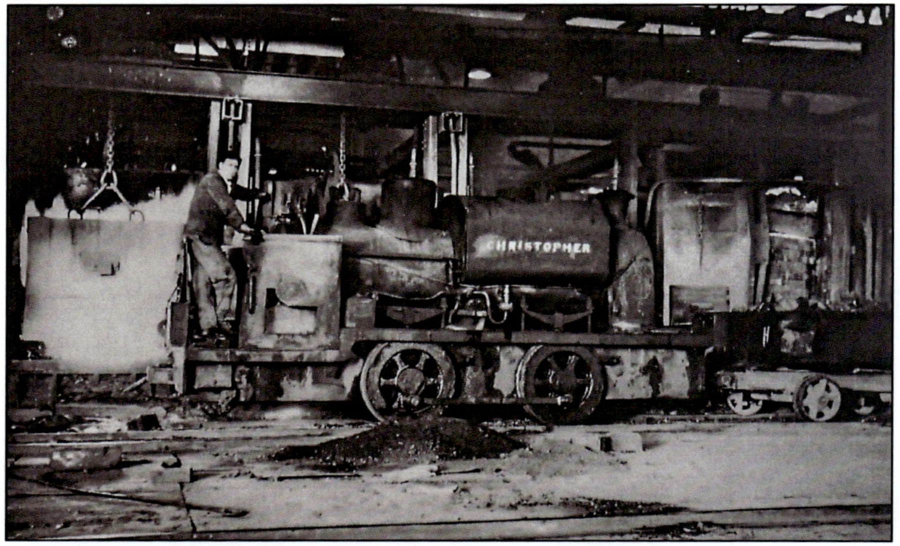


**Left:** 'Christopher' was the last brand new steam loco purchased by Llanelly Steelworks in 1956. It had a comparatively short working life, being withdrawn in 1968 and laid up until the chief engineer, W.S. Van-Arkle (Bill Van-Arkle) himself a steam enthusiast decided to have it overhauled and reinstated. New boiler tubes were fitted, but the boiler failed its re-certification test in 1969, and was subsequently scrapped after delivery of two new diesel locos. 'Christopher' is captured, here, at the melting shop, working in front of a furnace that was going full blast- note the flames passing the furnace door on the left! I wonder what the health and safety executive would say if these working practices existed today. It would all be closed down, especially if they saw a bricklayer standing on top of a furnace roof, plugging a hole in the roof whilst the furnace was still going full blast. Some people call it 'the good old days of the steelworks'. What was good about all those safety issues?

(V. Morgan collection).

**Right**: As a point of interest, all the steelworks locos were named after company directors children. However, after 55 years of 'yeoman' service, working three shifts per day in the steelworks, the two steam locos 'Lindsey' and 'Nora' await their fate – the breakers torch. Here, they were captured outside the steelworks' loco shed, situated at the old Llanelly Foundry site in 1969. This view was taken by the author a day before their scrapping. The building on the left, constructed from timber was originally the foundry office, and was used as an archive by Duport Steelworks. It was completely gutted by a fire in January 1982, losing all the company's records.

(V. Morgan).

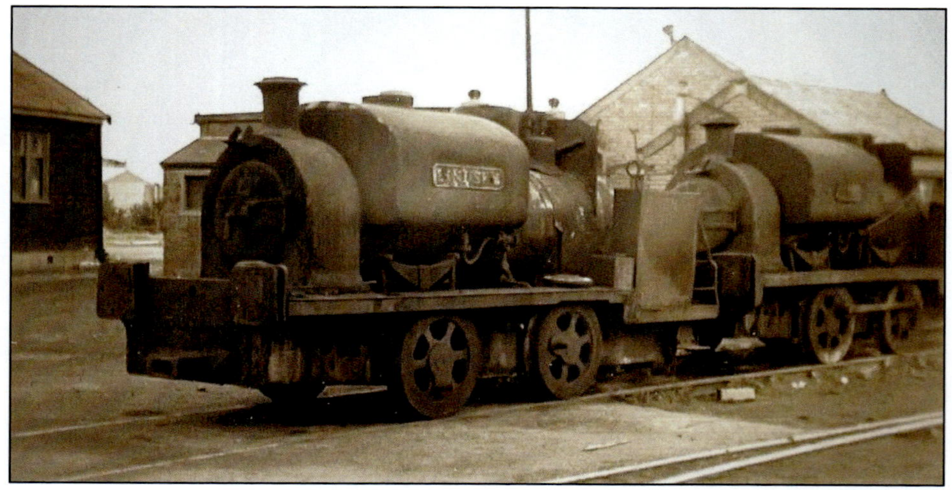

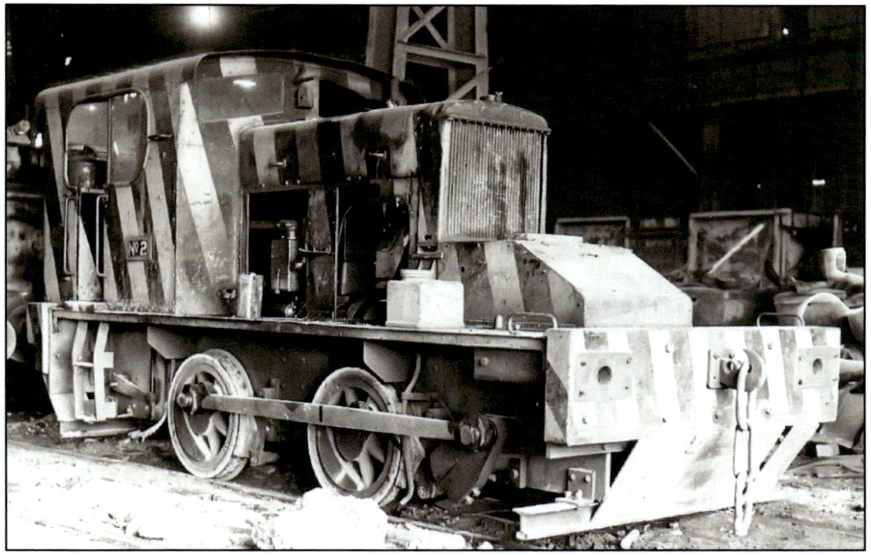

**Left:** New to the Royal Ordnance Factory at Pembrey, this 1939 Fowler 80hp diesel-mechanical loco, only worked for a short while in Duport Steelworks, in 1969. It was involved in a fatal accident and subsequently withdrawn.

(V. Morgan collection).

**Right:** Far superior to the Fowler and Ruston–Hornsby diesel locos used in the steelworks melting shop in the late 1960s, were a pair of 95hp Clayton diesel–hydraulic locos, specially built to meet the company's requirements, working in front of the furnaces They were built in 1969 as replacements for the steamers that had worked in front of the furnaces. 'Clayton' No. 2 is pictured, here, outside the loco shed in 1970, having received its weekly maintenance; done on a Saturday afternoon when the furnaces were closed down for maintenance.

(V. Morgan).

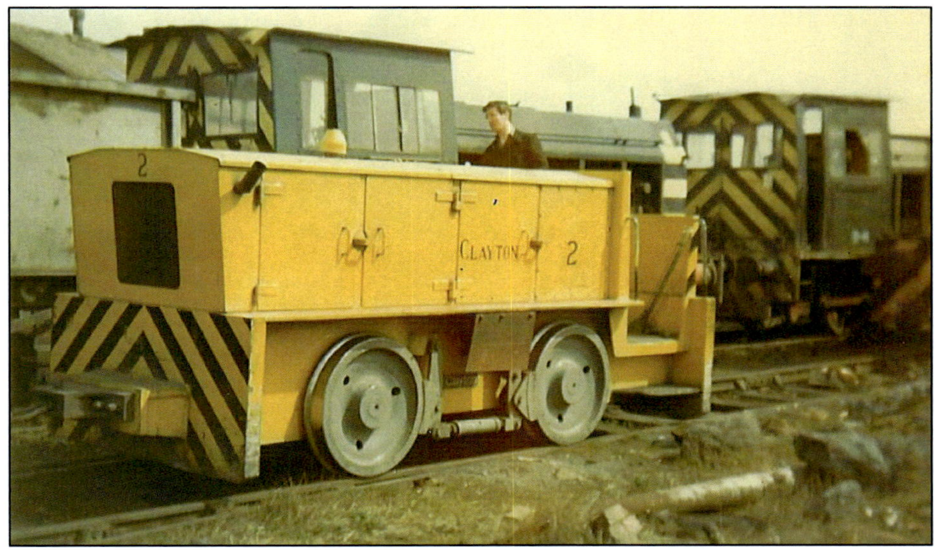

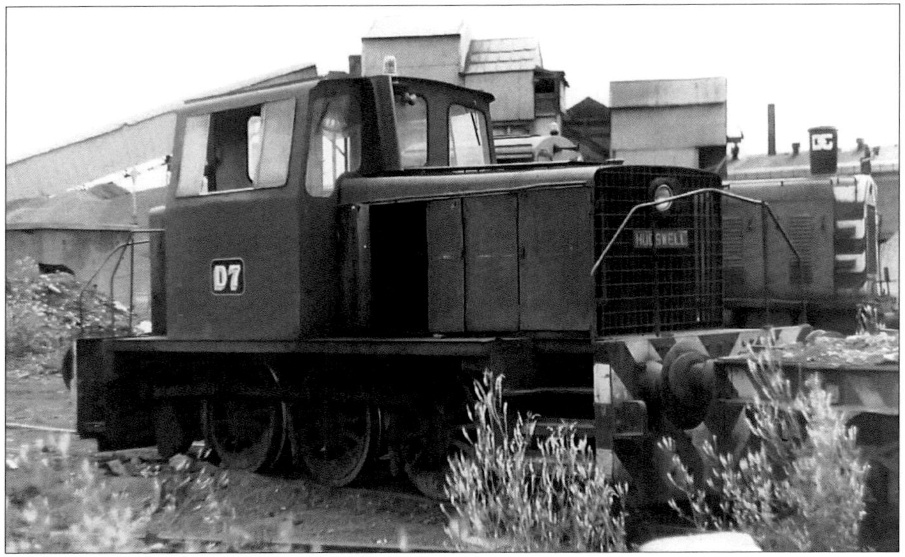


**Left:** Awaiting its fate after Duport Steelworks' closure in 1981, is this Hudswell-Clarke diesel-hydraulic loco (D7) pictured here at the Slag Reduction Company's yard, which was part of the steelworks land. This area of land, now redeveloped, is where the lake of Sandy Water Park is situated, along with Curlew Close.

(V. Morgan).

**Right:** A sad end; two of Duport Steelworks' locos being cut up for scrap in July 1981, at the mould preparation bay (formerly Sandy Sheetworks). Their Gardner 8L3 engines (straight 8 cylinder, 204hp) were sold at £1,000 each and exported along with 8 others to Hong Kong where they were fitted into fishing boats. Other makes of loco engines, Cummins and Dorman were unsaleable.

(V. Morgan).

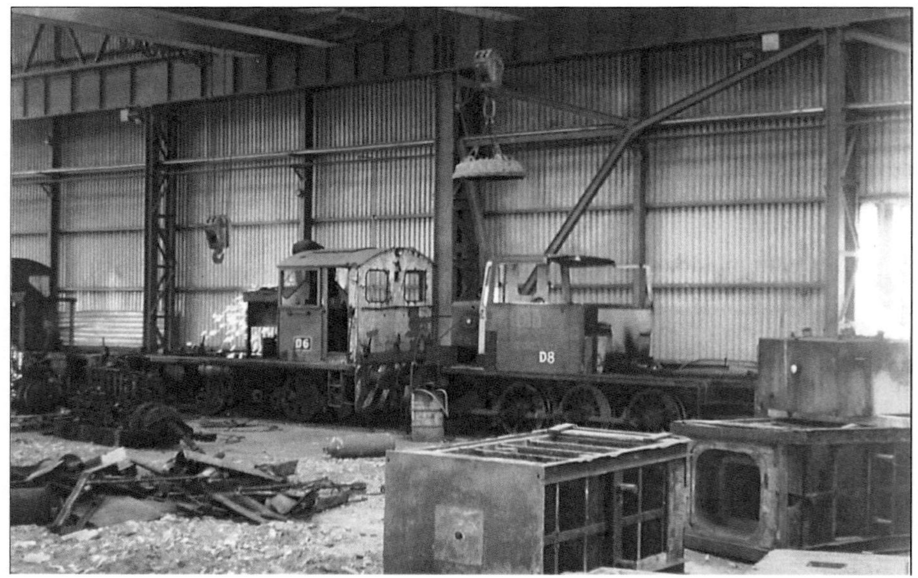

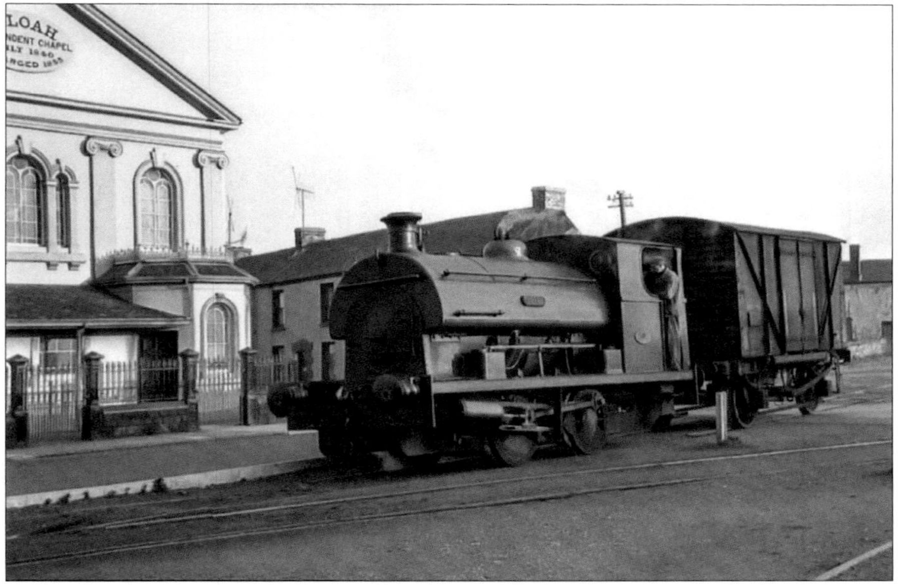

**Left:** This Peckett steam loco, named 'Betty', was owned by the Nevills Dock & Railway Co. Ltd, Llanelly; proprietors of the Copperworks, Nevill Druce & Co. It is captured drawing a goods van over the unmanned level crossing at the junction of Copperworks Road, Glanmor Road and Marine Street, passing Siloah Chapel in the Seaside district of Llanelli. There were a network of tram-roads in this area of Llanelli, linking up all the heavy industries of the town. This particular privately-owned branch line, ran along Glanmor Road in front of the houses (which was common place), to the Wern area of Llanelli, serving the Bres Pit; South Wales Pottery; Gas Works; Nevills Foundry; Waddles Foundry; Wern Ironworks; Llanesco's tram depot; Old Lodge and Marshfield tinplate works, and the Glanmor Foundry. The system closed in 1969. However, it requires a little imagination, nowadays, to consider the hazards of these locomotives trundling through the town's streets!

(T. S. Powell collection).

**Right**: Another view of Siloah Chapel from a different angle shows the South Wales Transport bus crossing the same junction at Glanmor Road and Copperworks Road in 1969, after the railway crossing had been removed.

(V. Morgan collection).

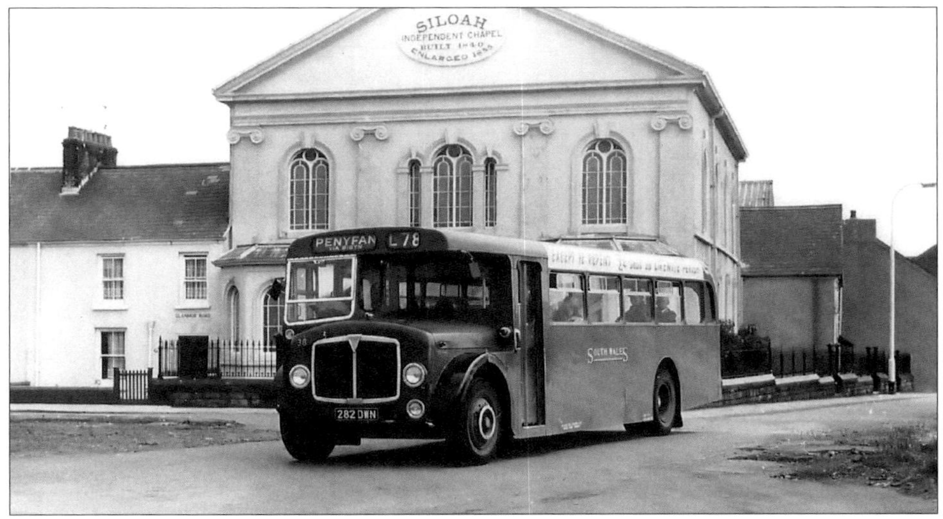

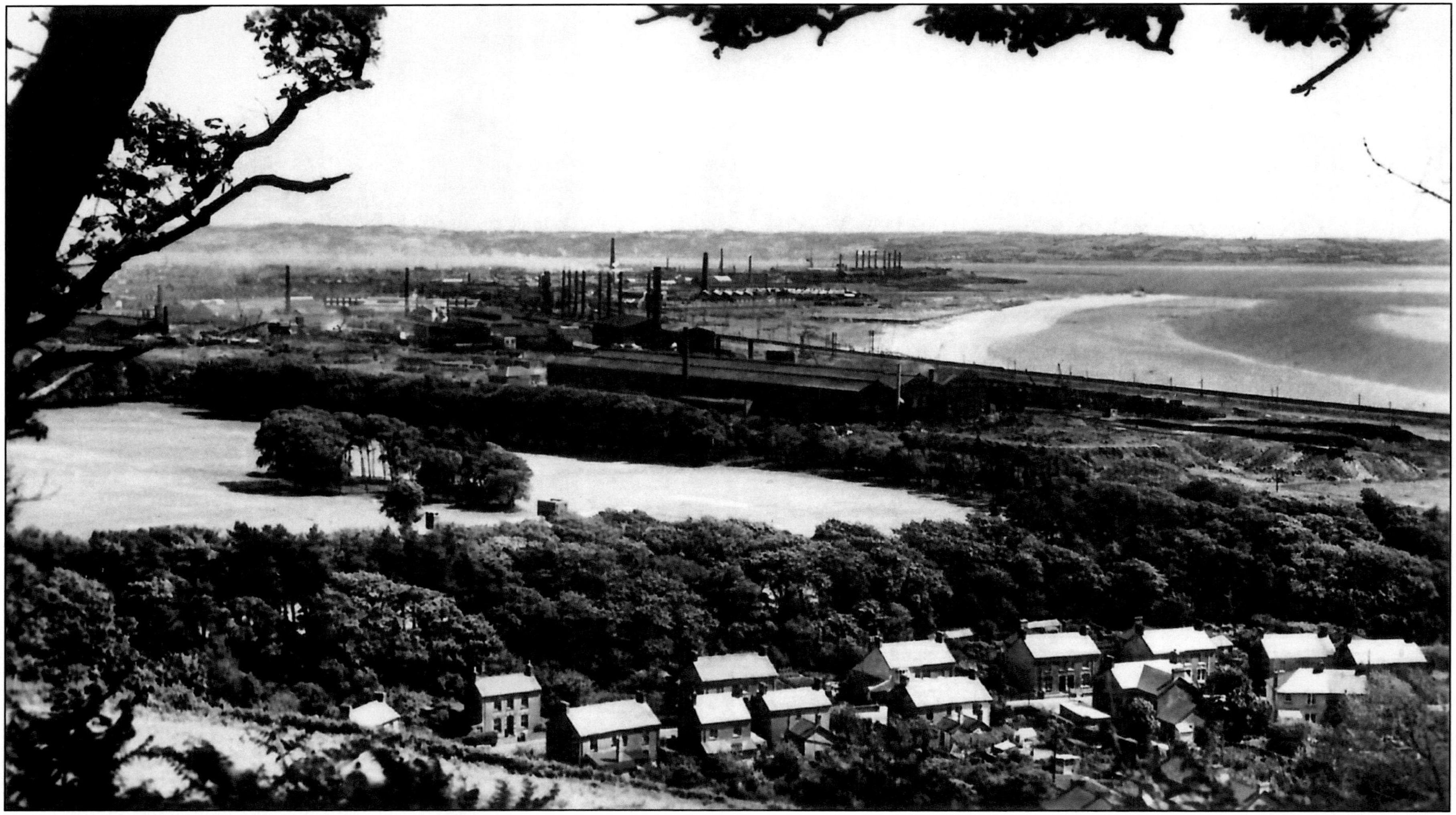

The sky-line of south Llanelli has certainly changed since this photograph was taken in the late 1940s. The view was taken from The Graig in Pwll, with Stepney Road in the foreground, before the boys Grammar School was built (now Coleg Sir Gar, Graig Campus). All the works visible in the background have since disappeared, the area now forming part of Llanelli's Festival fields and Millennium Coastal Path. The works visible in this view are: Llanelly Sheetworks; Llanelly Steelworks; Llanelly Foundry & Engineering Co; Old Castle Tinplate works; Pemberton Tinplate works; Copperworks; Glanmor Foundry; Llanelly Power-station; South Wales Steelworks (Morewoods); Batchelor Robinson metals; Burry Works; Morfa Tinplate works, and Machynys Foundry.

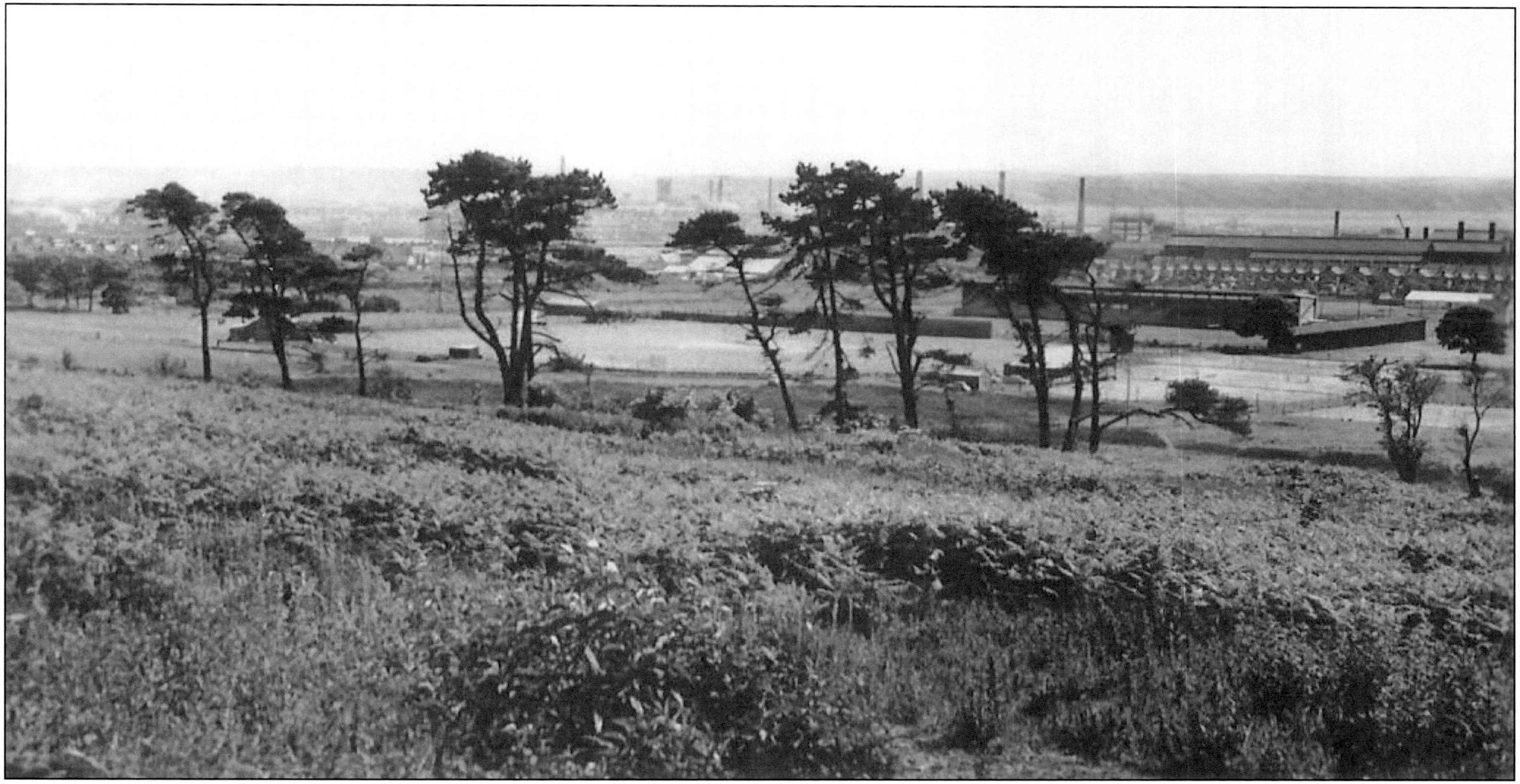

Stradey Park rugby ground Llanelli, is viewed here from Cwmbach Road during the late 1940's, long before St. Margaret's Drive was built.
Sandy Road is the row of houses just visible behind the rugby ground's only stand, and the roof of Llanelly Foundry can be seen just behind Sandy Road.

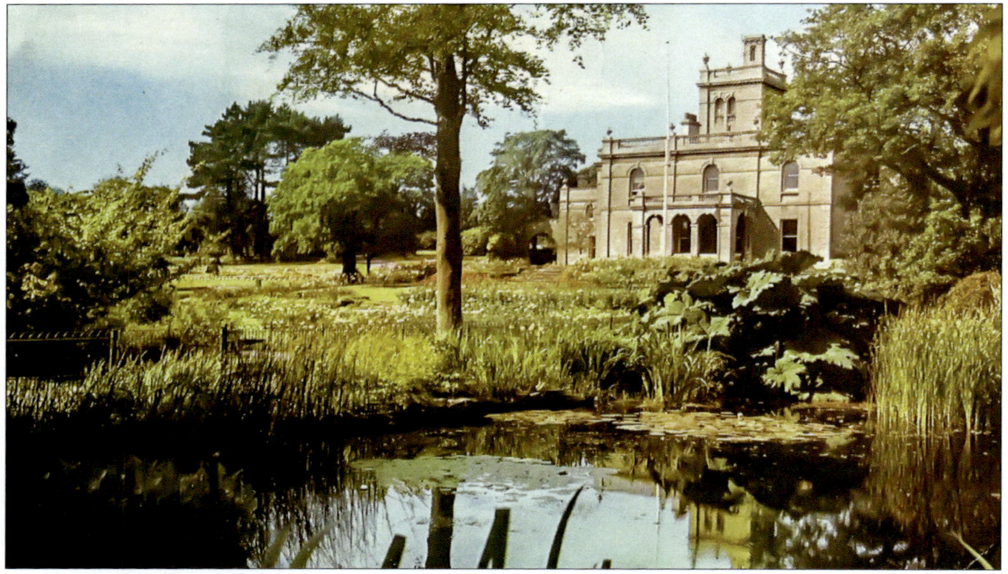

**Left:** The Mansion House at Park Howard, Llanelli, was built from Bath stone in 1882-6. This 18[th] century 'Italianate' architecture country house was originally named Bryncaerau Castle, and stood in its own 24 acres of land. Bryncaerau was the home of Sir Stafford and Lady Howard–Stepney. Sir Stafford had married Miss Stepney, daughter of the famous Stepney family in September 1911. However, after the death of Lady Howard-Stepney, Llanelli Borough Council acquired the whole estate, converting the Mansion House into a Museum and the 24 acres into a civic park.

(V. Morgan collection).

**Right:** This view of Llanelli's 'Intermediate School' was taken during Victorian times, circa 1896. The school situated in Marble Hall Road, close to the junction with Alban Road, later became Llanelly Boys Grammar School, ending its days as part of Llanelli Technical College, latterly C.C.T.A. After demolition of the site in more recent times, a new housing development has been built there. Note the absence of houses in the foreground. The houses built later (on the green), formed part of Marble Hall Road.

(V. Morgan collection).

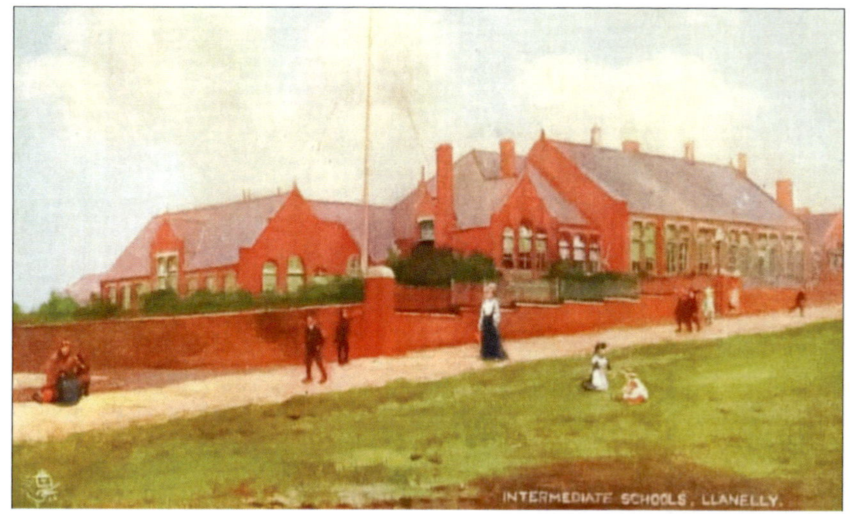

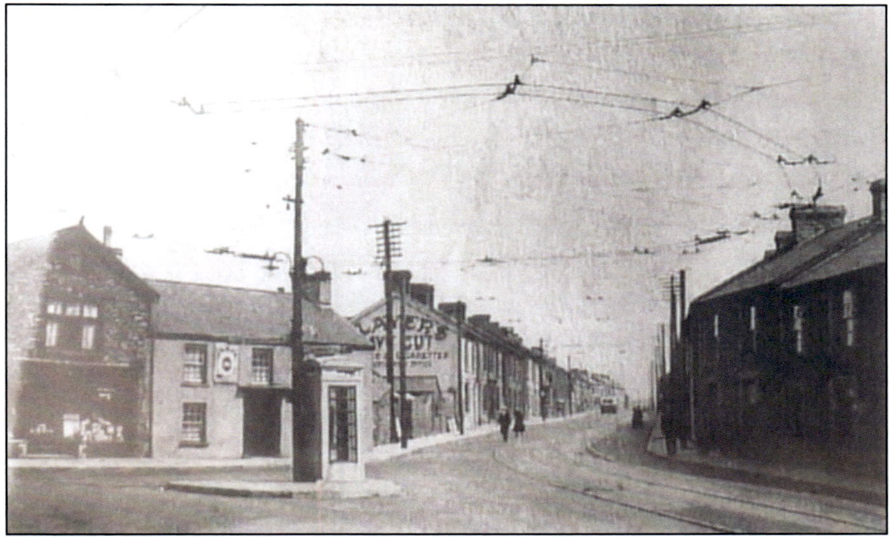

**Left:** Pemberton Square has altered a little since this photograph was taken in the 1930s. The shop on the left, and the Pemberton Arms (next door), are now private residences. The tramlines and electric overhead lines have gone, along with the telephone box. Now there is a set of traffic lights to control the traffic. Worthy of note, is the trolleybus overhead, wiring in the shape of a turning circle. This was the terminus for trolleybuses on the Llanelli Station to Pemberton route.

(V. Morgan collection).

**Right:** The village of Furnace obtained its name from the 'iron furnaces' built here in the hamlet, at Cwmddyche in 1793. The Cwmddyche Iron Furnaces, built by John Givers and Thomas Ingman, were sold to industrialist Alexander Raby in 1796. In this postcard view of Furnace village, taken around 1900, the square is quite prominent, along with Old Road leading away in the background; Stradey Road is in the foreground; New Road to the right and Ynys-y-cwm Road to the left, but there is a vast absence of houses in the area.

(V. Morgan collection).

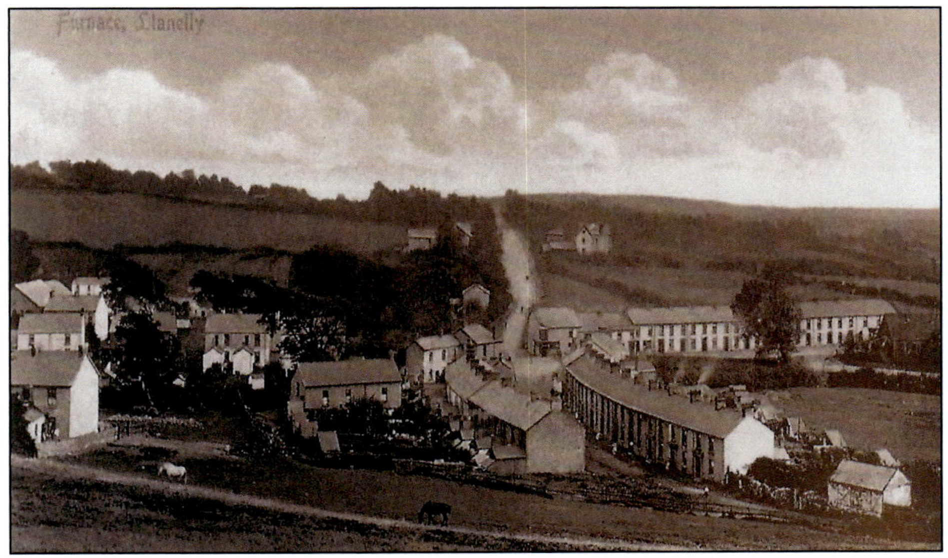

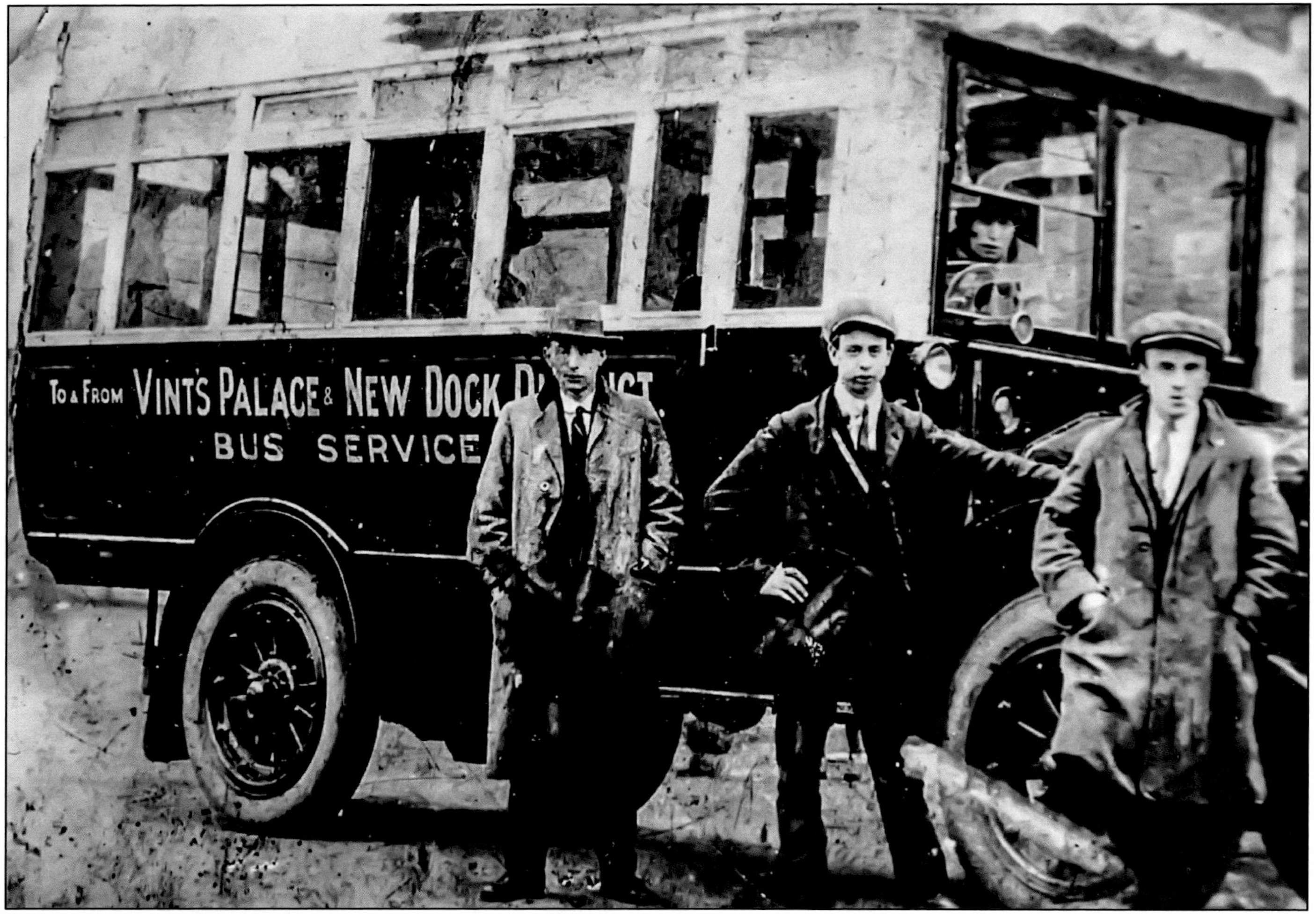


George Frederick Austin (left), of 15/16 Havelock St, New Dock Llanelli, was the owner of this Garford 20 seat bus. Mr. Austin, who also owned a bakery in Havelock St., began operating a bus service from the New Dock district; Morfa, Machynys and Bwlch-y-gwynt via Seaside to Llanelli in 1920, first of all using cars. The cars were run on an hourly service from 5.30am to 5.00pm, and then half hourly in the evening until 10.45pm. The minimum fare was 2d, and the fare from Bwlch-y-gwynt was 4d. Terminus of the service was the Vint's Palace Cinema, at the junction of Market St., Pottery St., Murray St., and Stepney Place (where St. Elli shopping centre is now located). One car owned by Mr. Austin, an American 'Bethlehem' 20hp of 1919, was converted into a charabanc during 1920, enabling the carriage of goods and passengers. In those days, it was commonplace to name the charabancs, and Mr. Austin named his 'The Lark'. A short while later, a proper bus (the Garford pictured here) was purchased, built on a surplus W.W.1 American lorry chassis. Continuing with the bakery business, Mr Austin sold the bus in 1922 along with the passenger service to James Donoghue of Llanelli, who quickly sold it to H. G. Sage of Burry Port. Sage, assisted by members of his family, continued the licensed service unchallenged until 1927, when Gimblett Motors obtained a licence for the same route, resulting in fierce competition. However, in 1936, Gimblett, and later Sage, sold their services and vehicles to The Llanelly & District Traction Co, the trolleybus undertaking. Sage then reverted to tours and private hire, operating from his garage at Burry Port (see pages 43-5).

(V. Morgan collection).

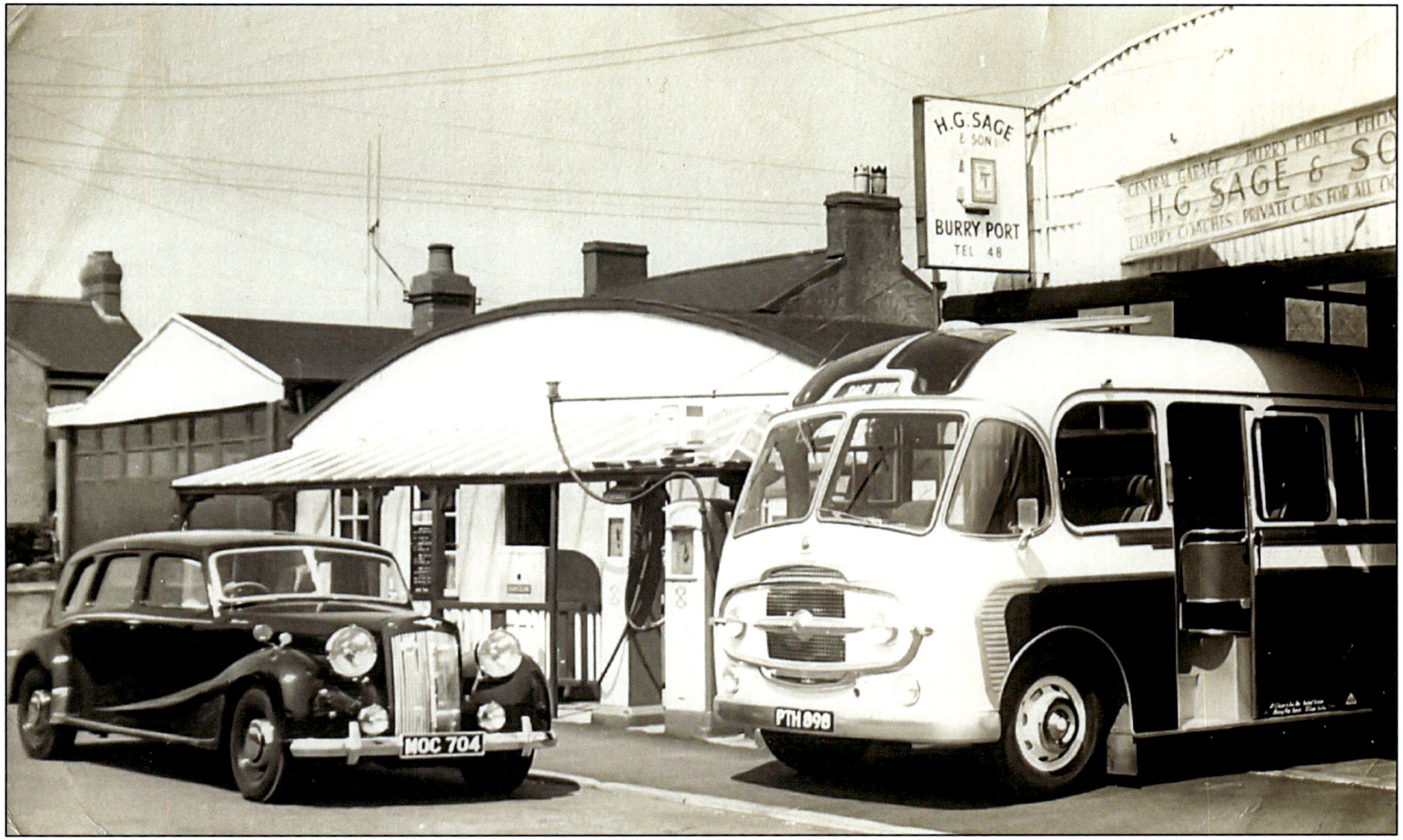


Henry George Sage was a Cornish man, and started a haulage business in Burry Port, soon after W.W.1 ended. In 1922, Sage bought his first bus (pictured on opposite page) from G. F. Austin (via. James Donoghue), together with a service from Llanelli (Vint's Palace Cinema) to New Dock and Bwlch-y-gwynt. Plagued with on-going problems, some self-inflicted, he sold the service to Llanelly & District Traction Co, in 1936, (the Trolley-bus undertaking) and continued with touring coaches and cars from his garage, pictured here, at Sea-view Terrace, Burry Port. Sage's house was the rounded roof building located between his two garages, complete with two petrol pumps selling Regent petrol over the forecourt. The limousine is an Austin Sheerline, complete with massive P100 headlamps. The coach is a rare Plaxton 'Embassy' bodied Bedford SB3, with a petrol engine that ticked over like a watch. Sage's vehicles were always in pristine condition.

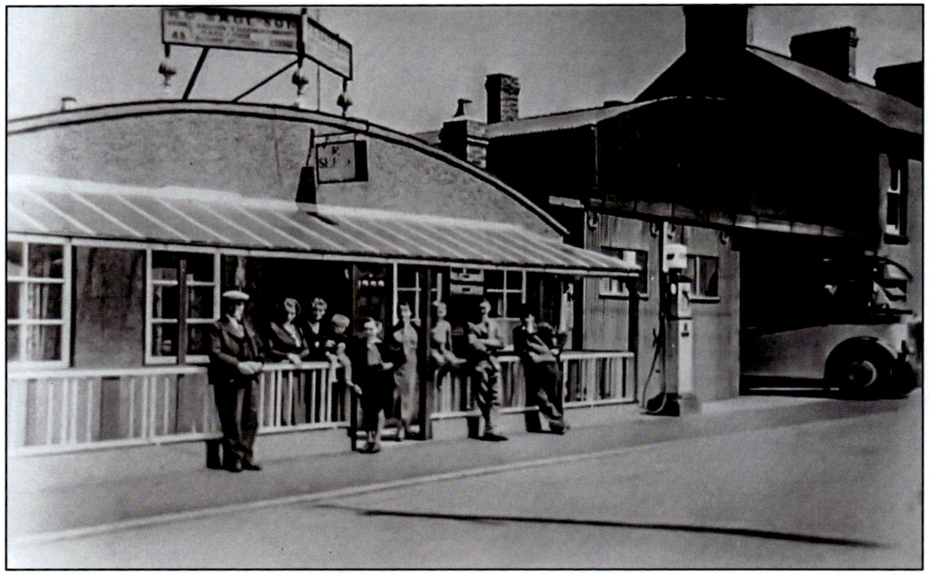

**Left**: This view of H. G. Sage's premisses was taken in the late 1930s, with one of his coaches parked in the garage entrance. This is a family photograph, with Mr. Sage standing nearest the camera.

**Below:** The ticket pictured below, is an eight-penny return ticket, issued by Sage on his New Dock to Llanelli service in the 1930s. This would have been the return fare from Bwlch-y-gwynt to Llanelli.

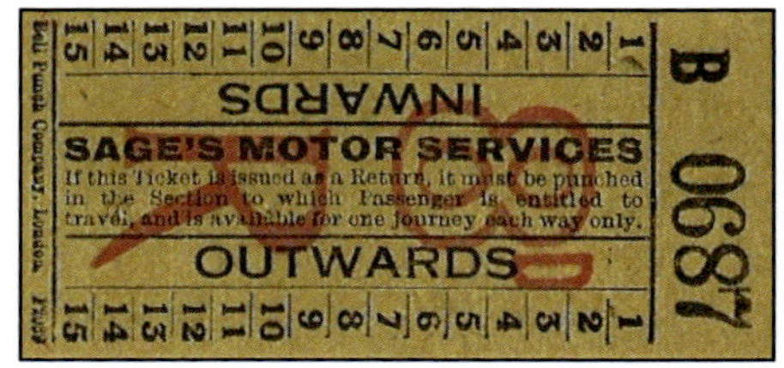


**Right:** Mr. Sage poses, here, in front of his new Albion Viking 'Sunshine Coach', in 1931. The normal control 26 seat coach was bodied locally, by Thomas & Thomas Coachworks, of Fair Lane Works, Carmarthen (by the old cattle market). It passed to the Llanelly & District Traction Co, in December 1936, with Sage's New Dock service.

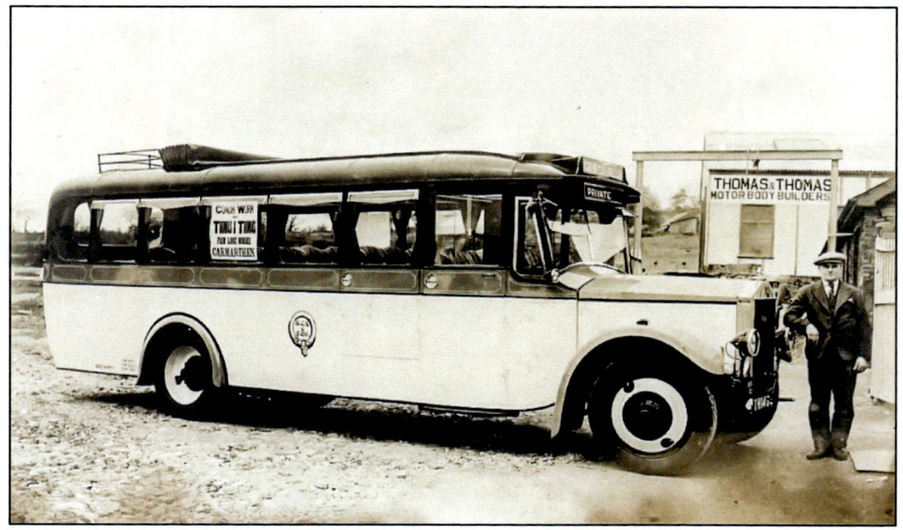

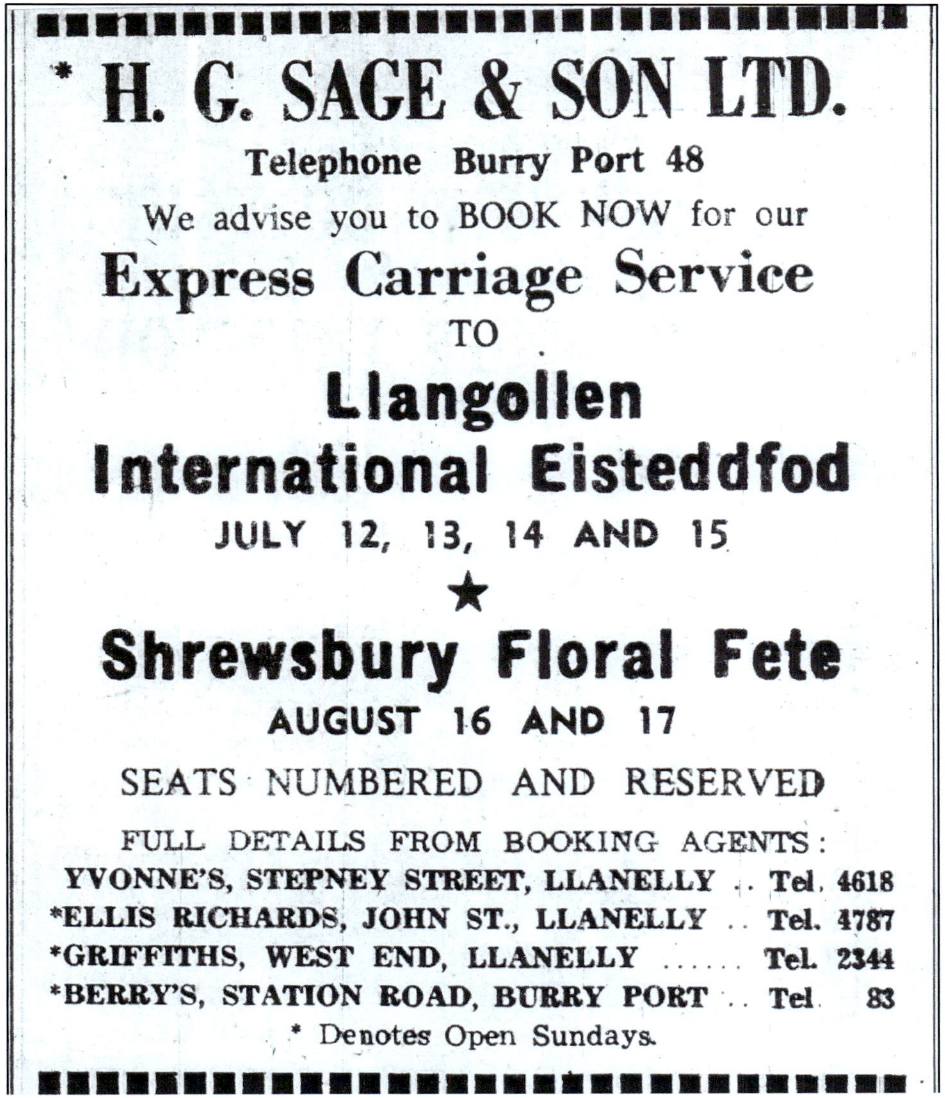


**Left:** An advertisement for Sage's tours, which was published in June 1961.

**Lower:** Burry Port railway station in the late 1930s, with a steam train departing for West Wales. Station Road in the background has changed very little, except for the demolition of the Railway Hotel at the junction of Stepney Road, in the centre of the view.

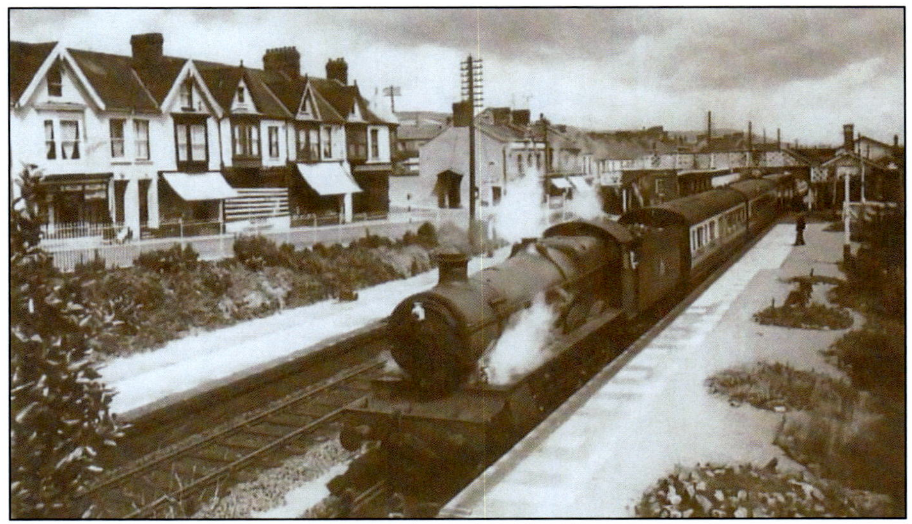

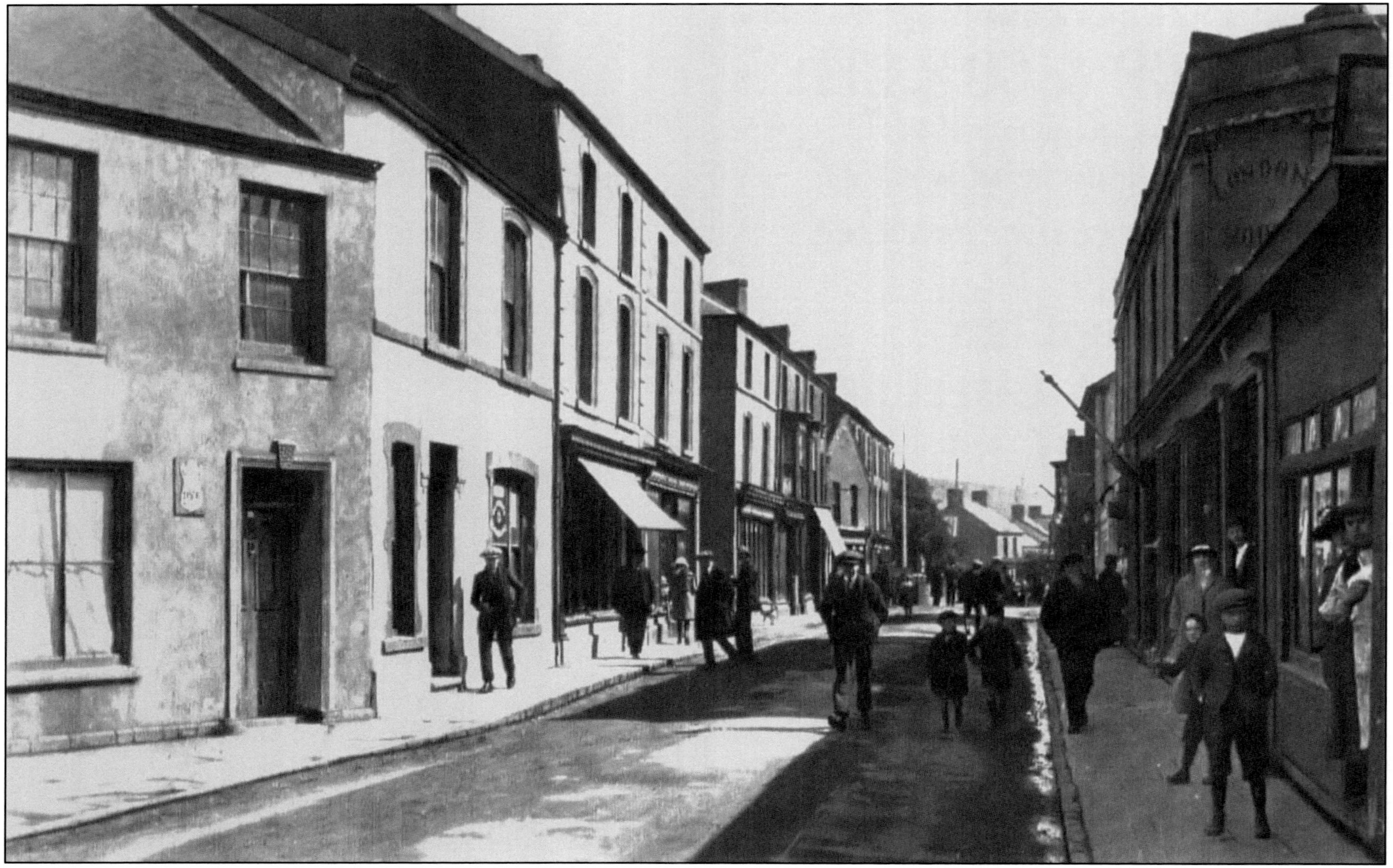

Station Road, Burry Port, doesn't appear to have changed much in 100 years, as seen from this view taken in 1913.
The single storey building, on the extreme right, is the only building that has disappeared.

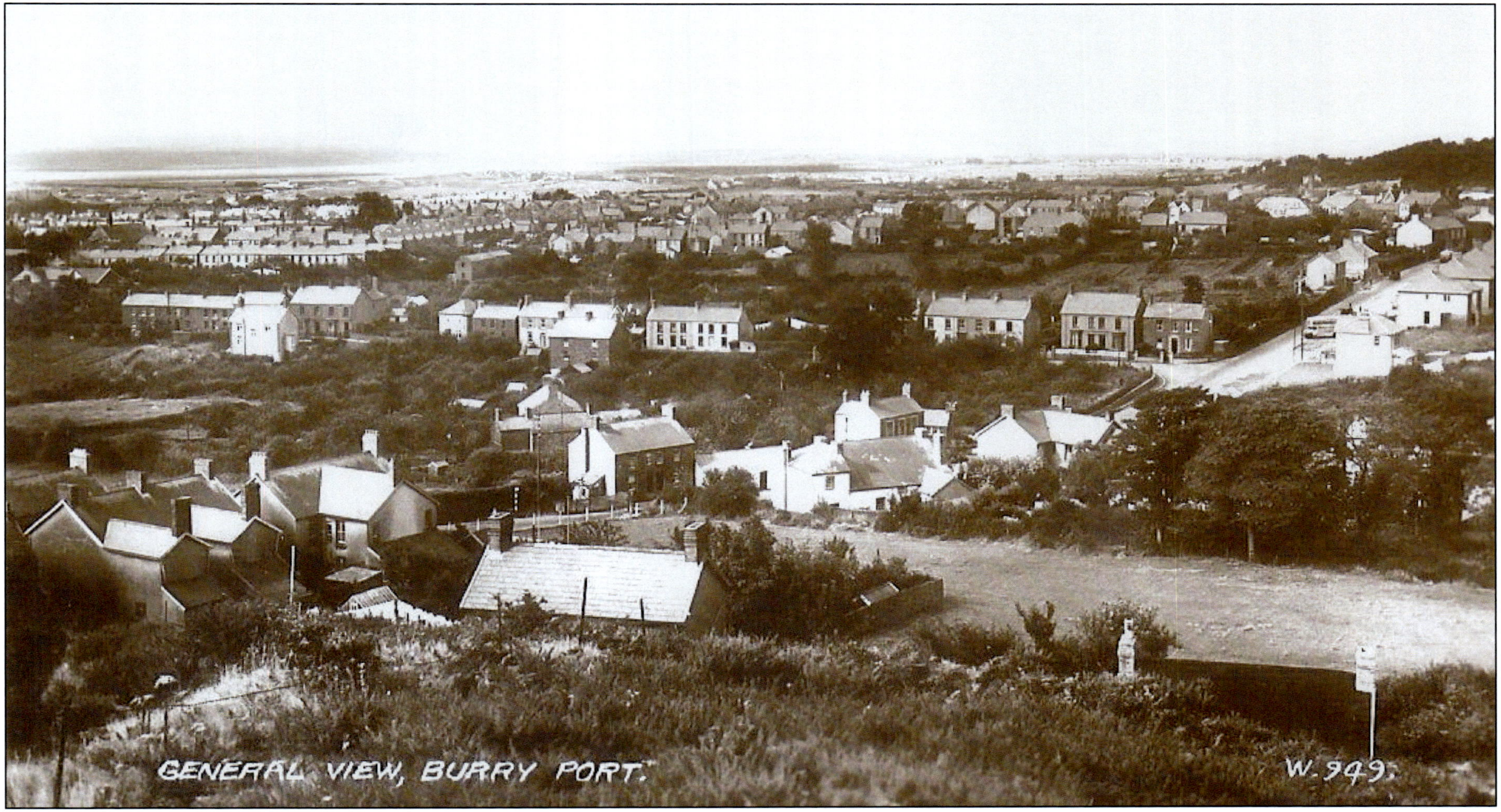


An interesting view of Burry Port, taken in the late 1940s, shows Colby Road (A484) running from left to right; Achddu in the top right hand corner, with Pencoed Road (centre). Stepney Road is just visible in the background. The Pemberton Arms is also seen here, in the centre of the picture. Note the absence of several streets: Parc Tyisha; Dolau Fan; The Crescent, and Brynhyfryd plus several houses along Colby Road and Pencoed Road.

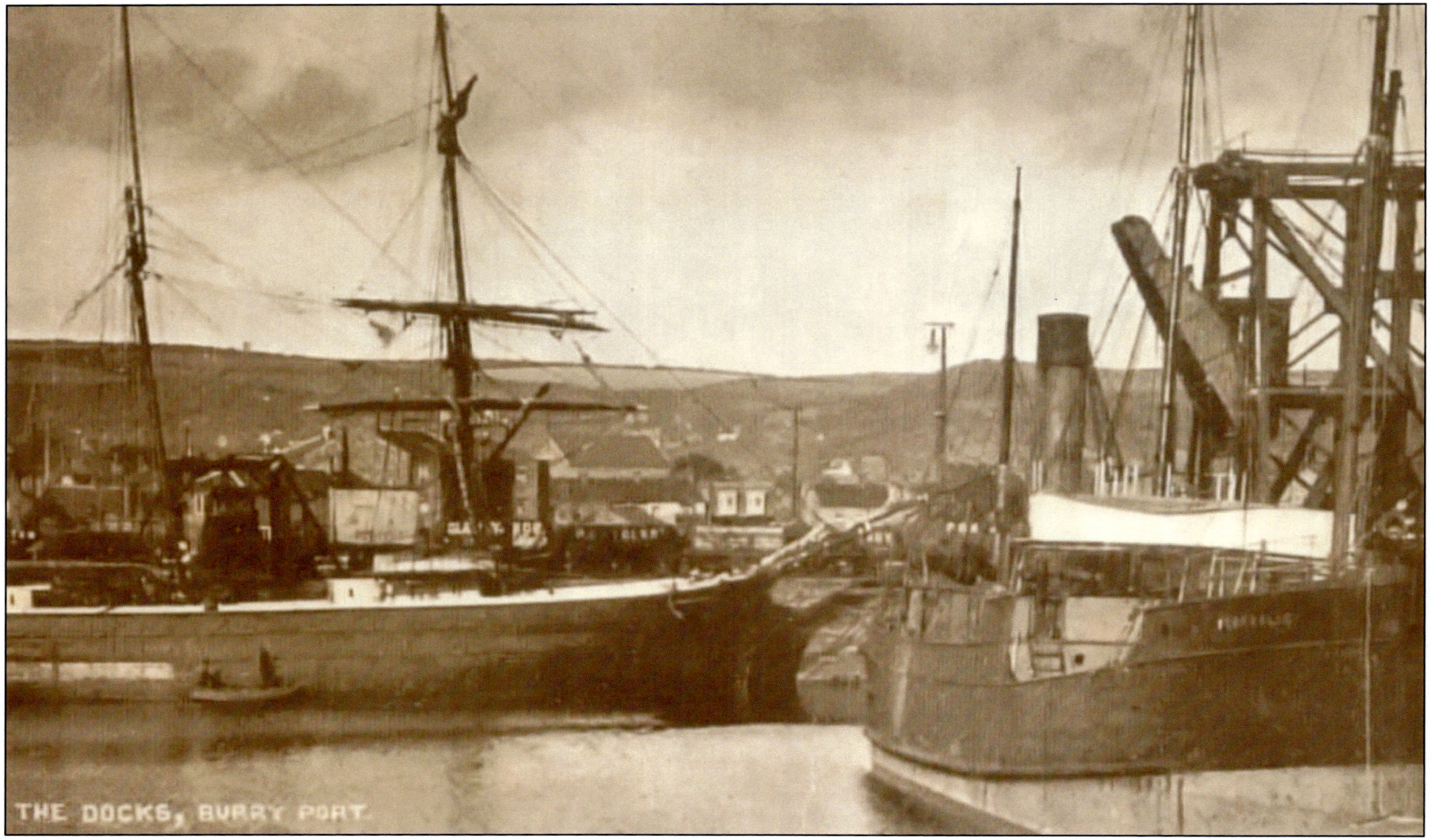


Coal export began as early as 1540, from Burry Port (Pembrey). With the huge demand for Welsh anthracite coal, a new harbour was built at Burry Port in 1832, to cope with the larger ships.
In this view of Burry Port's East Dock taken in 1908, S.S.'Ferguslie' and a two-masted brigantine, 'Mildred' can be seen loading up with coal emptied from the railway wagons visible in the background.

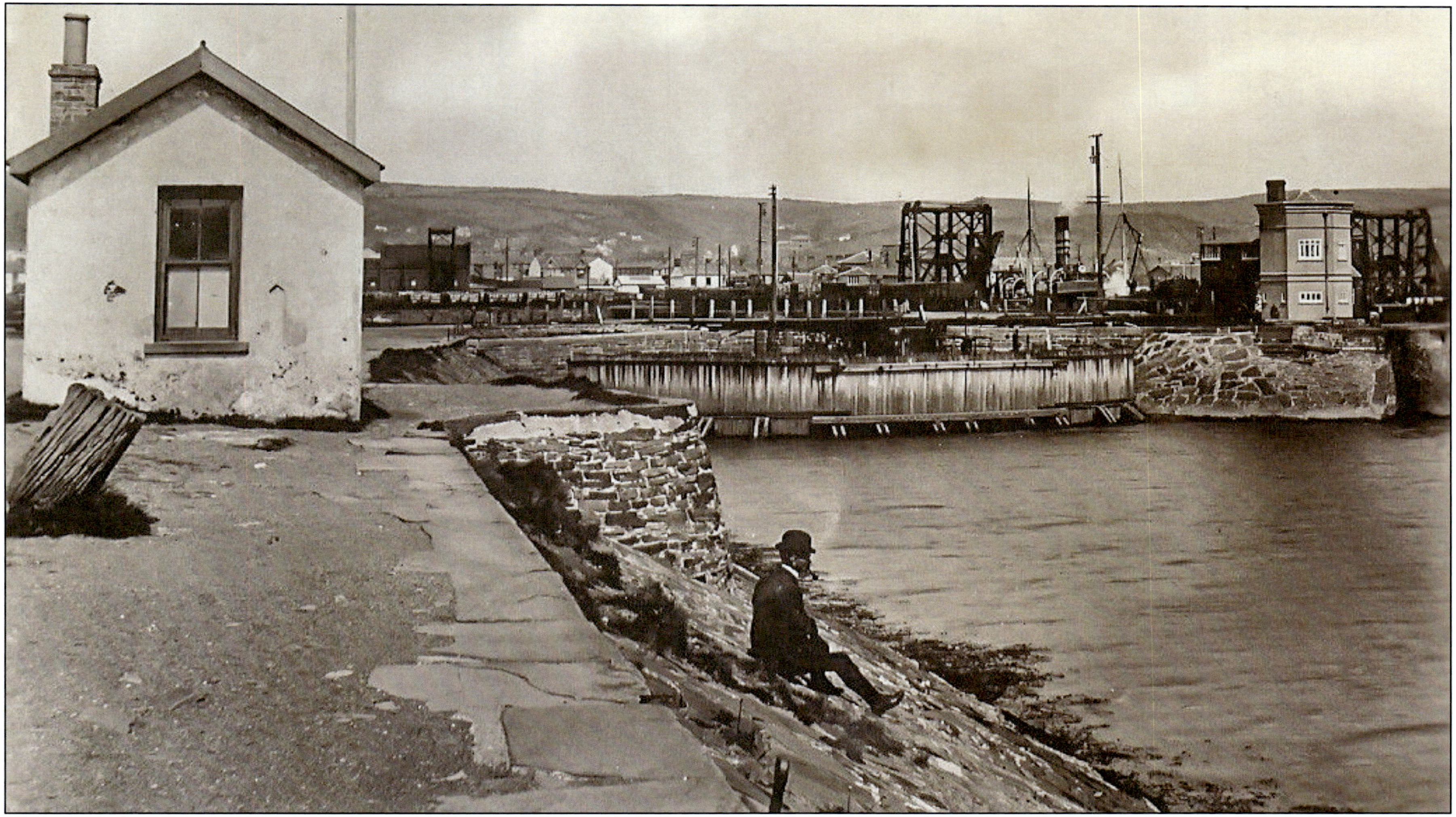

Another view of Burry Port Docks, or harbour as it's known today, was taken by a local photographer Ernest T. Bush in 1910. The Dock-master's office (later harbourmaster) is the building on the left. A Coffer Dam is prominent in the centre, with the Custom House to the right hand side. A steam ship is just visible, loading up with coal in the East Dock, or inner harbour (background). The two steel structures, visible in the background, were coal hoists; devices which emptied the coal from the railway wagons, via a chute, into the ships.

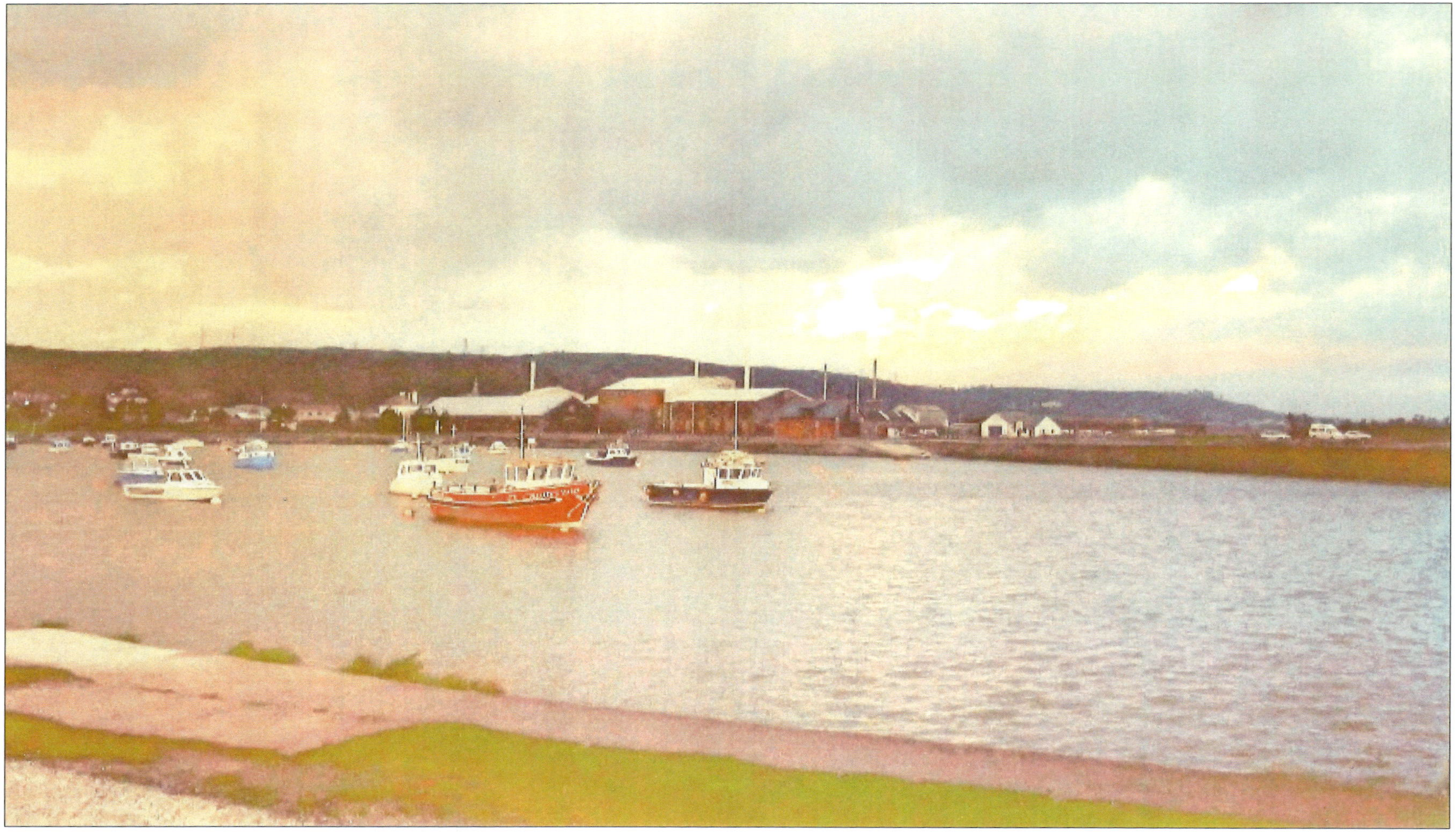

This is a far more recent photograph of Burry Port Dock (Burry Port Harbour), taken in 1993, before the area was redeveloped into a marina.

**Right:** This panoramic view of Burry Port (circa 1955), viewed from Mumbles Head, Pembrey mountain, takes in the newly commissioned Carmarthen Bay Power Station, the Burry estuary, and the Gower coast. The power station opened in 1953, closed down in 1984, and was demolished 1991-2.

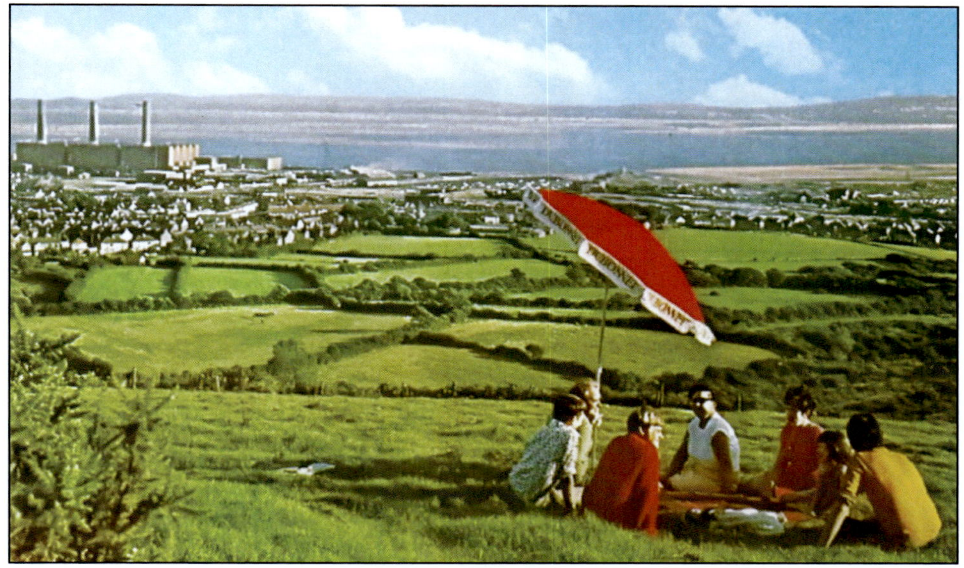

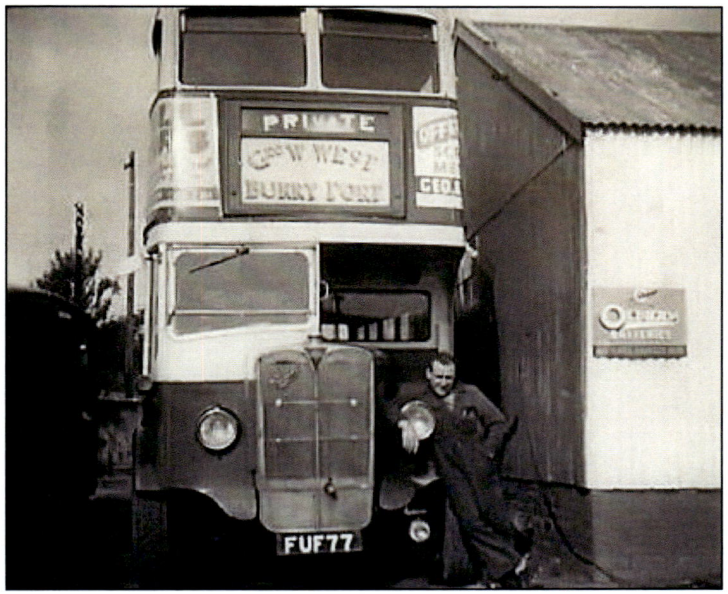


**Left:** George W. West, former harbourmaster at Burry Port, operated a small fleet of buses from his garage, here at Ashburnham Road, during the 1950's. The fleet of 3 double-deckers and one coach, operated workers services to the construction site of Carmarthen Bay Power Station. Investing in a new garage, Mr West moved into Chivers Corner Garage in the mid-1950s, also moving the buses there. The old garage at Ashburnham Road then passed to a boat builder, and later to its present occupier, Harbour Tyres. The bus, a 1939 A.E.C. Regent, originated from Brighton, having worked there as a tram replacement vehicle for the Corporation, carrying fleet No 77.

(George W. West).

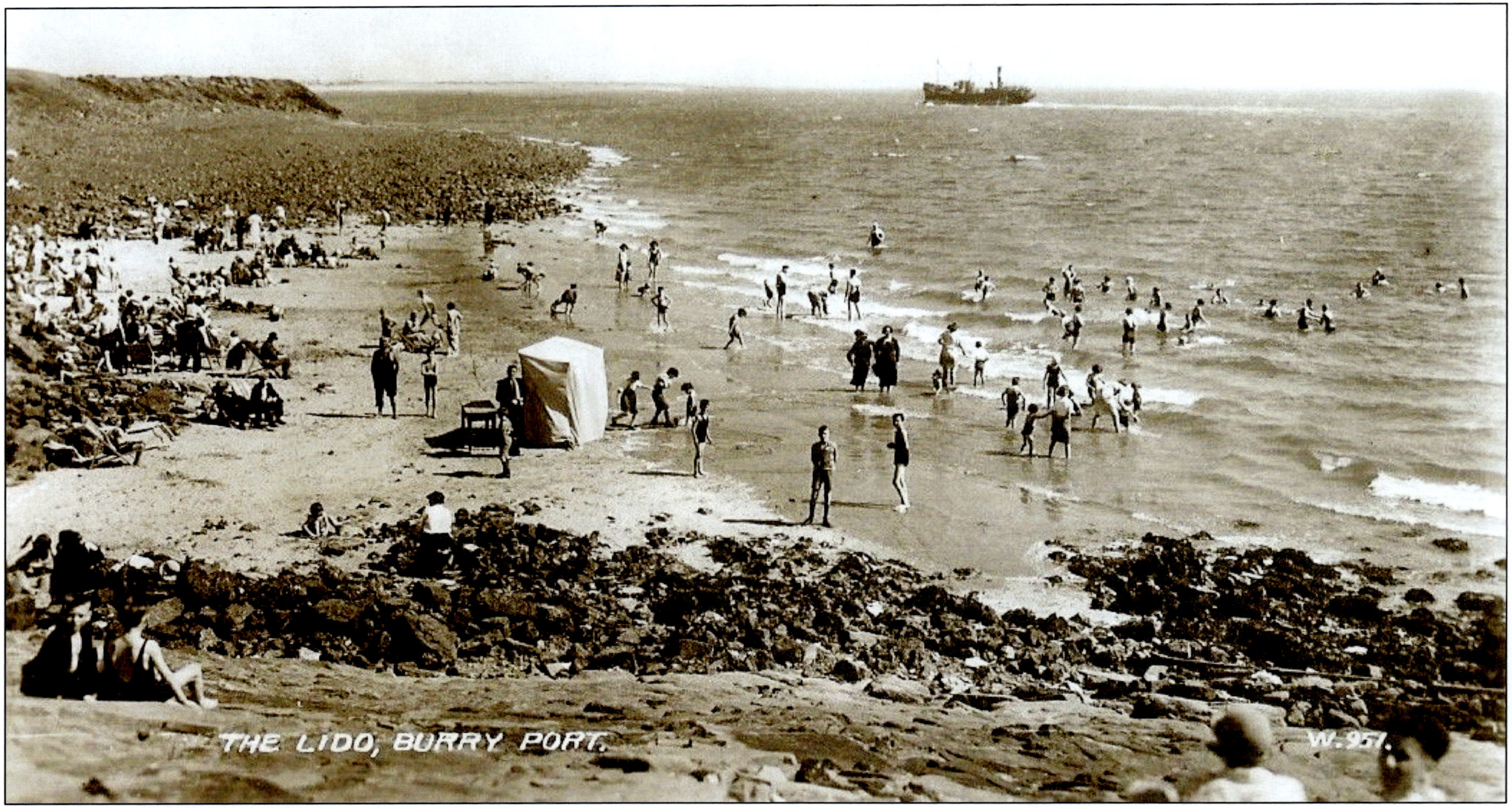


A very popular beach in the 1930s was this beach to the east of Burry Port harbour, even with all the pebbles and slag from the Copperworks located out of sight to the left of this picture. It was frequented by large numbers of Gwendraeth Valley people making day excursions from the valley villages by train. The cargo boat in the distance would be a 'Collier', heading for Llanelli North Dock.

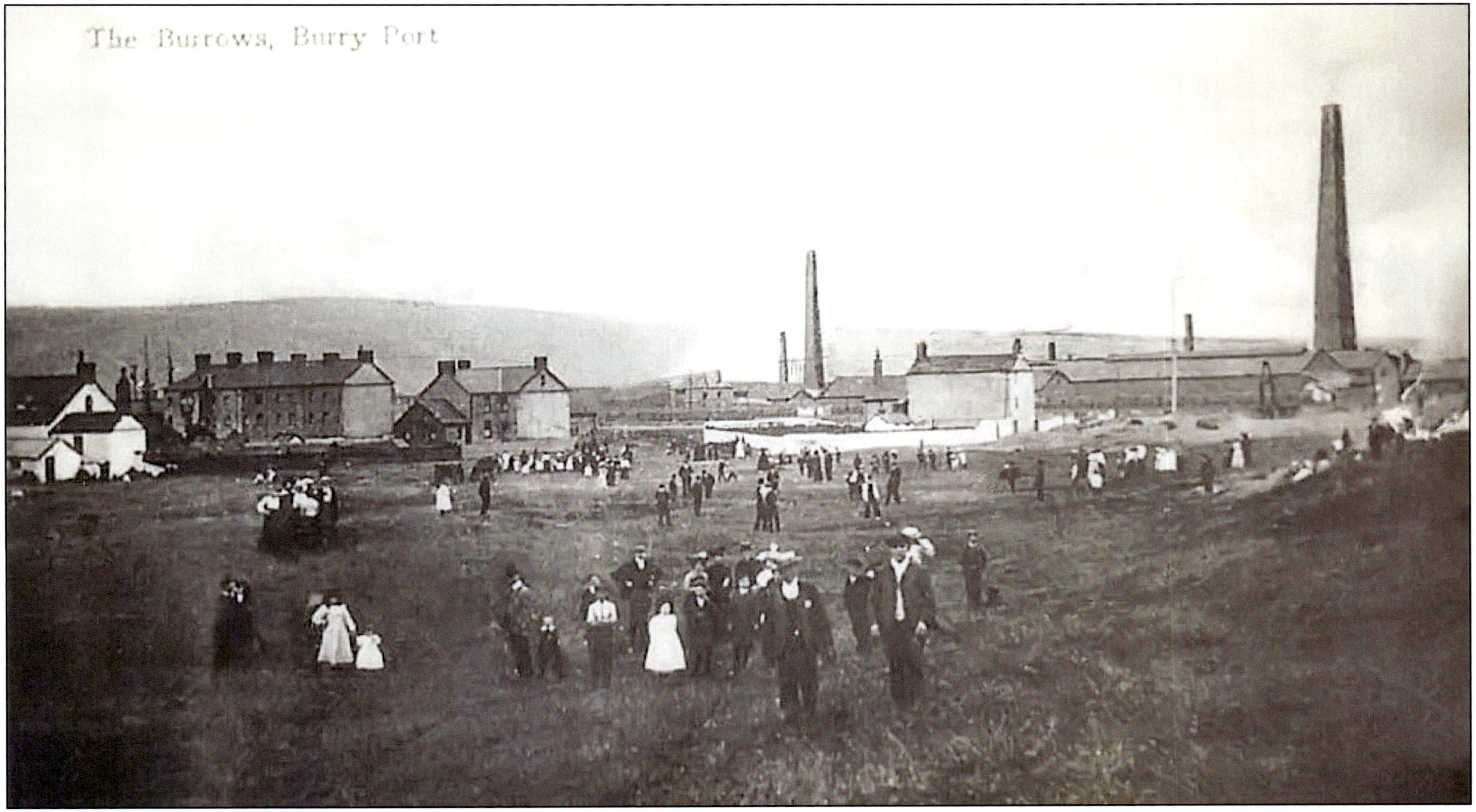


The Burrows, Burry Port, circa 1890, shows the Copperworks in the background. This area of Burry Port later became the site of Carmarthen Bay Power Station, which was demolished in 1991-2.

(Mrs. C. Ridgeway collection).

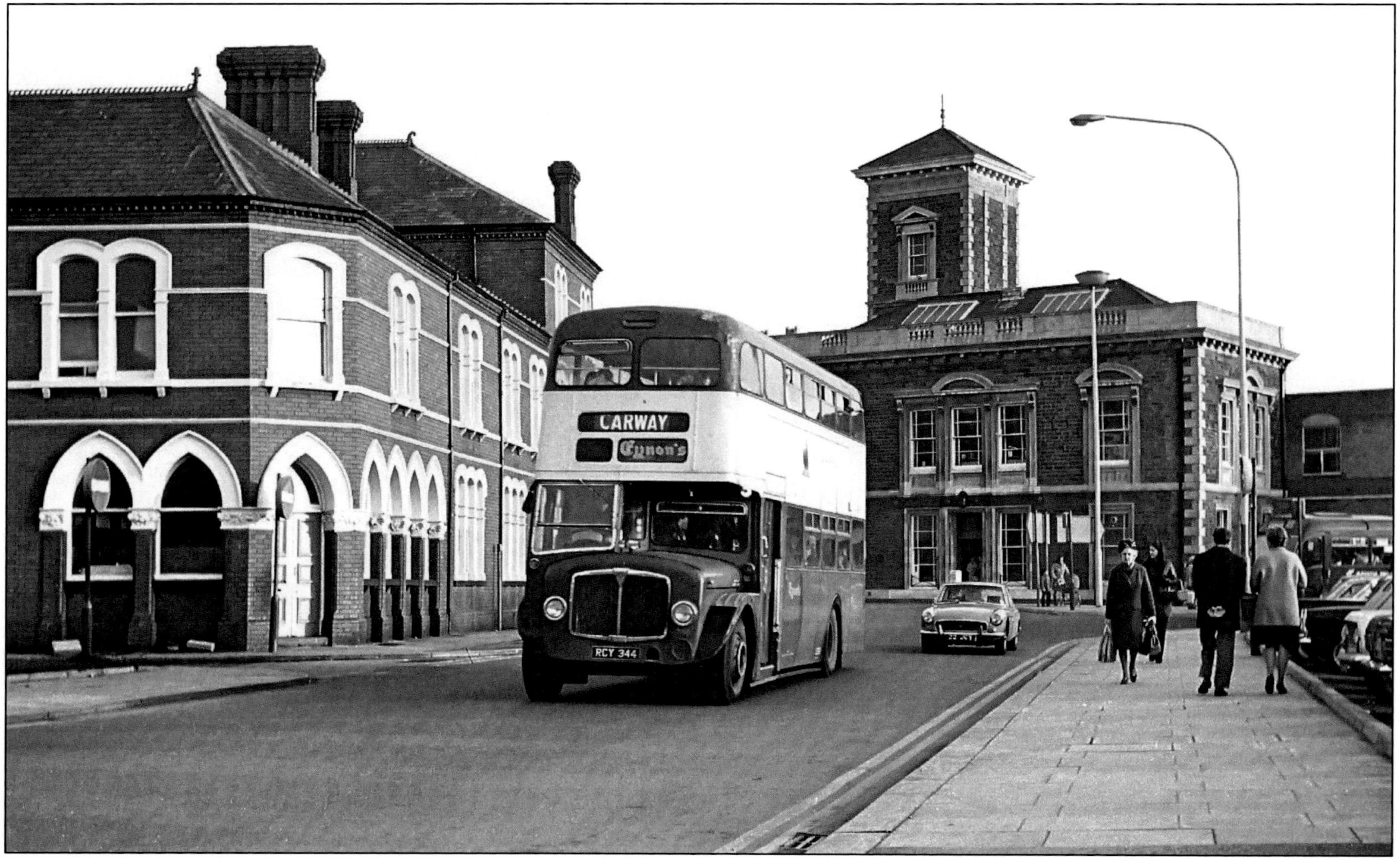


This view of Hall Street, Llanelli is dated December 1973, and shows the Mansel Hotel on the left, before its devastating fire. The section nearest the camera was badly damaged in the fire, and was subsequently rebuilt to single storey layout. Nowadays, the building is a restaurant, called 'Red Apple'. On the right hand side of the picture is the Llanelli Public Library, which at one time was the Athenaeum Hall. This particular section of Hall Street, at that time, had a one-way traffic system, operating in a westerly direction.

(Tony Moyes).

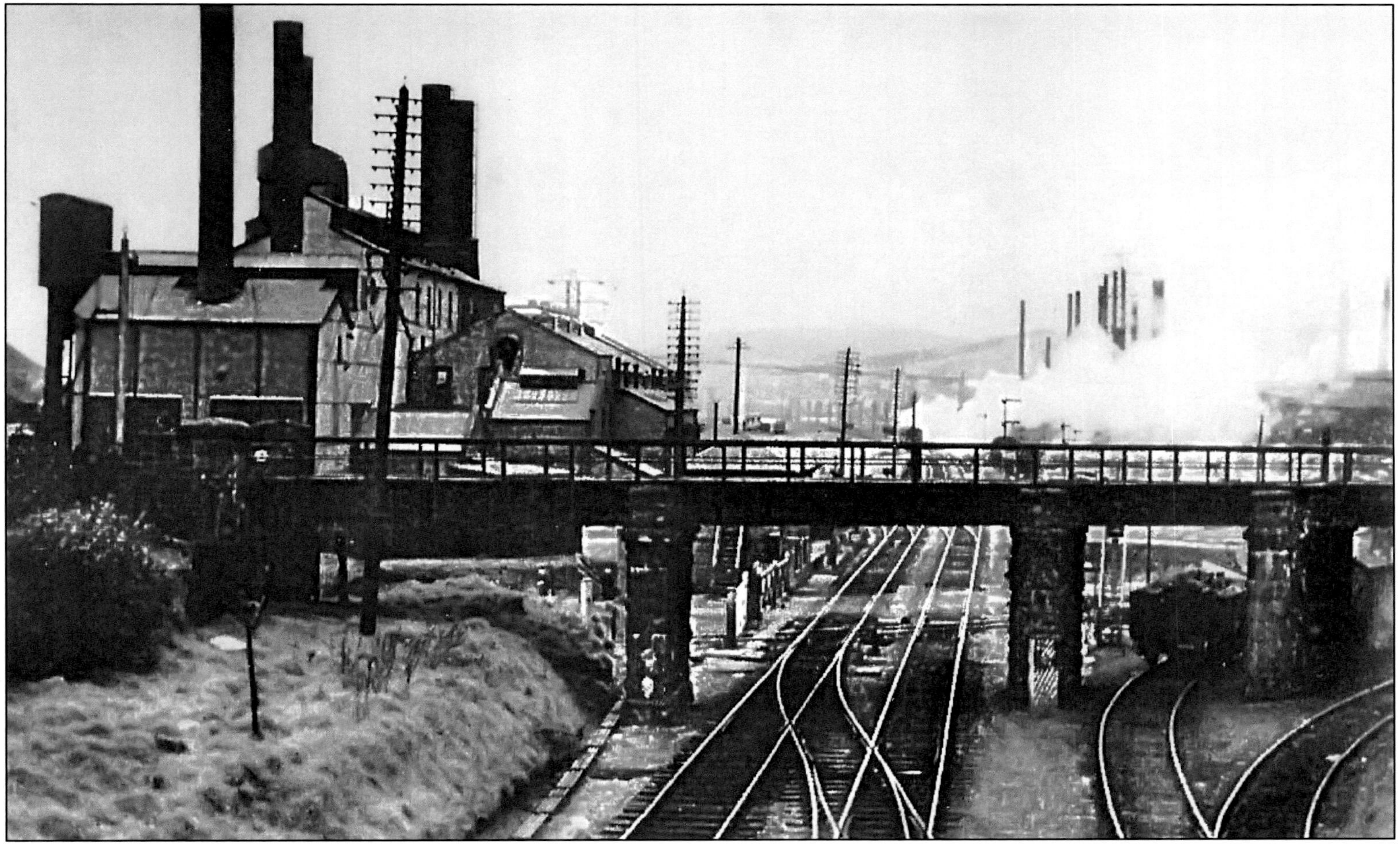

The building to the left of this picture is Llanelli power station, which was owned by the Llanelly Electric Supply Co., (LLAN-E-S-CO). Commissioned in 1910, this power station supplied Llanelli with electricity, until the commissioning of Carmarthen Bay Power Station at Burry Port in 1953. It also powered the Llanelli tramway system, and later the trolleybuses. Initially coal fired, it was converted to oil, becoming the only oil fired power station in Wales. The railway line in the centre of the picture is the Fishguard to London line, at the point of the Old Castle crossing, and viewed from Union Bridge. On the right hand side, the Llanelly to Mynydd-mawr railway line is just visible, and the viaduct in the foreground was a mineral line to Llanelli North Dock. Llanelly Steelworks is just visible behind the steam in the right hand background.

(V. Morgan collection).

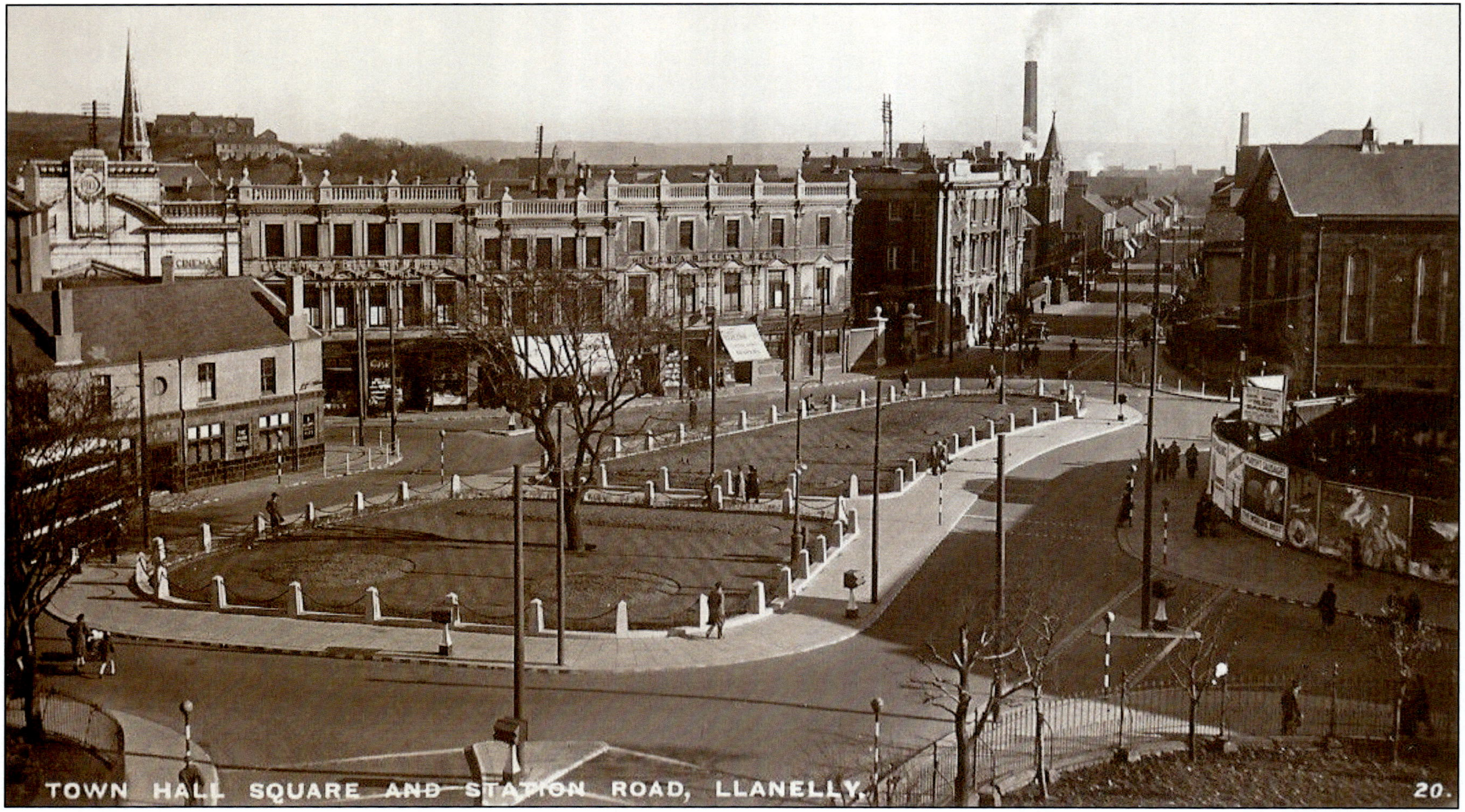


This postcard, postmarked 1949, shows the Town Hall Square and Station Road, Llanelli, viewed from the Town Hall clock tower. Llanelly Cinema is visible over the rooftop of the York Hotel, on the left hand side of the view, with Lucania Buildings (centre) advertising their billiard hall with 14 full size tables and free admission. The shops on ground level were: a bookshop; J. Allegri & Son (Allegri's Café); Jenkins, (bakers); entrance to billiard hall; Bevan Brothers; Tom Charles (tobacconist); Jelf's (herbalist); M. Green & Co. (draper), and the Cooperative Stores. The General Post Office is the first building on the left of Station Road, with Moriah Chapel directly opposite. Visible on the sky-line (from left to right) are: Bigyn primary school; St. Pauls Church; the Old Lodge tinplate works chimney stack – with the smoke coming out. Taking into consideration that the Old Lodge ceased operating in 1941, this photograph was probably taken the year that this pear shaped roundabout was opened, in 1939.

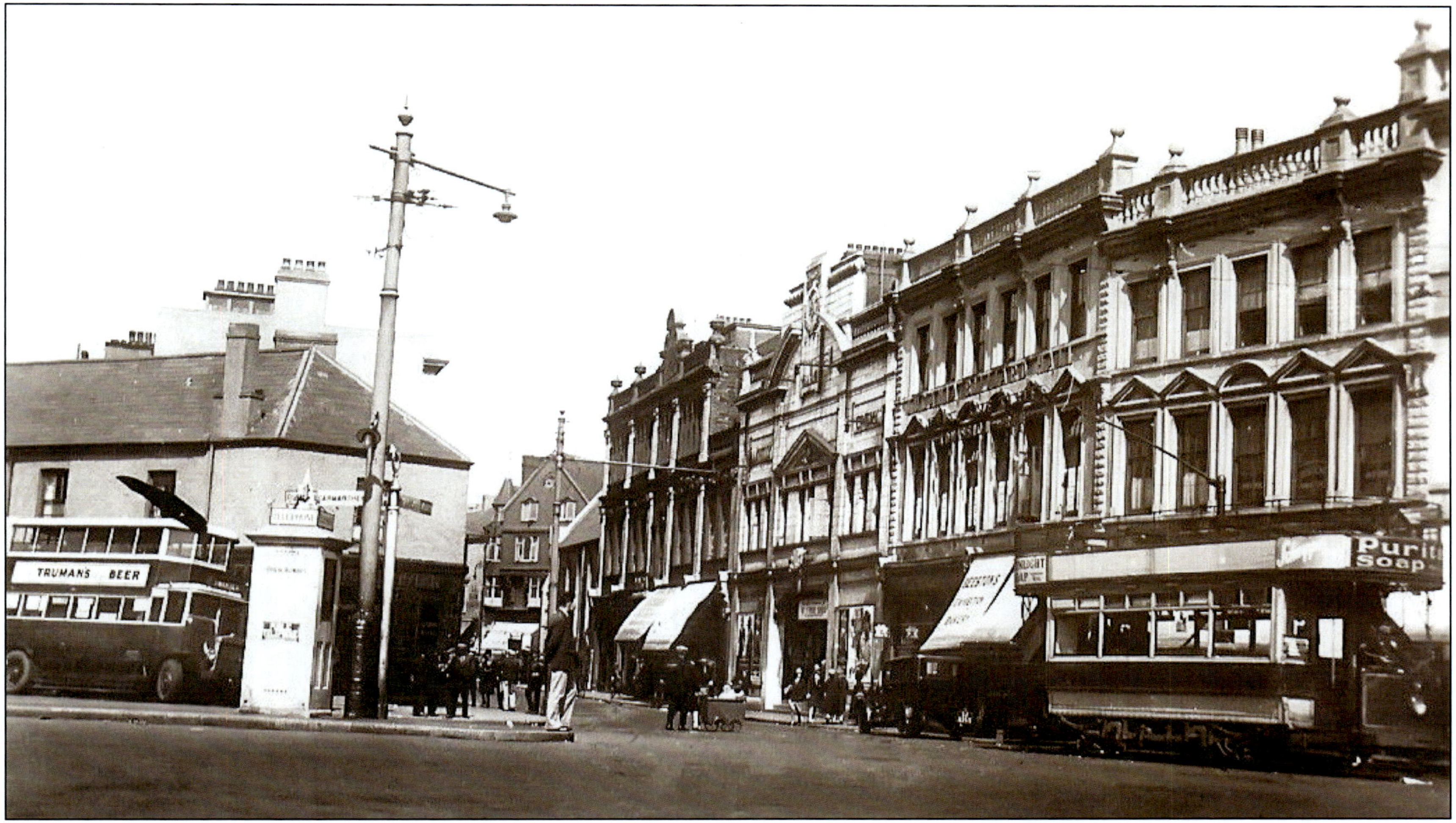


This view of lower Stepney Street, Llanelli dates from the late 1920s, and features the York Hotel on the left, and a very unusual public telephone box on the traffic island, in front of the South Wales Transport 1926 AEC bus. Beestons Bakery shop is forming part of the group of shops beneath Lucania Billiard Hall, with the Llanelly Cinema next door (nowadays a Weatherspoon's bar), and the YMCA building. The Llanelly Electric Supply Company (LLAN-E-S-CO) tram No. 7, is captured heading for the railway station terminus, with a large motor car (BX 5263) of unknown 1925 manufacture, parked outside Beestons Bakery. Note the vintage pram in the centre foreground, crossing a very quiet Stepney Street.

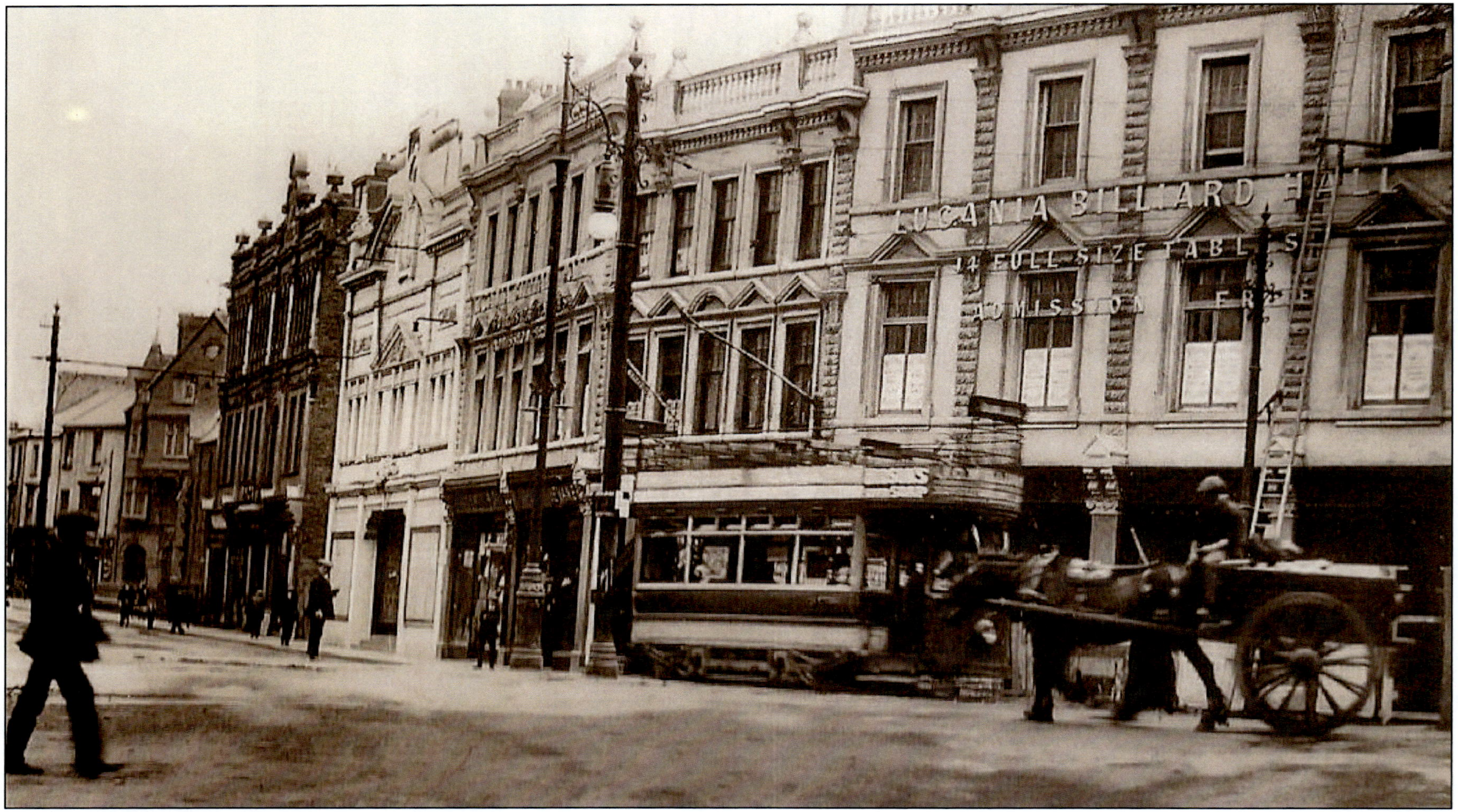


An almost identical view of lower Stepney Street, but taken earlier than the preceding photograph, probably circa 1913. It shows that the shops beneath the newly constructed Lucania Billiard Hall were still unoccupied.

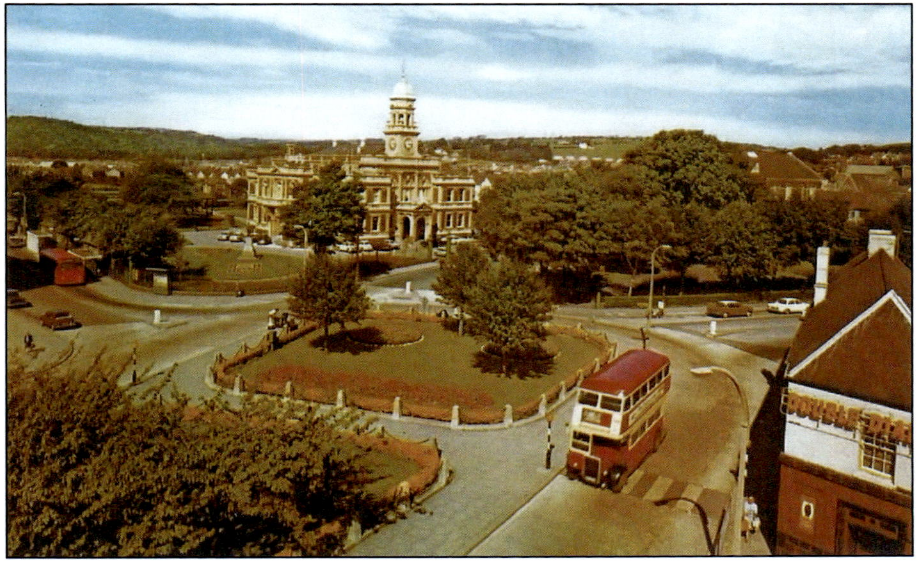

**Left:** Llanelli Town Hall (built in 1896) and Town Hall Square is viewed, here, from the roof top of Lucania Buildings, at the bottom of Stepney Street in the mid 1960s. The York Hotel is the building on the right hand side of the picture, with the 'Double Diamond' neon sign – a popular 'watering hole' for the thirsty steelworkers of Llanelly Steelworks. It can honestly be said that several tons of steel were 'tapped' inside the York; it was the general topic of conversation between the furnace-men as they met here on shift change-overs.
The bus, owned by Eynon's of Trimsaran, was about to terminate at the bus station just visible on the left hand side of the picture.

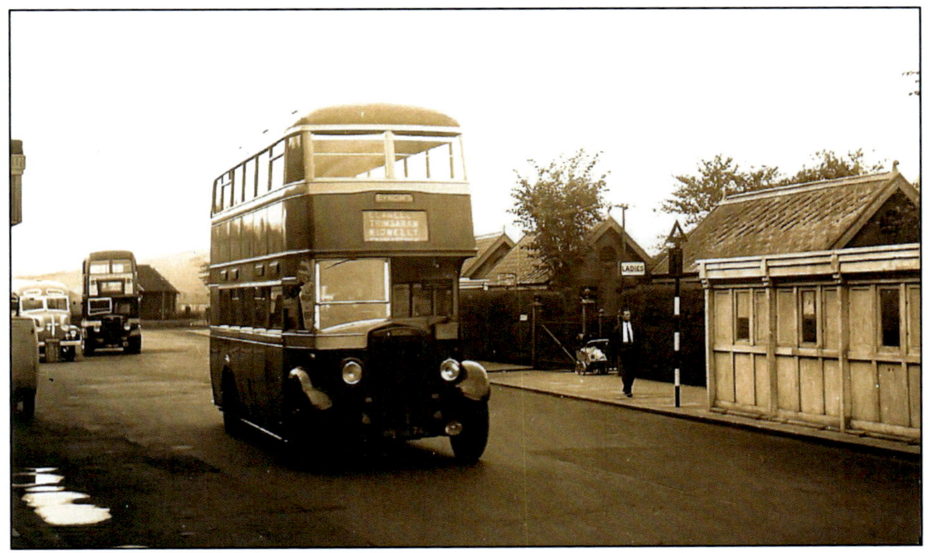

**Right:** Llanelli's Town Hall Square was the town's main bus terminus for 78 years, before moving to Island Place in 1997. In this view, dated 1951, Eynons' Leyland double decker is seen leaving for Kidwelly, with a South Wales Transport AEC Regent double decker behind, and H. G. Sage's Leyland Comet coach, complete with 'A' board, advertising their day excursions. It was a regular feature at this location with Sage, Jenkins Tours, J. James & Son Burry Port, and South Wales Transport, all advertising in the same manner. The fares charged by the group of operators were set by the Traffic Commissioners, after the operators had failed to agree on set prices in 1933. Tenby was set at 5/6 return (27½ pence), Barry Island at 6/0 (30 pence) and Cheltenham at 12/6 (62½ pence).

(D. A. Jones).

# JENKINS TOURS
## (LLANELLY) LTD.
**Telephone 3230**

## YOUR HOLIDAY TOURS

**Blackpool (7-Day)**

**Fare** .......................... **£11-15-0 Inclusive**
**Departures** ........... **July, August, September**

**Cheddar and Weston Tour (3-Day)**

**Fare** .............................. **£6-0-0 Inclusive**
**Departures** ......................... **July, August**

**Morecambe (4-Day)**

**Fare** .............................. **£7-7-0 Inclusive**
**Departures** ......................... **July, August**

**Book Now for Blackpool Illuminations**
**SEPTEMBER 8 to OCTOBER 28**
**3-Day** ........... **£4-12-6**
**4-Day** ........... **£5-12-6**
**Accommodation at Good Class Hotels**
**(Coach Fare only, if required)**

Call or write for full details at:
OFFICE, 5, SWANSEA ROAD, LLANELLY

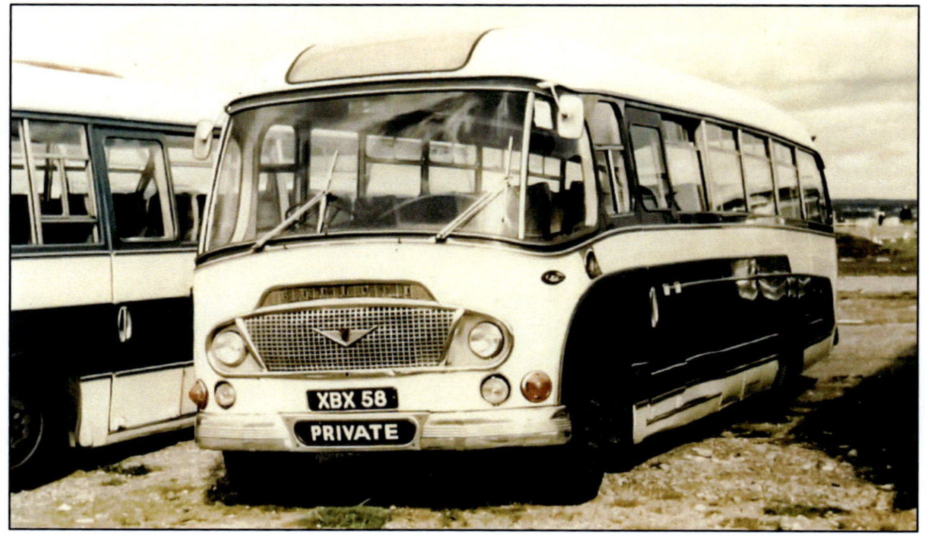


Jenkins Tours of Llanelly was founded in 1936 by Thomas Stanley Jenkins of Brynallt Terrace. 'Holiday Tours' commenced in the 1950s, and were very popular with their regular clientele, Blackpool being one of their favourites. The advertisement, seen here, was published for the 1962 season, and bookings were made at their office, No. 5 Swansea Road. Their luxury coach fleet was updated on a regular basis, and this Bedford SB3, above, with a petrol engine was the new coach purchased for the 1961 season. Petrol was cheap enough in those far gone days at 4/2d per gallon (20½ pence per gallon).

(John Jones).

**Left:** The South African Fallen Heroes Memorial, situated in the grounds of Llanelli Town Hall, is dedicated to the local men who had laid down their lives in the Boer War, 1898 – 1900. It was unveiled on 26th August, 1905, by Lord Roberts the Commander-in-chief in South Africa. Although the cannons have disappeared, the monument is still intact in the south-east corner of the Town Hall grounds, overlooking Ty-Elwyn.

(V. Morgan collection).

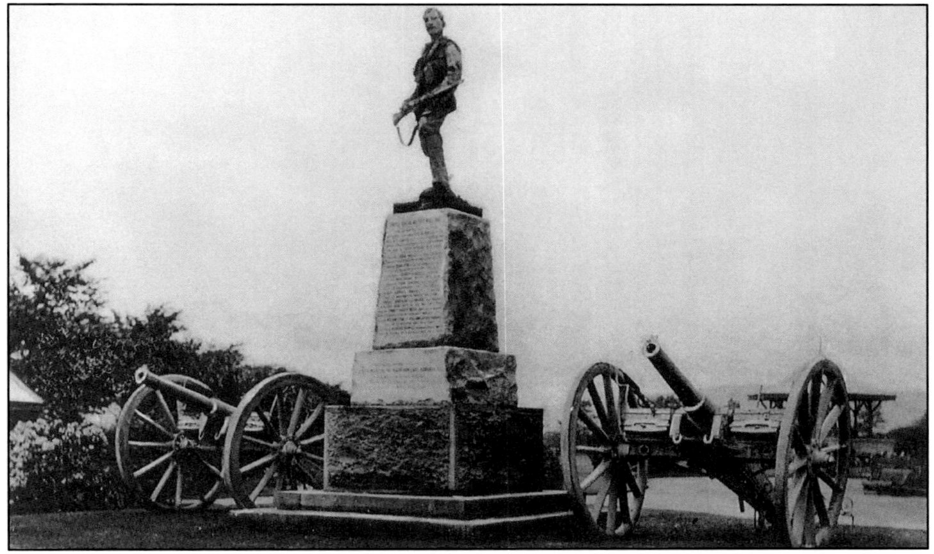

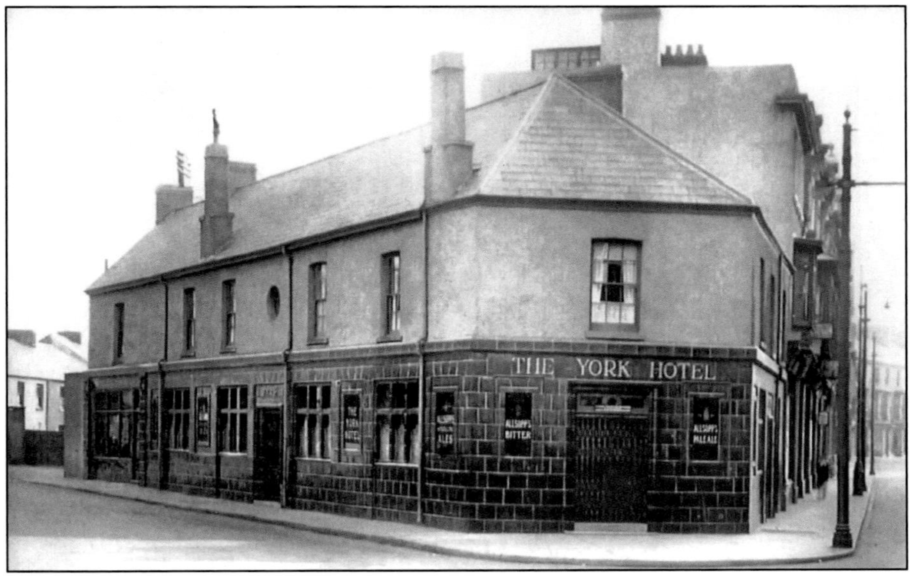


**Right:** It is difficult to put a date on this excellent picture of the York Hotel, but it would have been taken sometime before 1931, as the houses in the left hand background – Spring Gardens, were demolished in 1931. Earlier photographs of the York Hotel (in 1915) show Buckley's Brewery signs, but by the time that this view was taken, it had received a face lift and had changed ownership to Allsops Brewery – So when did the change take place?

(John Phillips collection).

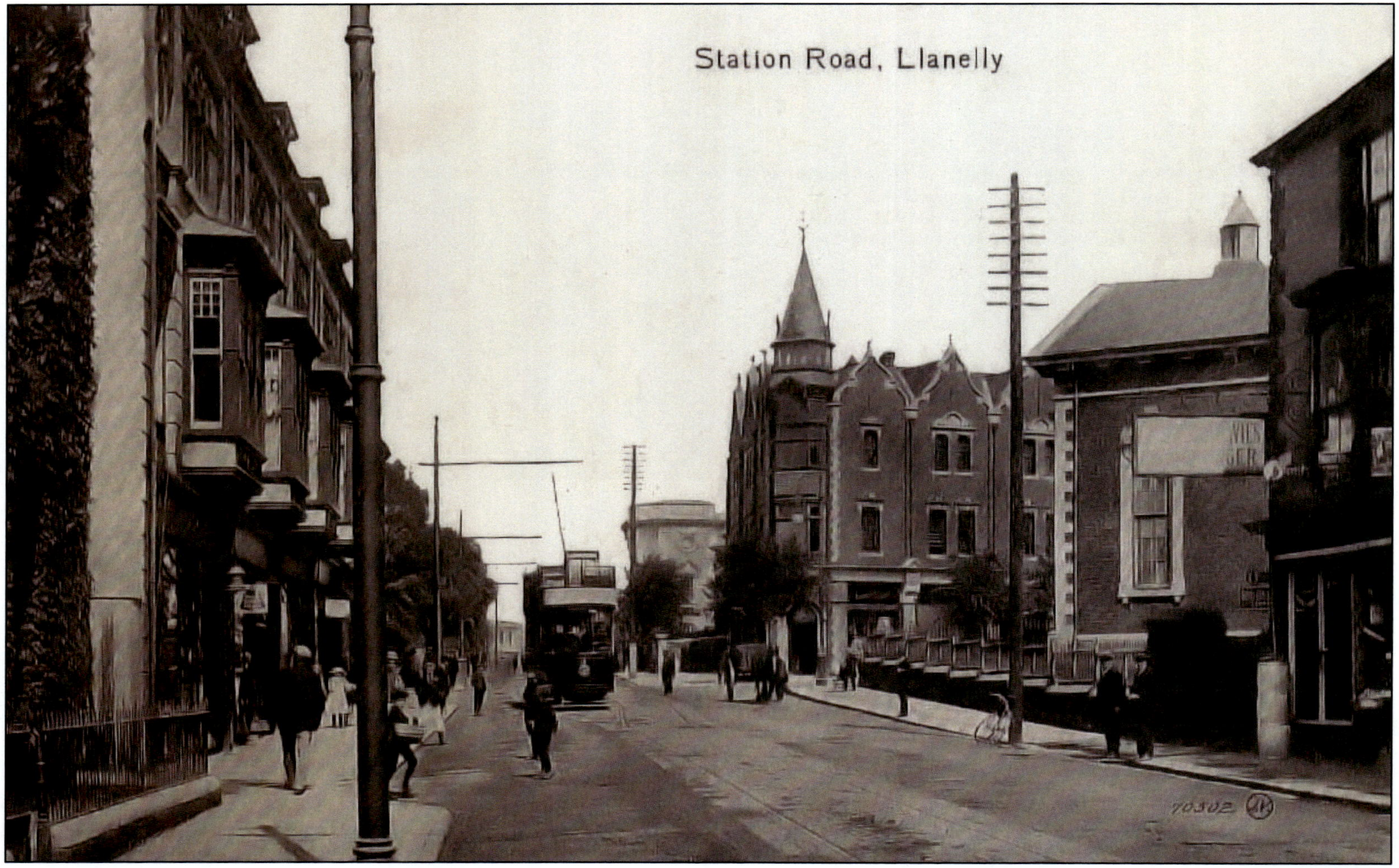


There has been very little change to this part of Station Road, Llanelli over the last 100 years. All the buildings visible here, still stand today - virtually unchanged. The trees, to the left of Station Road, were removed to make-way for the Odeon cinema, which was changed to the Classic Theatre in 1971. Additionally, the Midland Bank had not been built. The Bank was built in a space directly opposite the cinema (centre background), in the space between Castle Buildings (now Vista Lounge) and the General Post Office (centre of picture). The ironmongers shop, on the right hand side, owned by T. Brabyn Davies, has long gone. This building is now the Llanesco Social Club. However, the noisy trams which rattled through the streets, disappeared in 1932, making way for the 'modern' silent electric trolley-buses.

**Right:** This was one of Llanelli's early horse drawn trams, which operated between the railway station and the town centre. The horse drawn trams, also known as J. Andrews' patent cars, were replaced by more modern electric tramcars, with extensions to their routes in March 1908. The tram depot and stables were situated at Robinson Street, Llanelli, which is the present day depot of First Cymru Buses Ltd.

This view was taken in 1905 by J. Vaughan Evans (photographer) Murray St., Llanelli, who also advertises his business on the tram!

(V. Morgan collection).

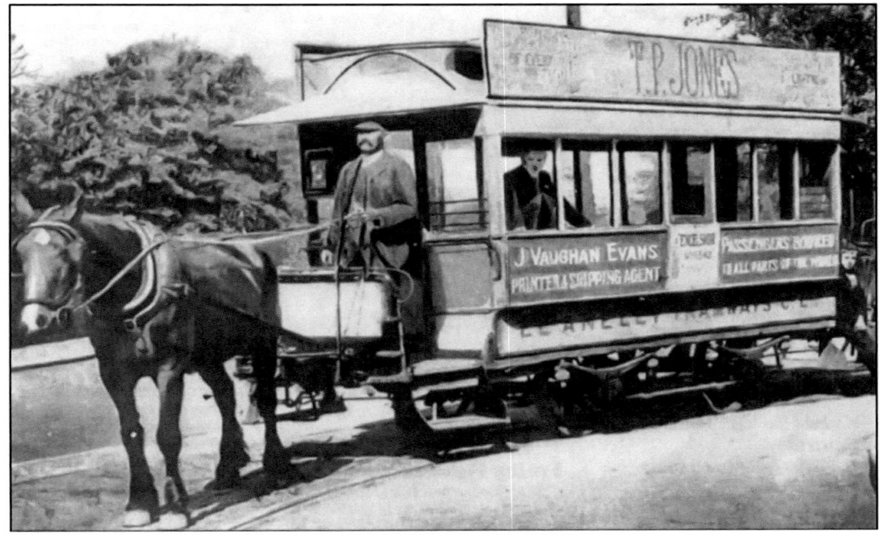


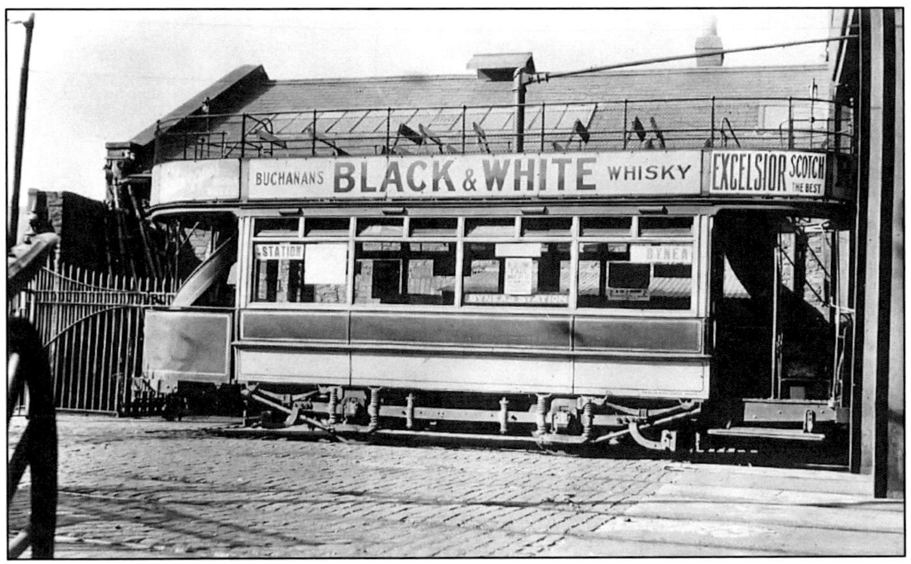


**Left**: Llanelli had a fleet of sixteen open top electric tramcars, which had replaced the horse drawn trams in 1908. This electric tramcar is pictured at the entrance of the tram depot in Robinson Street, soon after delivery, with a destination board displaying 'Bynea to Station'. It seated 64 passengers; 24 inside and 40 on top, and had a wheelbase of just 8 feet. The old tram depot still stands today (2014), virtually unchanged, housing a fleet of buses owned by First Cymru. The tramlines are still visible, along with the old stables from over a hundred years ago, forming a grade two listed building.

(V. Morgan collection).

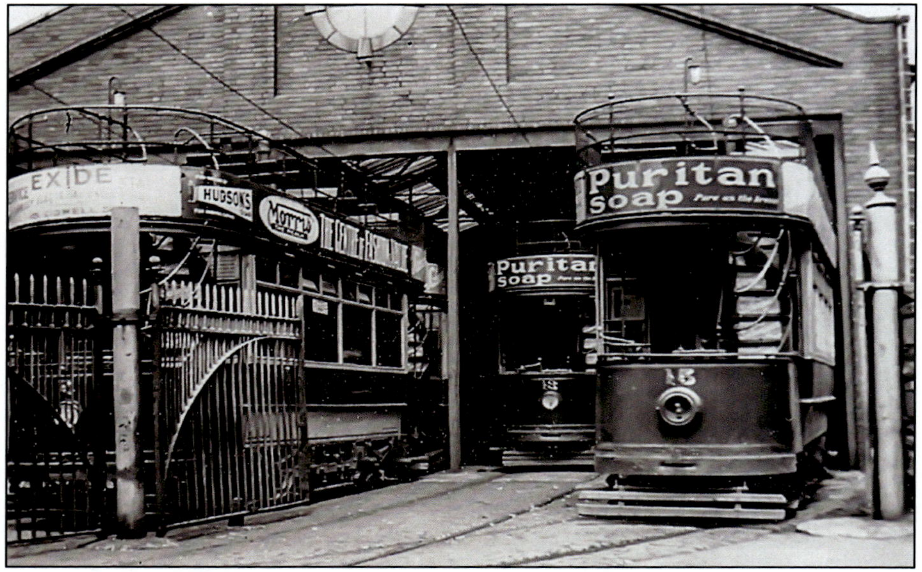


**Left:** An excellent view of the Llanelli tram depot at Robinson Street is seen here, sometime around their inauguration date in 1908. As seen here, the trams were initially not fitted with destination display boxes; they simply had paper displays fitted to side windows. The wrought iron gates at the depot entrance remained there for decades, but the façade above the entrance was removed to give increased headroom on arrival of the trolleybuses in 1932. The replacement frontage was built using corrugated asbestos sheets.

(V. Morgan collection).

**Right:** 'The old and the new'.
Poised for the camera on the cross-roads of Station Road, Murray Street, and Queen Victoria Road, in December 1932, are tramcar No. 4 and trolleybus No. 4. They are marking the occasion – the arrival of the new electric trolleybuses, and the departure of the last electric tram. The splendid architecture of Castle Buildings is just visible behind the two vehicles.

(V. Morgan collection).

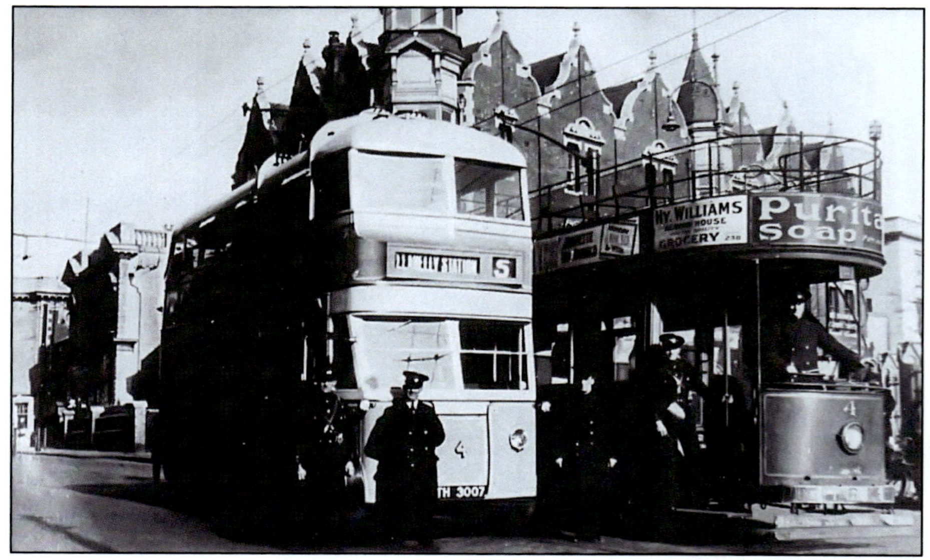

**Right:** This view, taken c.1915, looks eastward along Stepney Street, Llanelli, capturing an electric tramcar heading for the railway station. The tram is just passing the entrance to Llanelli market – on the right hand side of this view.

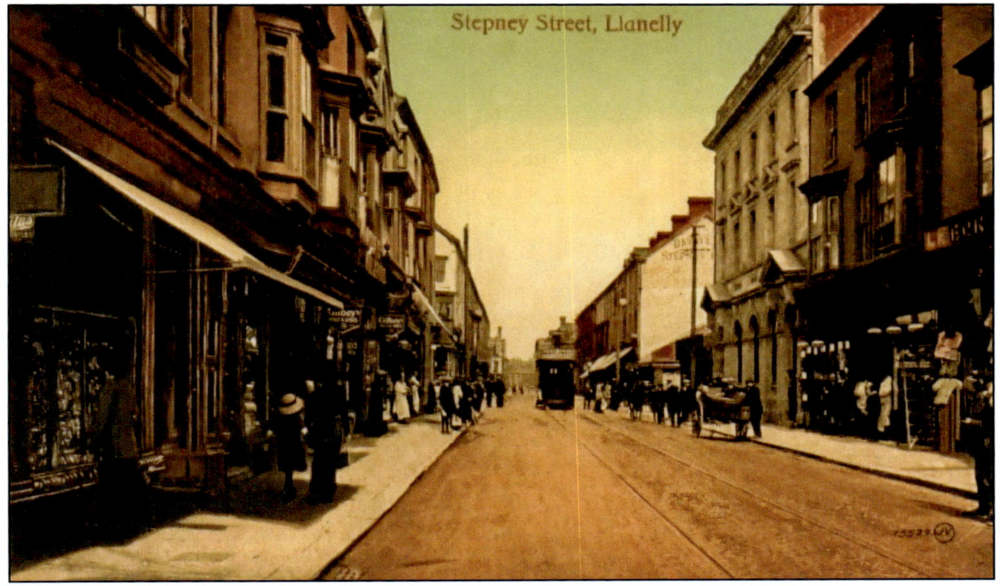


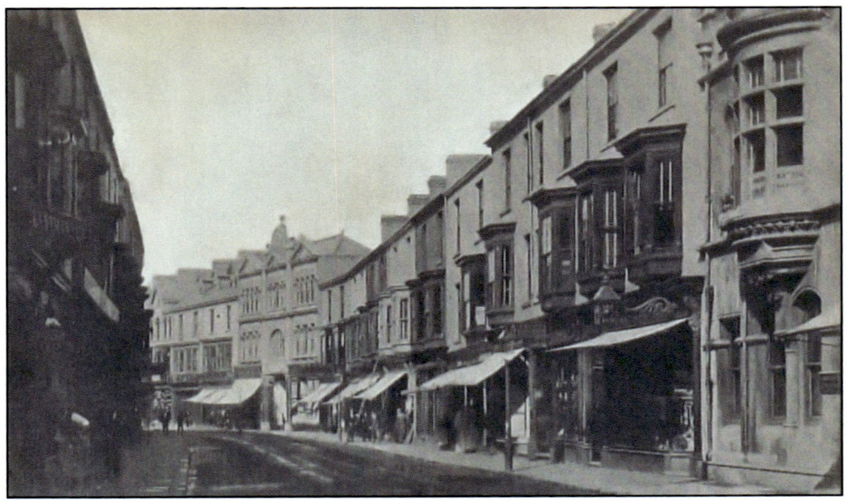

**Left:** This view looking westward along Stepney Street, Llanelli, is postmarked February 1903. The shops cannot be identified, but the fine architecture of the Arcade entrance is clearly visible in the background. The Arcade was built in 1894, linking Stepney Street to Frederick Street.

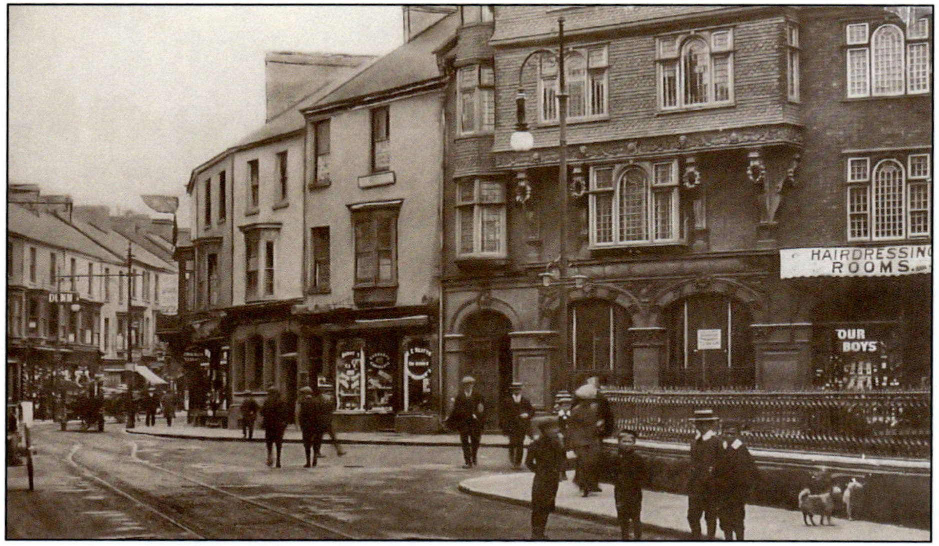


**Left:** The focal point of this view is the splendid architecture of the building, to the right of the picture. Built for the South Wales Union Bank in 1892, its façade was a fine example of Victorian design, and remains there today (2014), virtually unchanged and owned by the Halifax Building Society. This area of Llanelli was known as Presbyterian Square, a name derived from the church located at this junction. The hairdresser, 'Our Boys', was a feature in this building for almost a century. The roadway off to the right is Cowell Street, and the road ahead is the much photographed Stepney Street in 1911, now pedestrianised. This postcard view was published by J. Marker, Tobacconist, 7A Stepney Street & 94 Station Road, Llanelly.

(V. Morgan collection).

**Right:** Another view of Presbyterian Square and Stepney Street, taken around 1925, shows the confectioner's shop on the left of Stepney Street, with Thomas (Welsh Produce Store) next door to it. On the right hand side, Evans & Jones is just visible, with Tyrynis Thomas (Chemist) next door, and Lewis Norman (Draper) next door to that. The wrought iron railings, on the right hand side, are the railings of the Presbyterian Church. One of the Llanelli electric tramcars can be seen disappearing around the corner of Stepney Street.

(John Phillips collection).

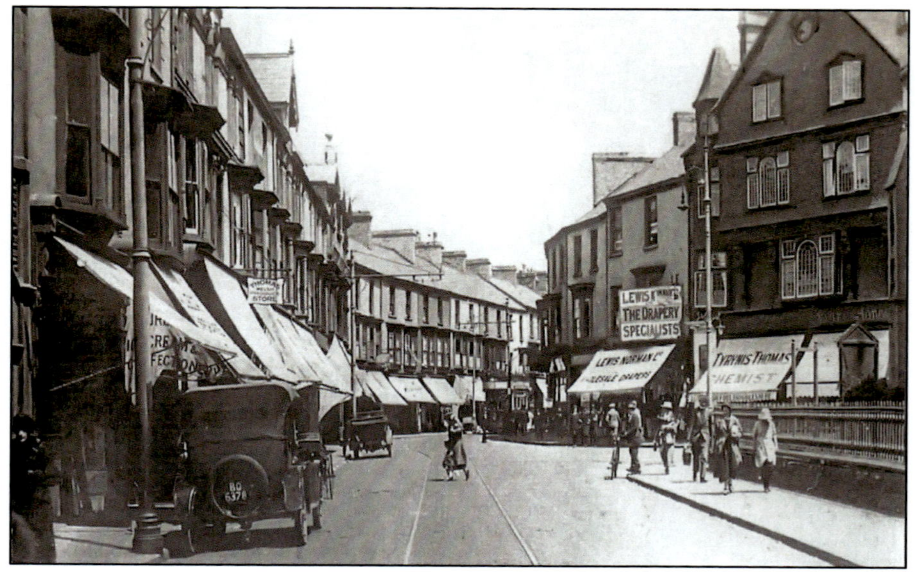

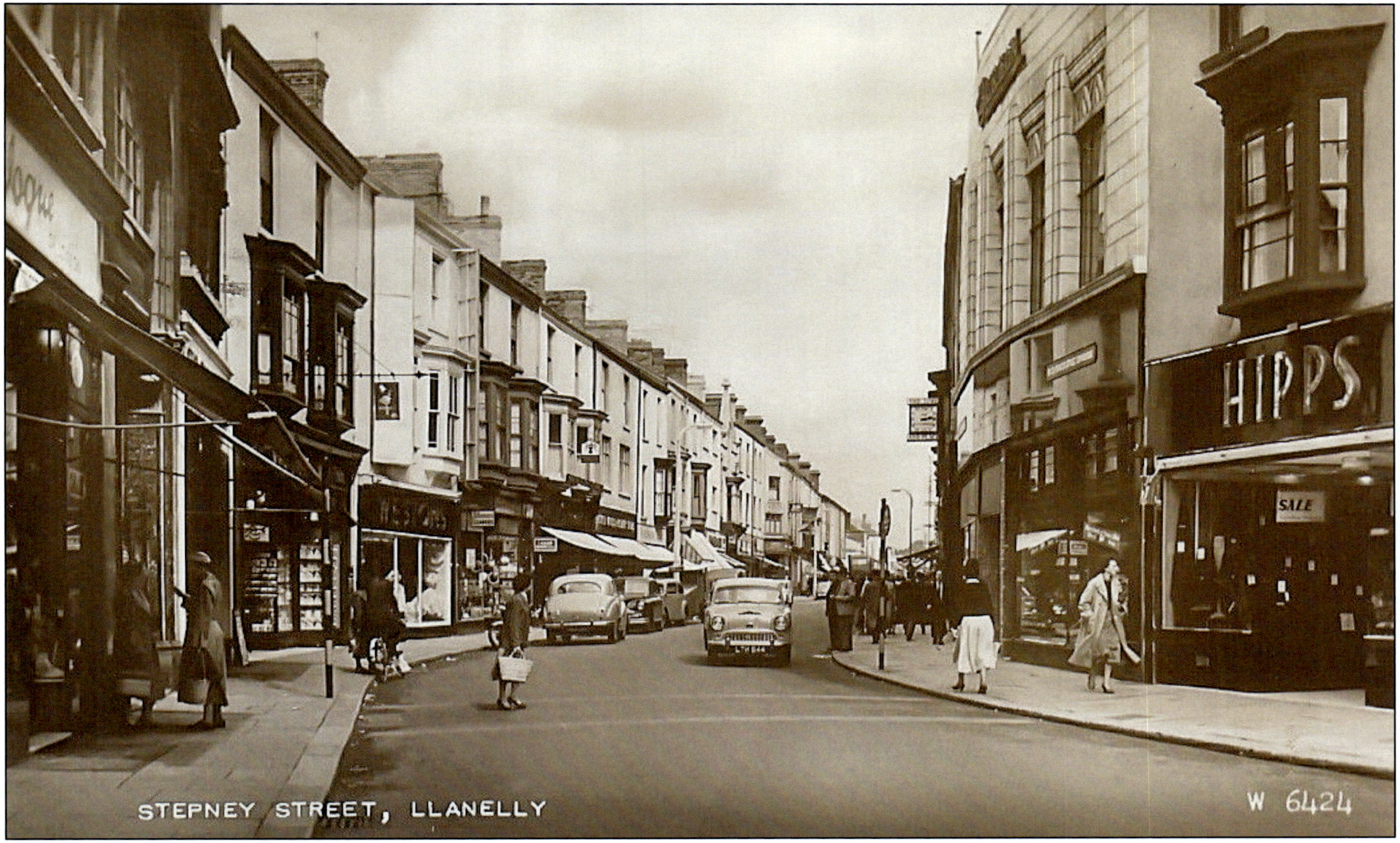


This view of Stepney Street, looking eastwards, was taken in 1956. On the left hand side of the street: Vogue of London; the Arcade entrance; W.H.Smith, Stationers; Weston's; Johnsons the Cleaners, and Paige. Visible on the right hand side are; Hipps (Gents Outfitter); Burtons (Gents Outfitter), and Morris The Realm, (General Store). This street is now pedestrianised at this point.

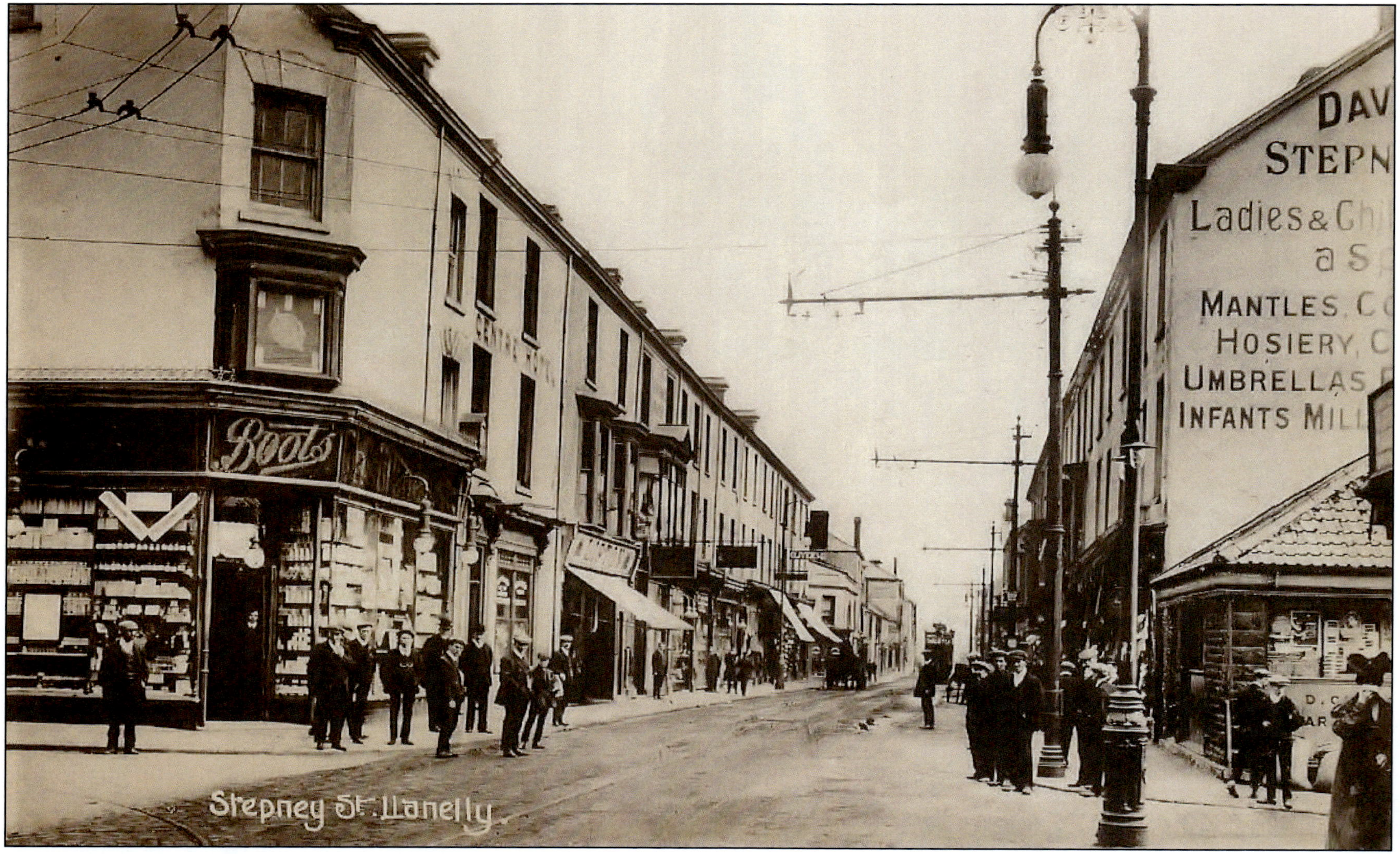


This view of Stepney Street, Llanelli, was taken during World War 1, in 1917, and shows on the left: Boots Cash Chemists; Centre Hotel; Lipton's (Grocer); J. Davies (Chemist); Olivers (Shoe Shop) and Peglers (Grocers). On the right hand side of the street is the entrance to Llanelli Market; David Evans, Stepney House (Outfitter); Bradford House (Drapers); etc. The postcard is by Thomas, 38 Thomas St., Llanelli.

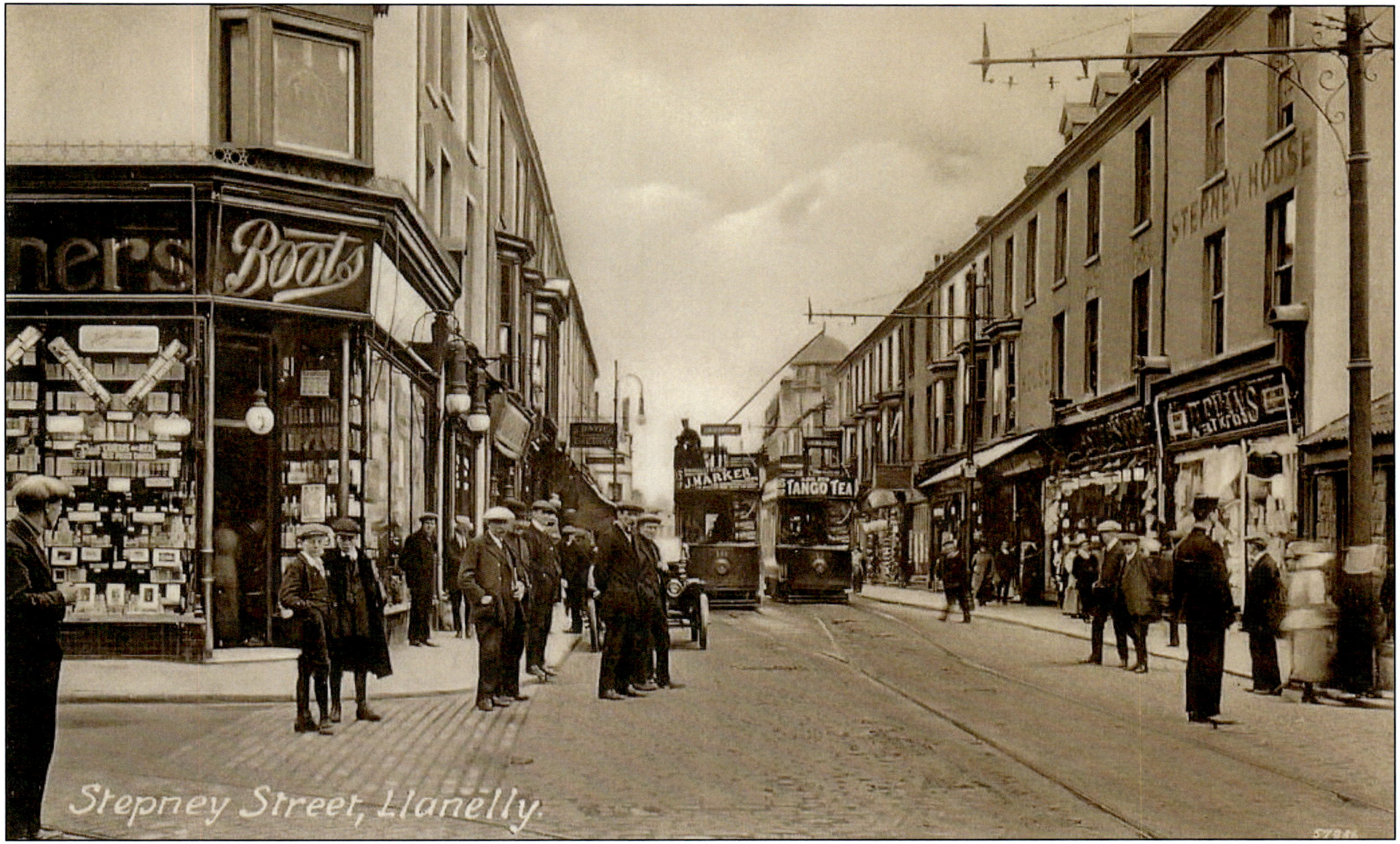


Numerous photographs of Stepney Street have been taken throughout the years, and many of them are quite similar. This one is quite similar to the previous page, but gives a good view of the electric tramcars passing on the loop, outside Bradford House. Tramcar No. 10, on the left, is heading for Bynea, which was the end of the line, whilst tram No. 13, on the right, is returning to Llanelli Railway Station from Bynea. Note the advertisement on tram No. 10, for J. Marker - the Stepney Street tobacconist. This postcard was produced by J. Vaughan Evans & Son, Printers & Stationers, Murray St., later 6 Cowell St, Llanelly.

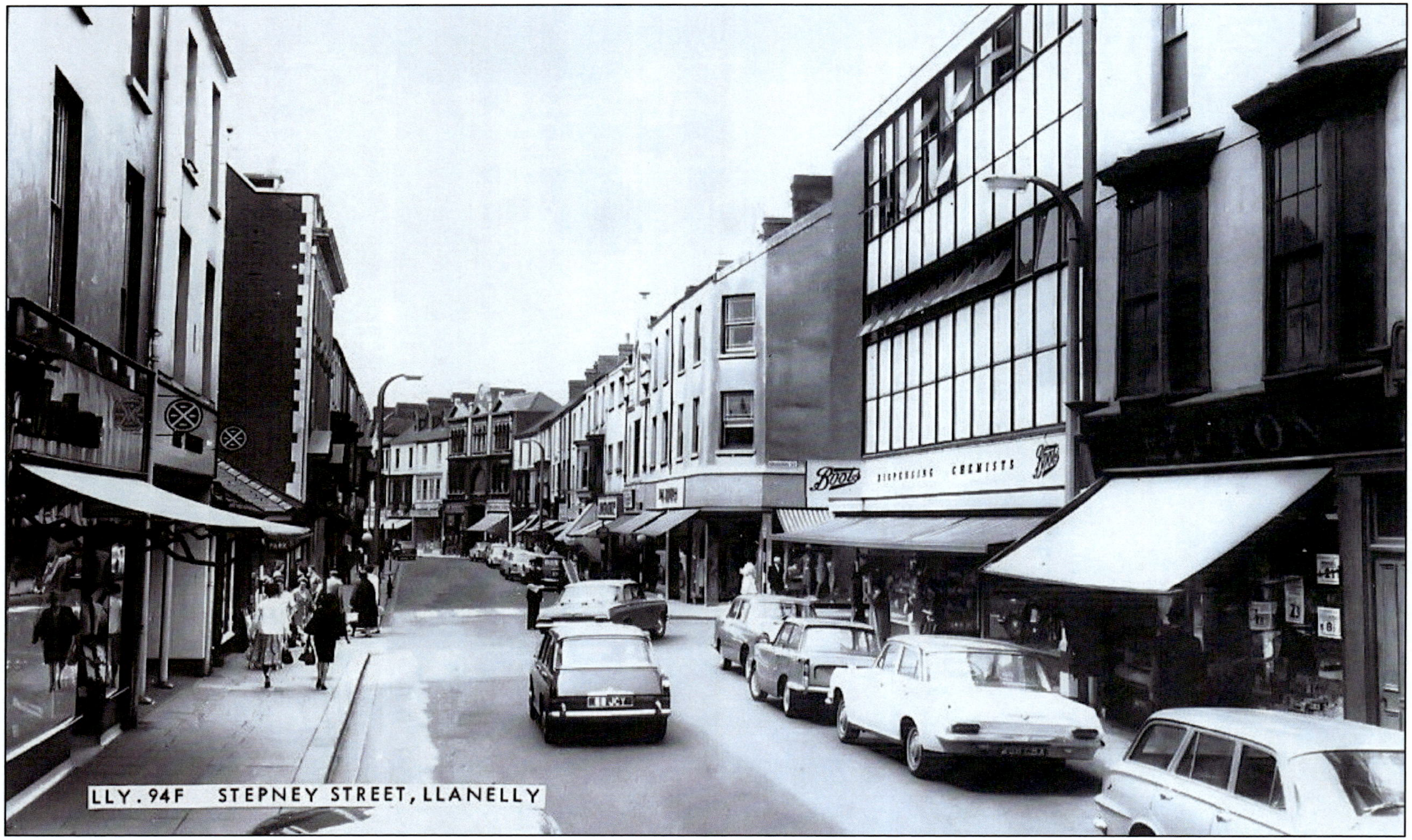


By the time this view of Stepney Street was taken in 1968, Boots the Chemists had been rebuilt and extended into what was previously the Centre Hotel, next door. Boots later vacated this shop and moved to a newly built store across the junction of Vaughan Street, where they remain today (2014). Lipton the Grocer is the shop nearest the camera, on the right hand side, and Masters the outfitters were occupying the old premises of Bradford House, on the left hand side, with Mac Fisheries (Fishmonger) occupying Stepney House next door. Note the Policeman on point duty on the busy thoroughfare outside Boots!

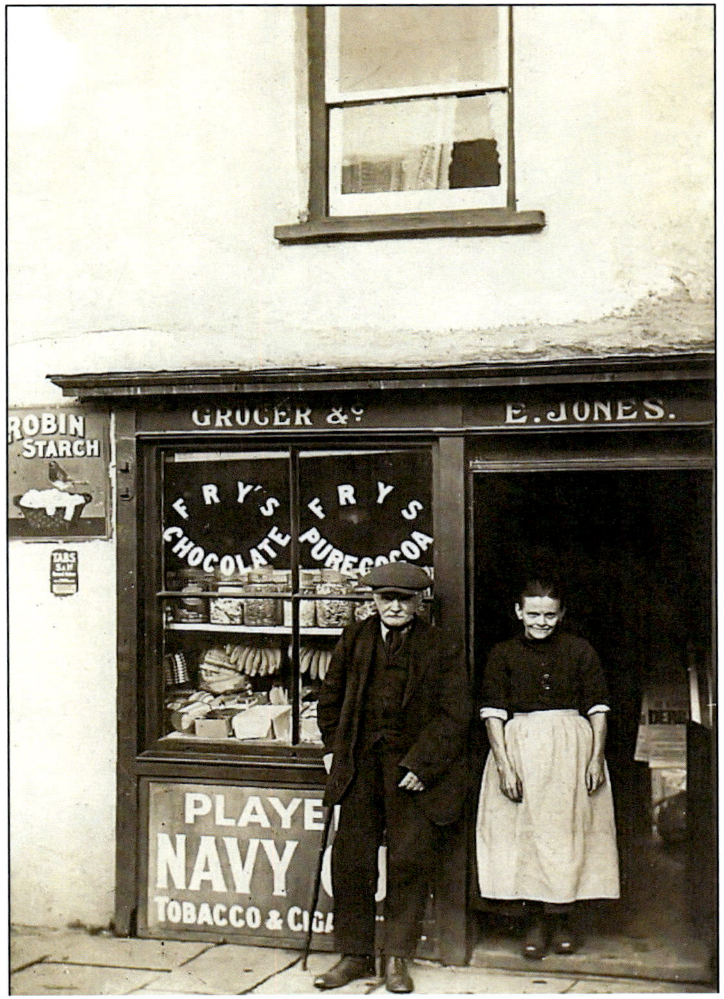


**Above:** A splendid view of a traditional corner shop which stocked items to suit everyone's day-to day requirements. This particular corner shop at 38 Swansea Road, Llanelli, was owned by Edward P. Jones, who poses here for the camera, circa 1910. The shop has received a tremendous face lift during the last 100 years, and today is a fishing tackle shop, in a street which has changed from being a busy thoroughfare, to a cul-de-sac.

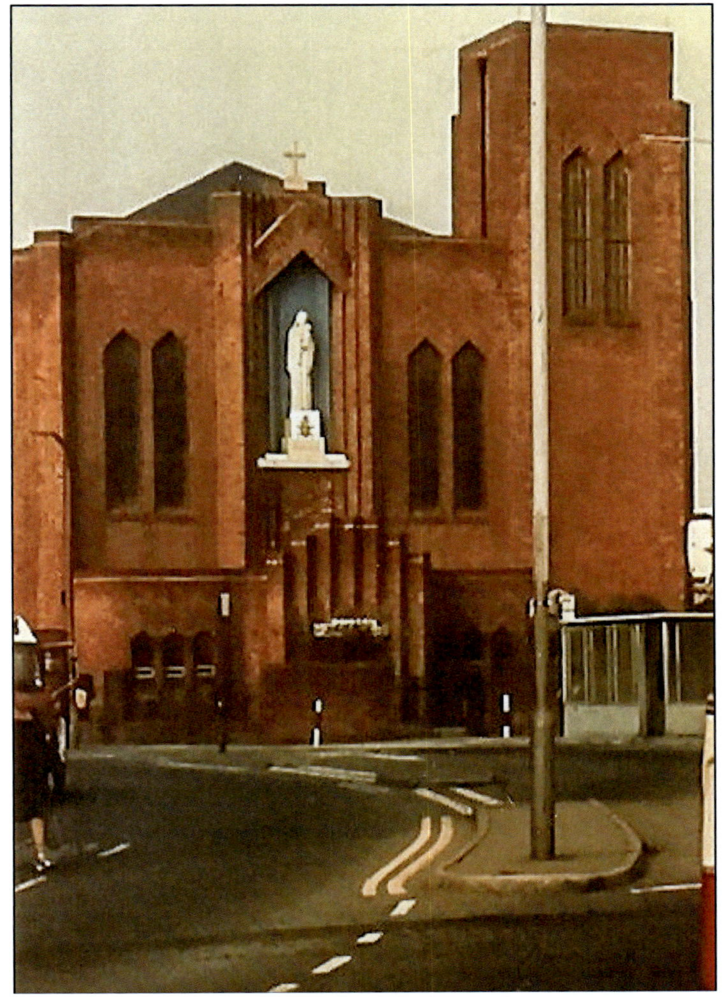

**Above:** Llanelli's Catholic Church in Waunlanyrafon, was a splendid looking structure when it was built in 1938-9, but unfortunately did not survive. It was plagued with structural faults and had to be demolished in 1988/9. It was later replaced by a new church named 'Our Lady, Queen of Peace'.

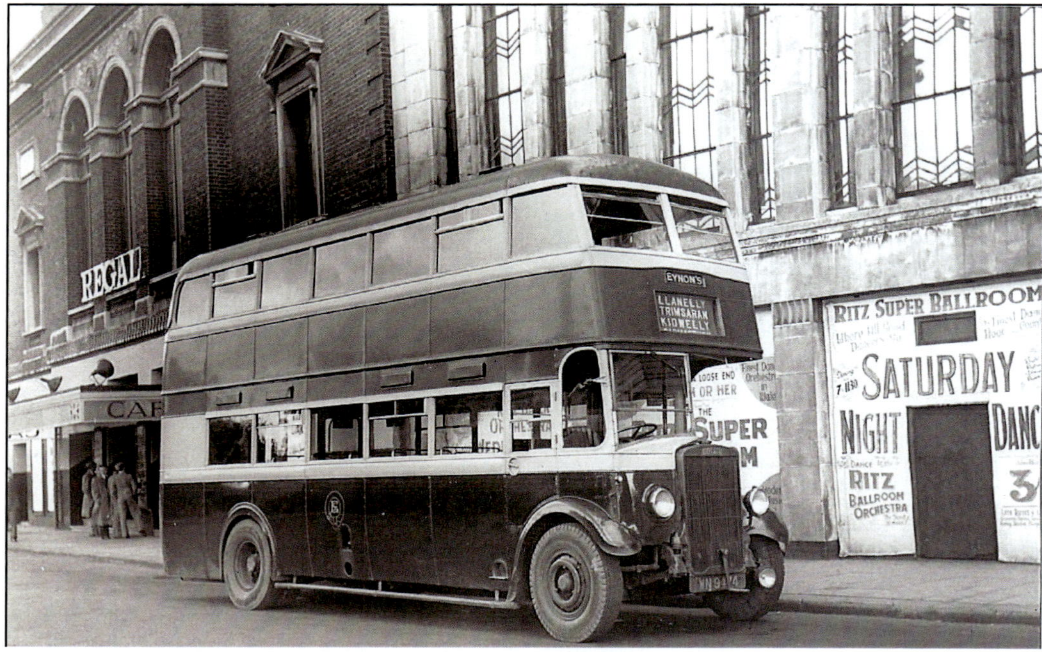


**Left:** This picture of the Ritz Ballroom in Llanelli's Town Hall Square was taken in 1952. The Ritz was a very popular dance venue in the 1950s, and was also used as a roller skating rink between 1959-62. The place was re-furbished in 1962-3 when an upper floor was added, becoming the new dance floor, and the ground floor was converted into a ten pin bowling alley - the first in Wales. The re-vamped Ritz was then called the Glen Ballroom and Scotts of Llanelli Tenpin Bowling (Scotlanes). Nowadays, the ground floor is a café and amusement arcade, and the upper floor a snooker hall. Next door was the Regal Cinema and café. The Regal was completely gutted by fire and demolished in the early 1970s. The site is now occupied by new council offices, built in 1982, known as Ty Elwyn. The bus, a pre-war Leyland Titan was working between Llanelli and Kidwelly for, the now extinct, 'Eynon's of Trimsaran'.

(V. Morgan collection).

**Right:** A complimentary entry ticket for the Glen Ballroom, dated 11th February, 1965; signed by the Ballroom Manager, Mike Monkton.

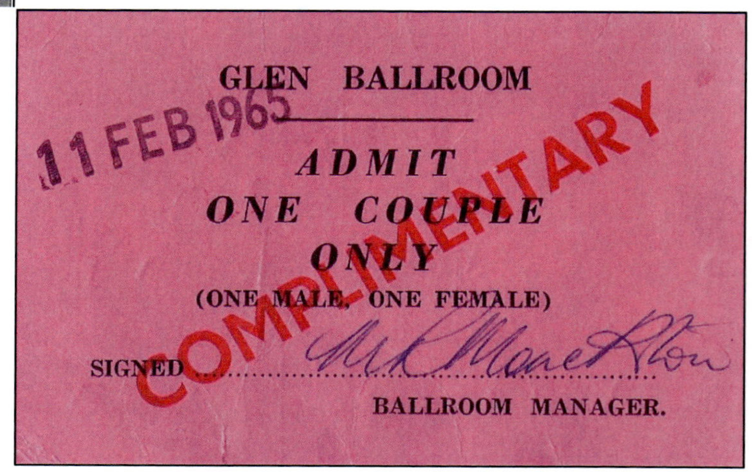

# HALLETT'S

**Service Station, William St.**

**LLANELLY**

We have much pleasure in announcing that we have been appointed official **Sole Distributors** for the famous . . . .

**Isetta and Messerschmitt Bubble Cars**

and invite you to a demonstration and trial run in these popular models, without obligation

| Now in our Showrooms<br>I<br>Latest<br>SKODA<br>Cars | HIRE PURCHASE<br>*<br>PART EXCHANGES | Our Modern Lubrication Bay Now in Operation |
|---|---|---|

Telephone **Mr. BIRT,** our Manager, at **LLANELLY 2980** for your appointment

THIS WEEK'S BARGAIN OFFER—1954, 350 cc. B.S.A.

**Left:** This advertisement is dated 2nd June, 1960.
Fred Hallett was a renowned Llanelli businessman who tried his hand at several types of businesses. Beginning with an ironmonger's shop in Murray Street Llanelli, on the site of what is now the Conservative Club, he diversified into tools and ironmongery, selling ex-Government surplus stock. He then moved to other locations in town, Thomas Street and Stepney Street, and also Castle Street, Swansea. Buying a plot of derelict land at William St., Llanelli, near the Island House pub, he built a garage, service station, and car showroom with car sales. Mr Hallett was the first man in Llanelli to sell 'cut-price' petrol, and cars would queue along the road to buy his 'cheap petrol'. Cut price tyres were another venture. However, a second garage was acquired a short while later, and was the former premises of F.W. Leason & Co., in Murray Street. A Ford car dealership was secured in 1965. Mr. Hallett later acquired an old timber yard at Pottery Street, Llanelli, where he opened another garage and petrol station.
When a colleague of mine began working at Hallett's garage in 1964, there was a famous Messerschmitt bubble car still there, brand new, which no one wanted to buy!

**Right:** David Williams of the Falcon Garage, Bridge Street, Llanelli, placed this advertisement for his dealership of Essex cars, into the Carmarthen Journal newspaper, on 11th December, 1925. Essex, however, was not a success, and soon fell by the wayside. David Williams subsequently switched to a dealership for Morris cars, and even ran a taxi and coach hire business. He also advertised a daily coach service to London in 1932, at nineteen shillings single, or twenty-nine shillings-and-six-pence period return. Compared with today's money, this is a 90 pence single, or £1.47 period return. Was that cheap? - Eynons' Coaches were charging just £3.00 day return in 1981, so that was a bargain!

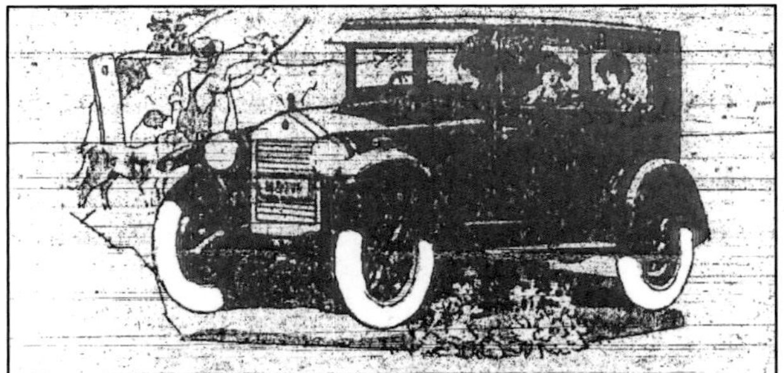

# ESSEX COACH

now **£280** now

*The price was reduced by £15 on November 23*

The Essex Coach with the acknowledged superiority of smoother, vibrationless performance of its 6 cylinder engine, and its all-year-round comforts and advantages, is now priced far lower than *many open touring cars of lesser quality and engine power.*
To-day's Essex, in all ways, is the finest ever built. Easier riding and driving, handsomer in line and finish, and lower in price than ever before. Essex represents the utmost in motor car value and satisfaction, because it offers the great combination of chassis quality, car performance and economy in maintainance

Distrib uto rs for the County of Carmarthen—

**DAVID WILLIAMS.**

**FALCON GARAGE——LLANELLY.**

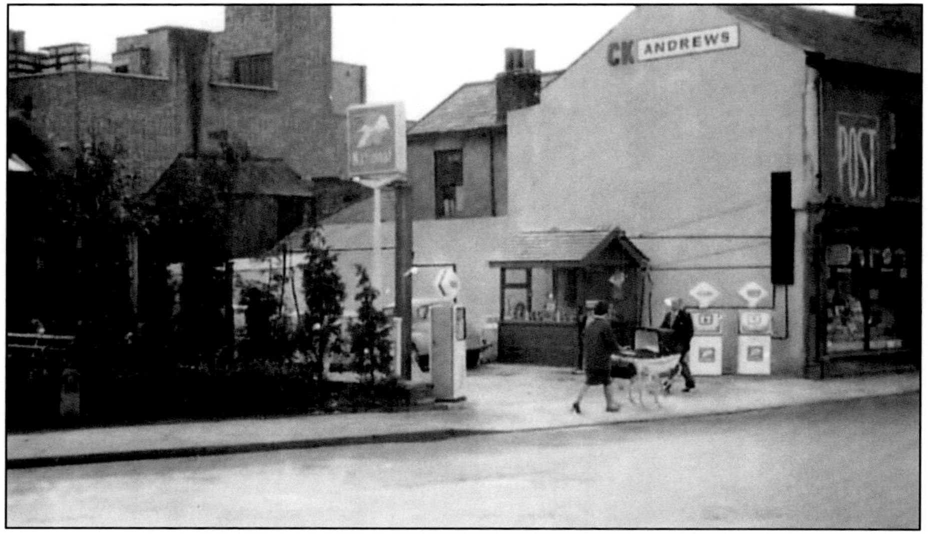


**Left:** C. K. Andrews were a Swansea based company, and main dealers for Morris; M.G; Riley; and Wolseley cars. They moved here to Bridge Street, Llanelli when they took over the business of David Williams, Falcon Garage in the 1950s (see previous page). Their small garage workshop was situated behind the petrol forecourt, selling National petrol (formerly National Benzole). Their showrooms, which were quite small, were situated across the road, at the bottom of Thomas Street. C.K. Andrews, however, closed down their Llanelli premises in 1972.

The tall building in the background was the newly built extension of Woolworth's store, built in 1962/3.
(V. Morgan collection).

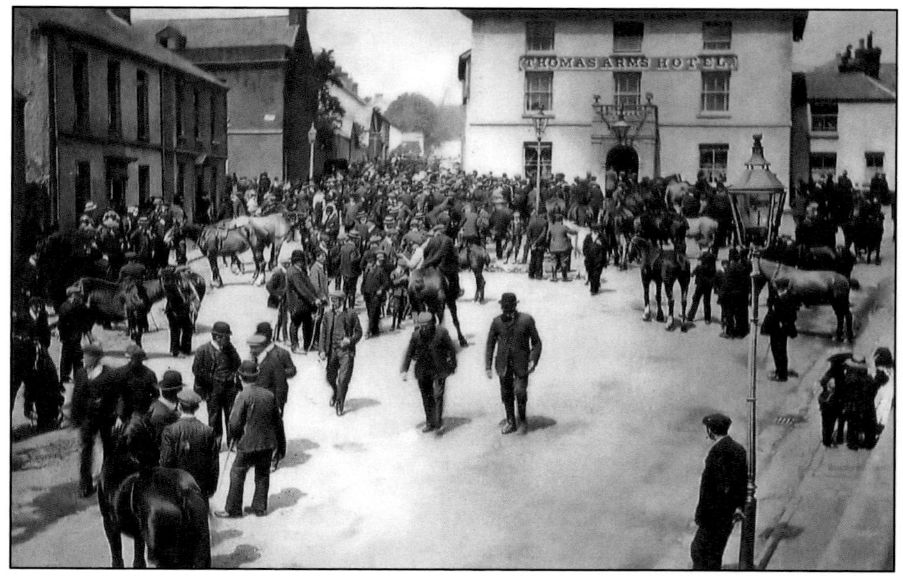


**Right:** The Thomas Arms Hotel and Thomas Street, Llanelli hasn't changed very much in the last century. This is a view of Thomas Street in 1911, when the annual horse fair was being held there. Note the absence of motor traffic – a rather different scene to that of today.
(John Phillips collection).

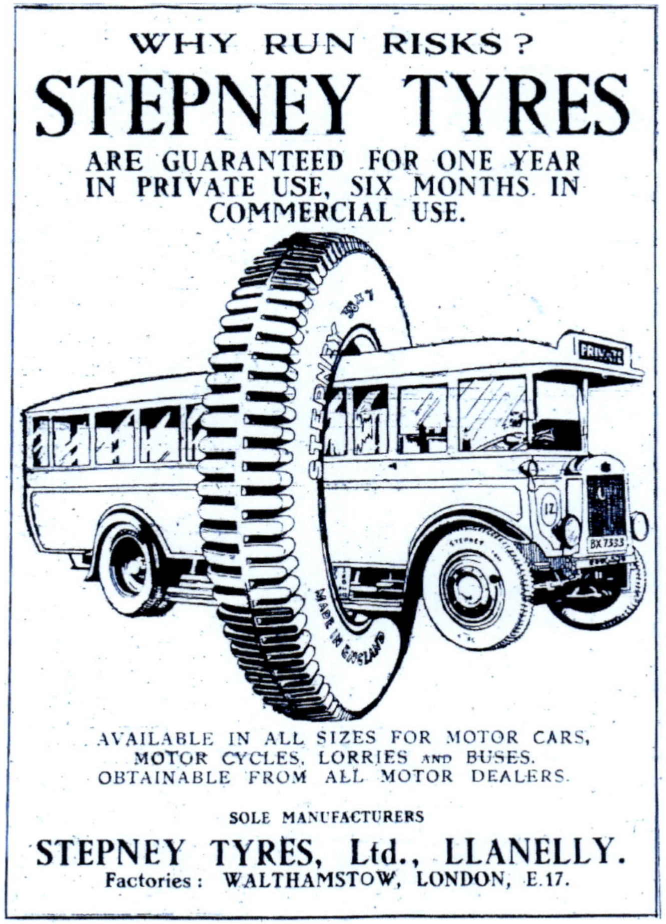


**Left:** A Llanelli man, named Morris Davies, invented and patented the spare wheel for motor cars in 1904. Forming a company called Stepney Spare Wheel Co., in partnership with his brother, they opened a factory adjacent to Llanelli railway station, where they manufactured 'clamp on' spare wheels. Re-forming the company as Stepney Tyres in 1922, they opened a new factory at Walthamstow, London, where they manufactured pneumatic tyres to suit all motor vehicles, as seen in this advertisement dated 1927.

**Right:** John Pryce Ferriday, of Coleshill Terrace, Llanelli, commenced a car hire and charabanc business in 1913. Joined later by his brother, the business became known as Ferriday Brothers, operating from Sandy Garage at Raby Street, Llanelli - a premises which still stands today at the bottom of Sandy Bridge. Their charabancs, named 'The Florence', were used for private hire parties and outings. In 1920, the brothers accepted a Ford motor car agency, as seen from this advertisement dated August 1920.
The business closed down in 1924.

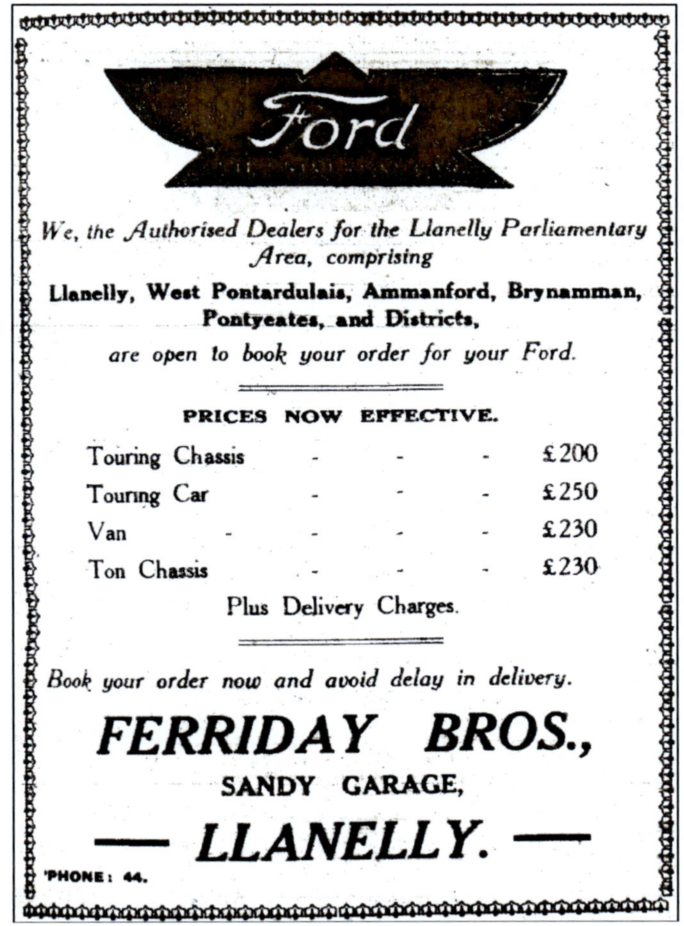

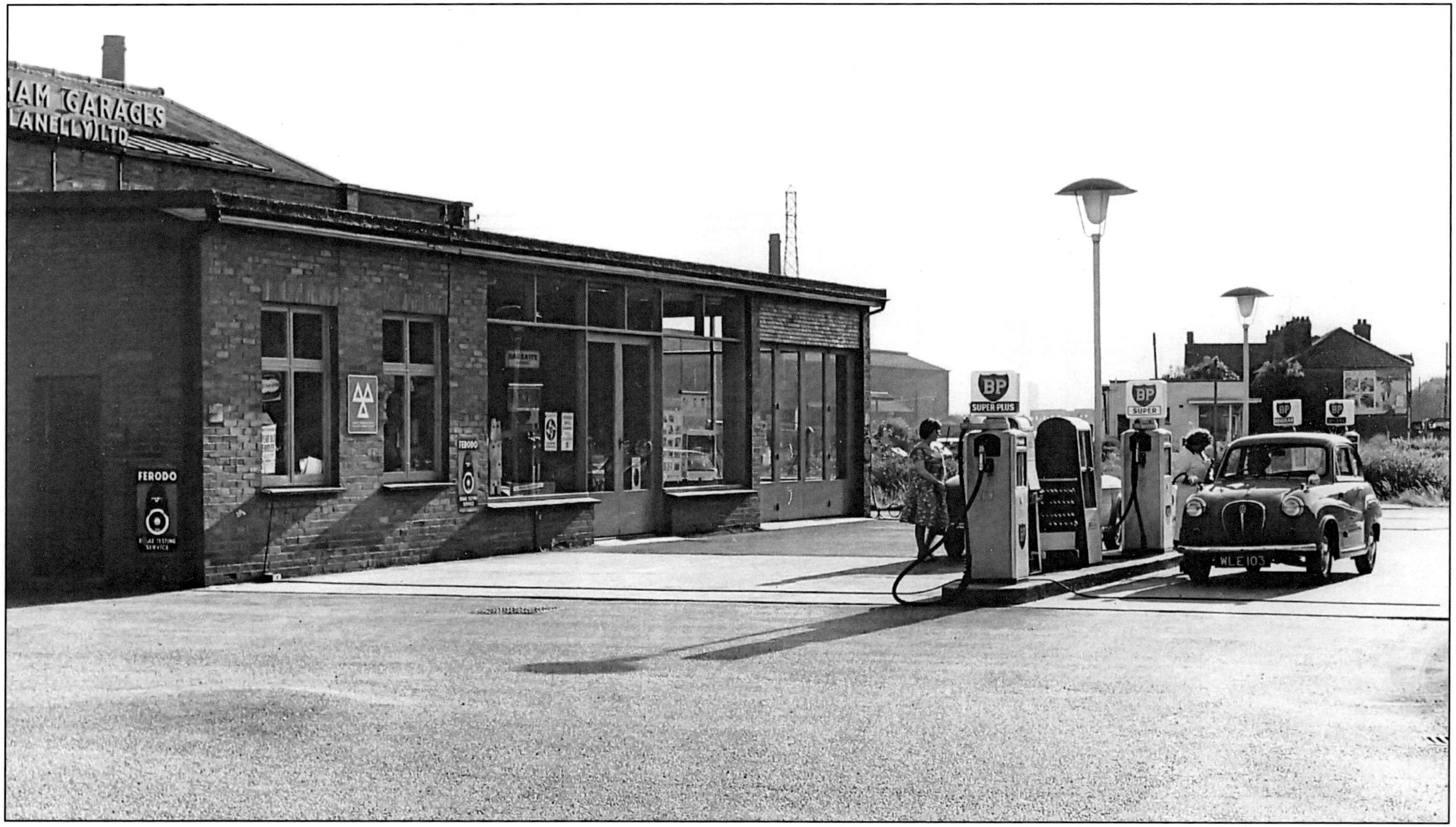


Denham Garages of Sandy Road, Llanelli, was originally built for John Evans & Sons (Llanelly) Ltd., a transport company formerly of Bancffosfelin, Pontyberem. The garage, built in 1957, had a franchise for Rover cars, which were sold from their showroom (pictured here) on the forecourt. After changing hands a few times, namely to George Rees (Ford) and J. B. Wheeler & Son Ltd (Vauxhall), the premises now has a modern rebuilt showroom, and a forecourt without petrol sales, which is owned by Cawdor Cars Ltd. The large building just visible behind the showroom is Sandy Sheetworks.

(Peter Evans Collection).

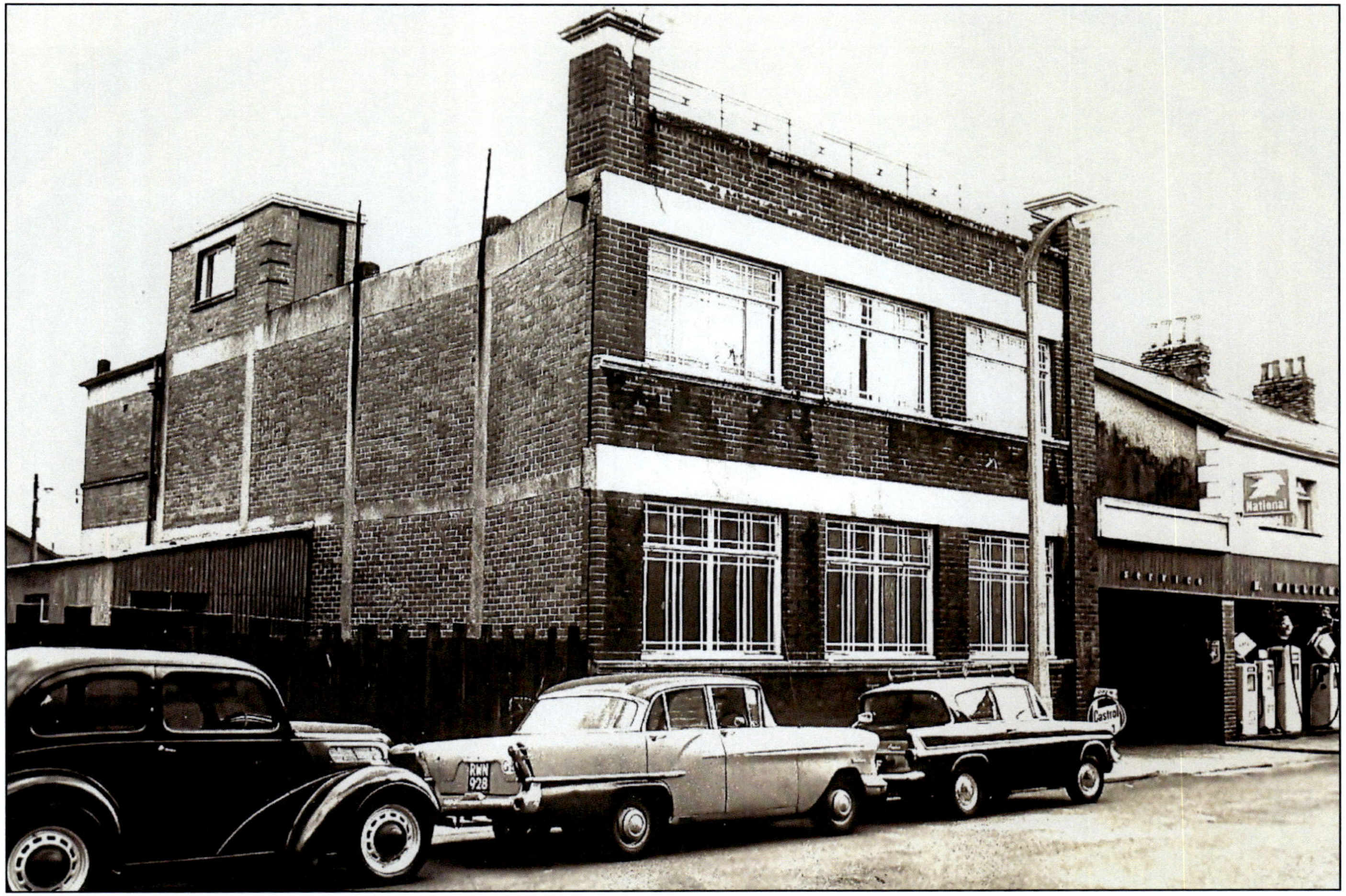


This office block in Inkerman Street, Llanelli, was built by the Llanelli & District Electric Supply Co., Ltd., (LLANESCO) and passed into the hands of the South Wales Electricity Board upon nationalisation of the electricity industry, in 1948. SWEB moved out in 1962, and the South Wales Transport Co., already sharing the adjacent yard, took over the complete premises. The building, now somewhat altered, is owned by First Cymru Buses, and is offered for sale along with the depot, at the time of writing (2014). The garage and petrol filling station next door, then owned by Ken Williams & Son, remains virtually unaltered today, except that no petrol is sold. The practice of selling petrol over the pavement became illegal many years ago.

(V. Morgan collection).

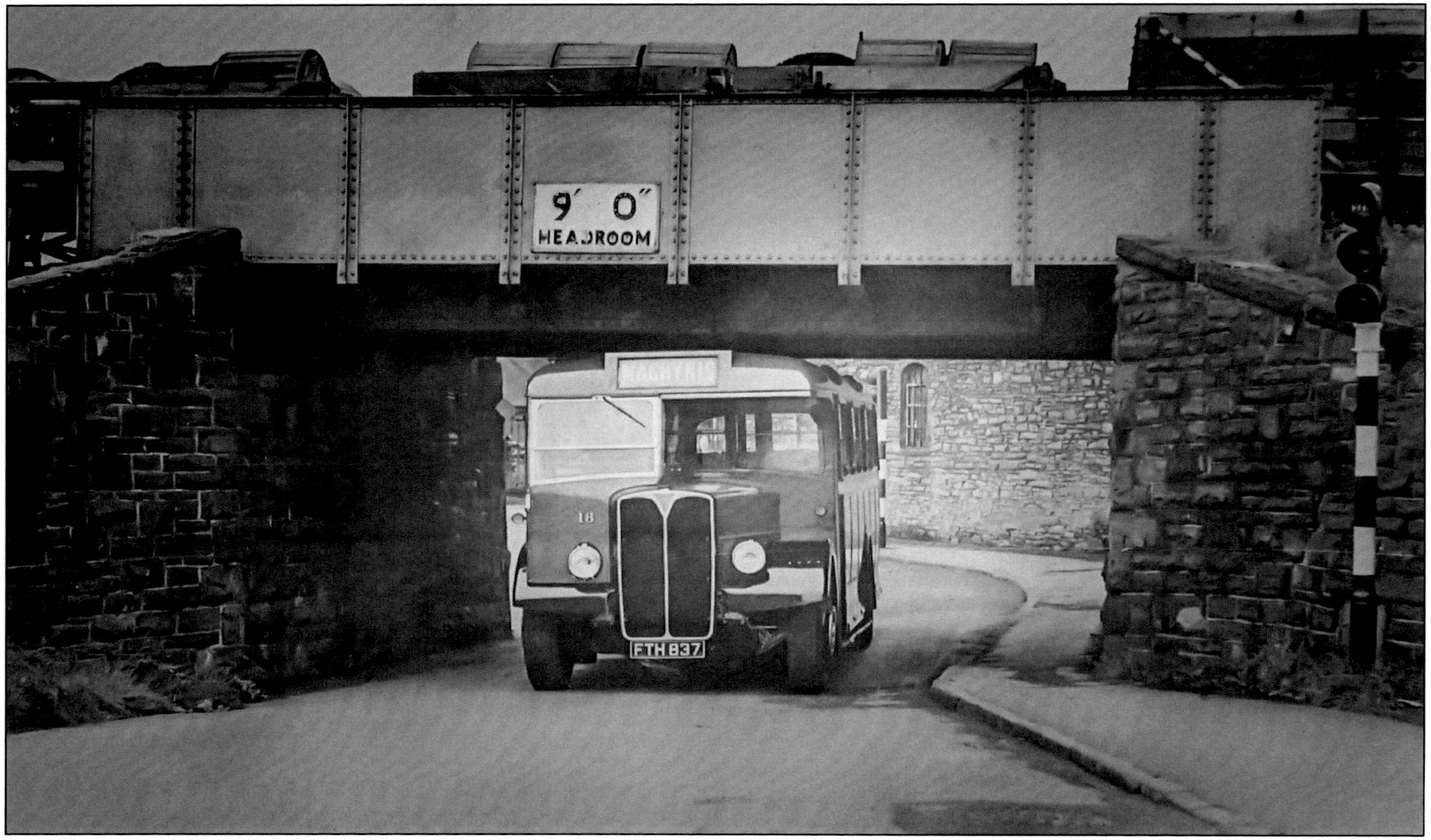


The New Dock district of Llanelli had a large network of railways in the community, serving the heavy industries of the area, together with the GWR loco sheds. As an alternative to having railway crossings, numerous low bridges were constructed in the neighbourhood, as seen here at Trinity Road. The clearance beneath these bridges was exceptionally low, varying between 7ft 9inches and 11ft 0ins, and through the years claimed several bridge collisions. Flooding beneath the bridges was an added problem, as some of the roads were lowered in order to gain extra headroom.

(V. Morgan collection).

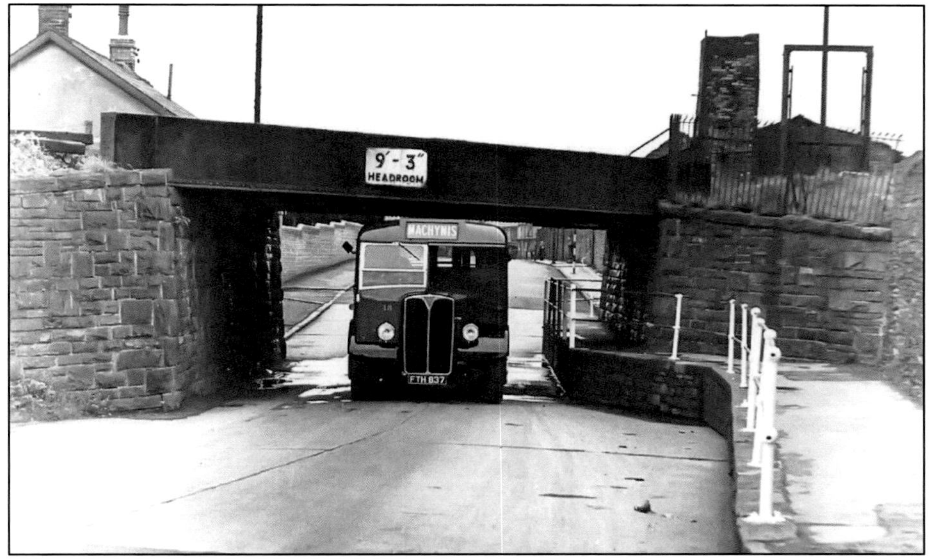


**Right:** This particular low bridge was one of two situated 200 yards apart on Trinity Road. It carried the Dolau branch line into Batchelor Robinson Metals Co. (later AMG Resources Ltd.), Benjamin Howells' timber yard and sawmills, Stanley Street Brickworks, GWR (British Railways) loco sheds, Great Western Dock, Copperworks Dock, and the Copperworks. This photograph features the original steel structured bridge, with 9ft 3ins headroom. It can be seen how much the road had been lowered to gain the extra headroom, by looking at the height of the footpath.

(V. Morgan collection).

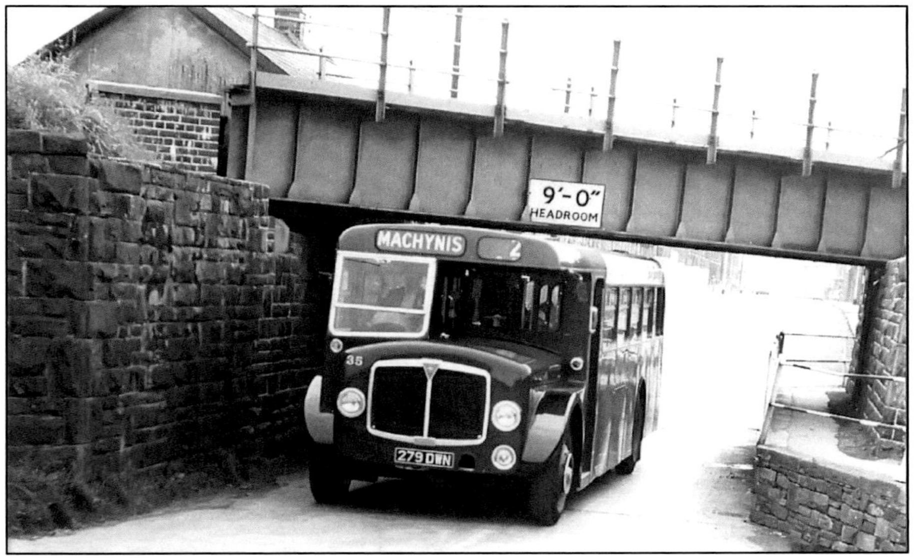


**Left:** This view is of the same location in Trinity Road, as the photograph above, but taken in the late 1960s, after a new steel structured bridge had been built with 3 inches less headroom. This railway line became redundant in 1991, and together with a bridge crossing Dolau Road, were the last remaining bridges in the district to be demolished. The bus passing under the bridge was one of eight specially built, low height single deckers used regularly on this route. They were unique – the only eight ever built on AEC Regent V double-decker chassis. The double-decker chassis had a lower frame than a single-decker, enabling a lower floor and lower roof structure to the vehicle. A sister vehicle to this one, 282 DWN (38) is now preserved in its original form, and can be seen at the Swansea Bus Museum.

(V. Morgan collection).

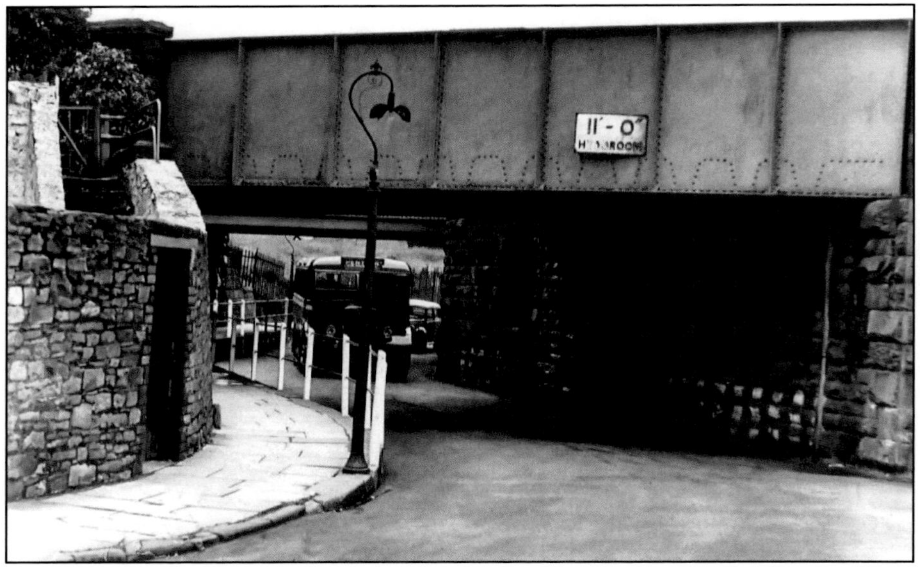


**Left:** Looking southward along Embankment Road, New Dock, Llanelli, this view shows the bridges with the greatest clearance in the district. These pair of bridges at the junction of Embankment Road and Dolau Road (foreground) carried the rail connection into the Great Western Dock, GWR (British Railways) loco sheds, and Benjamin Howells' timber yard. The photograph, taken in 1952, also captures the elegant Victorian cast iron lamp post in the foreground - a delightful piece of street furniture.

(V. Morgan collection).

**Right:** This part of Embankment Road has completely disappeared with the redevelopment of south Llanelli. The trio of bridges were situated on the southern end of Embankment Road, with the entrance to the British Railways loco shed (which closed in November 1965) on the immediate right of this picture, near the antique street lamp. The roadway up the gradient in the background is Embankment Road. Out of sight, behind the bus a lorry, is a street (which remains today) emerging from Dafen Row. This subway was filled in and the roadway diverted after removal of the bridges. Lidl supermarket has since been built close to this location.

(V. Morgan collection).

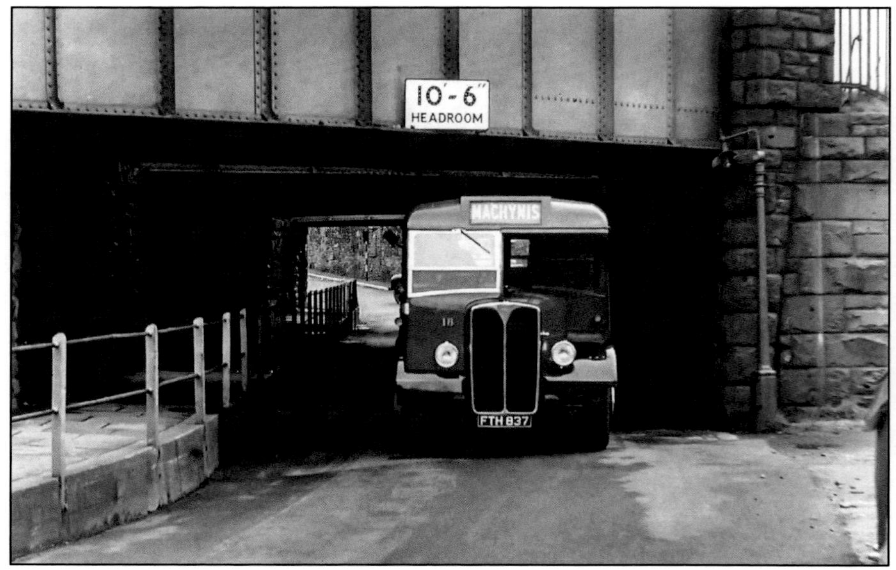

**Right**: This view of Murray Street was taken in 1964, when traffic flow was two way. The Albion Inn, a 'Buckley's public house, is on the extreme right. Martin's the gents hairdresser shop is next door, with Holloways Garage (Austin dealer) seen behind the bus, which is loading up for Penyfan. It is hard to believe that all these buildings, except the Drill Hall in the background, have undergone redevelopment. ASDA superstore and the St. Elli shopping centre now occupy this whole area.

(V. Morgan collection).

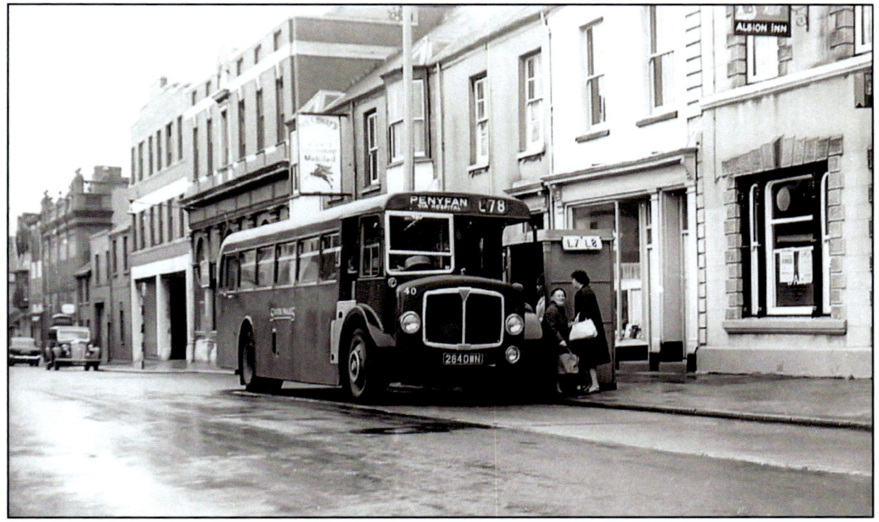


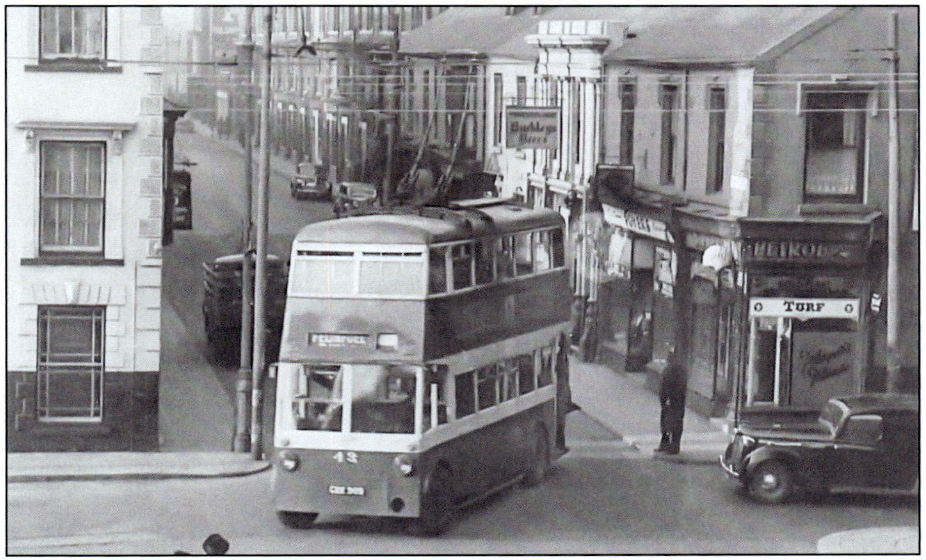


**Left:** Viewed from the footbridge on the eastern end of Llanelli railway station, is this utility built trolleybus of Llanelly & District Traction Co., making a right turn from Station Road into Gt. Western Crescent (Station Approach). The shop on the corner of Emma Street and Station Road, was owned by Poyer's, and also sold petrol. Note the petrol pump outside. The 'Buckleys' public house, next door, is The Apple Tree, and the building on the left hand side of Station Road is the Station Hotel.
The photo is dated March 1952.

**Below**: A 'Bell Punch' bus ticket used by the trolleybus undertaking.

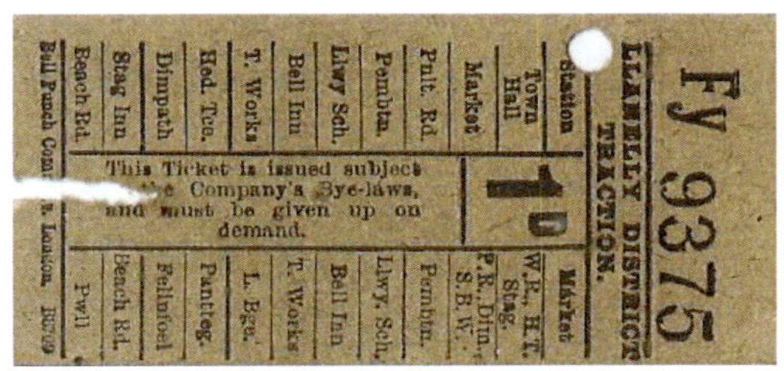

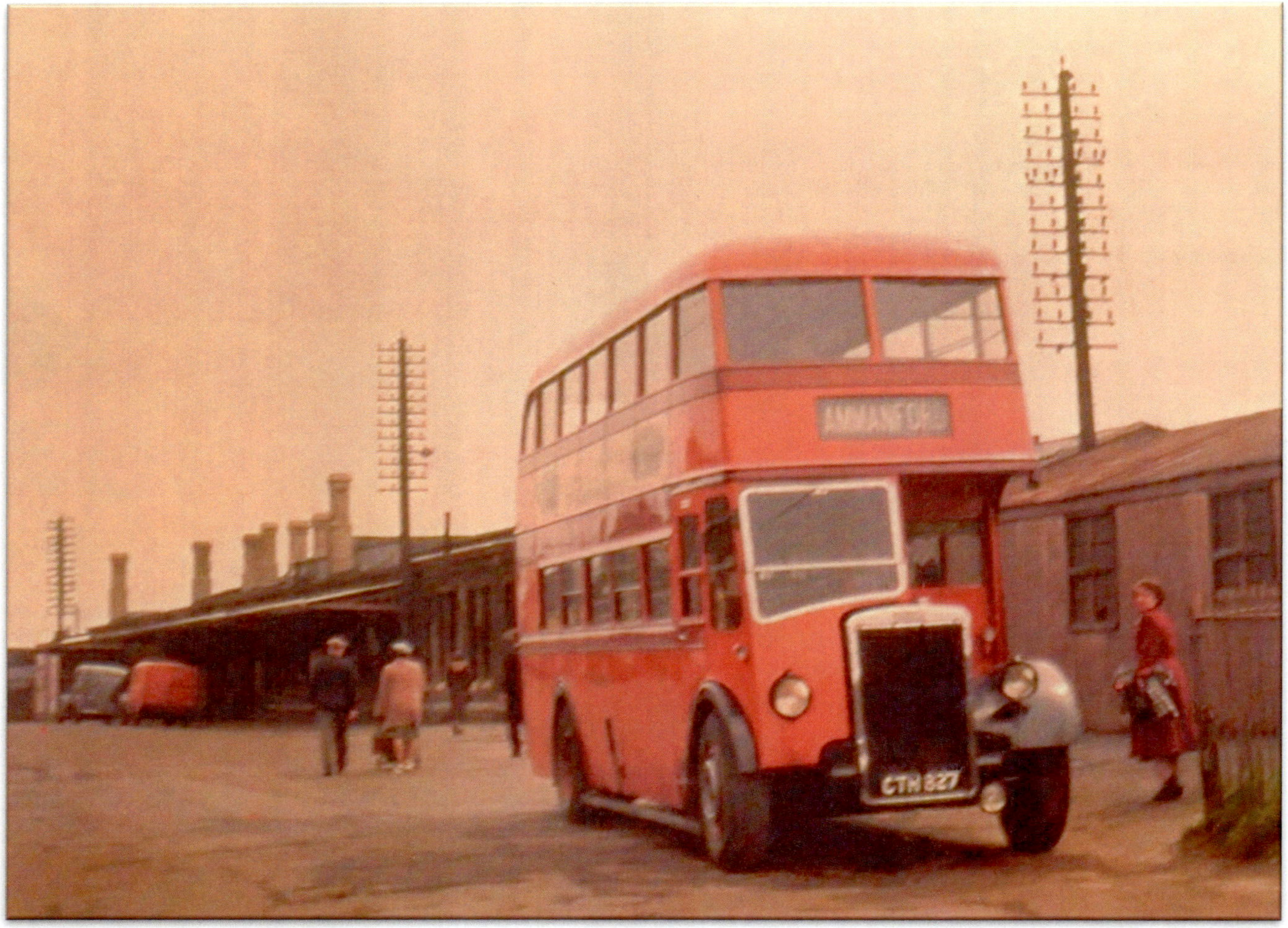


I am indebted to Chris Carter of London for this view of Llanelli Railway Station, taken at Gt. Western Crescent (the station forecourt) in June 1952. Chris came to Llanelli purely to photograph the Llanelli trolleybuses before their demise, and captured this view of James Ammanford's Leyland Titan about to leave for Ammanford. James acquired this service with the take-over of William Jones 'Brynteg' in the 1930's. A detailed history of James' business is still available from the publisher, www.vernonmorgan.com. The buildings visible in this view have changed considerably over the past 60 years, and nowadays, no buses call at the railway station, which was once a very busy bus terminus.

Pugh Brothers were a very reputable family owned furnishing company in Llanelli, and were well known for their high-class quality furniture throughout West Wales. In the early days, they employed their own cabinet makers to build quality furniture in their own workshops at Princess Street, Llanelli. Their shop at Cowell Street, Llanelli, stocked every item of household furnishings imaginable, from bedrooms to kitchens, and cutlery to carpets. They were also very competitive – look at the price quoted for an oak bedroom suite in 1929.

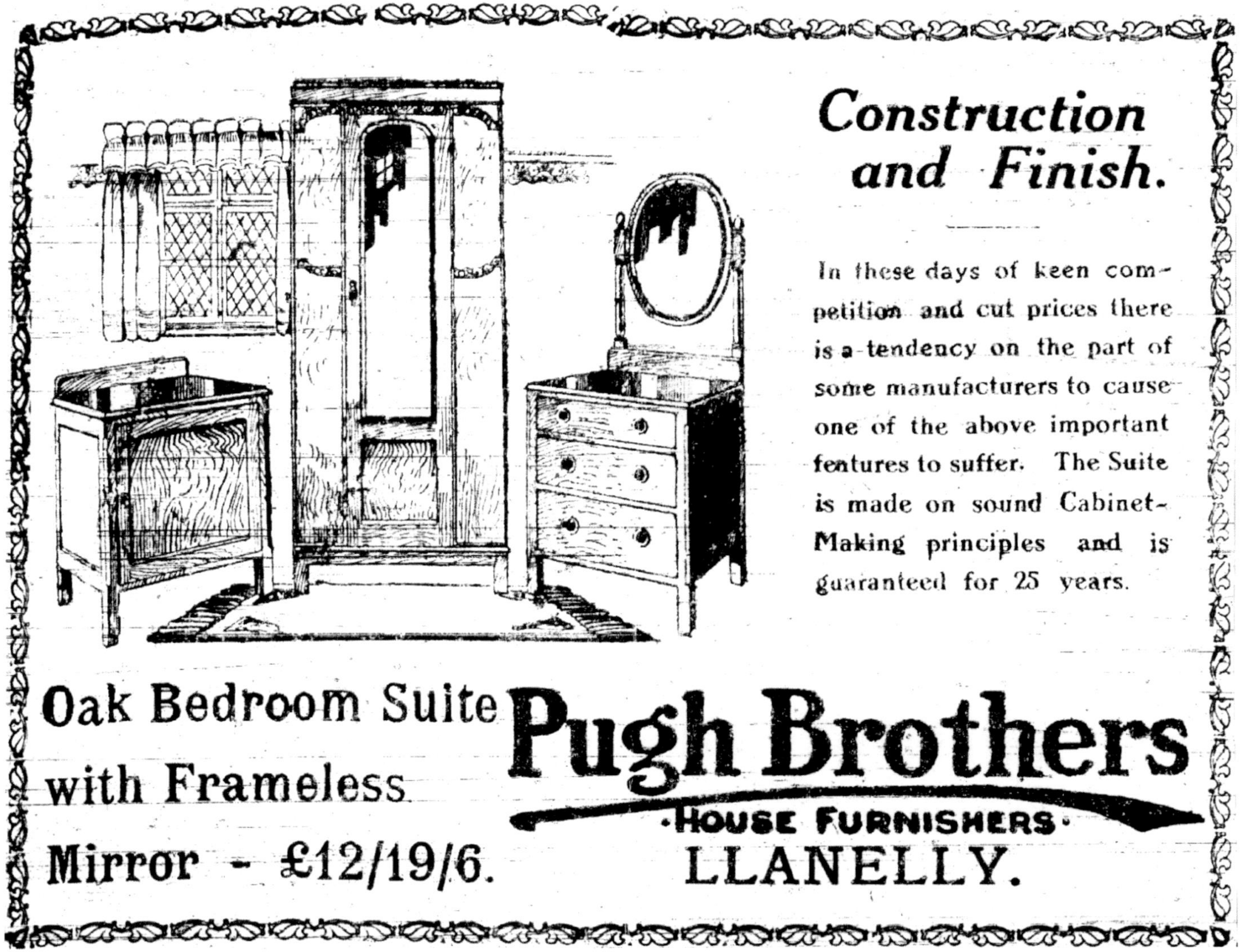

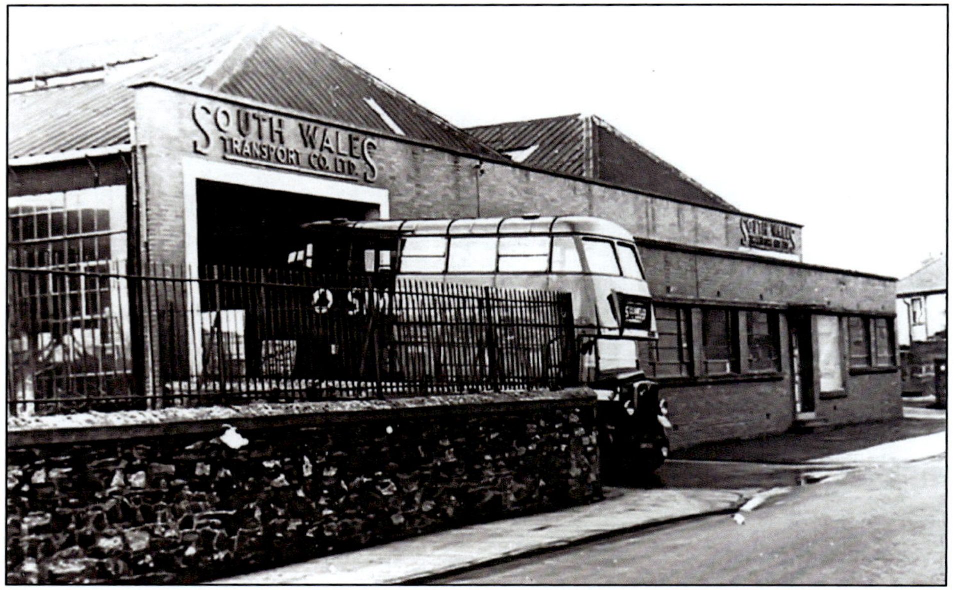


**Left:** The South Wales Transport Co. constructed this fantastic garage in Copperworks Road, Llanelli to house the entire fleet of buses allocated to Llanelli. The floor space of this building was free of structural pillars, and built in 1938. Previously, the fleet had been kept at Spring Gardens and Mina Street, with maintenance carried out in their garage at Erw Road, (the site of Avenue Villa surgery). Following the takeover of Llanelly & District Traction Co., the trolleybus undertaking in 1952, the both depots continued to be used until 1964, when under a rationalisation plan it was decided to house everything together at the former trolleybus depot on Robinson Street – the older of the two depots! Copperworks Road depot closed in 1964 and was eventually sold to the lessor, Neville Druce & Co., the Copperworks, for storage purposes and a social club for Copperworks employees.

(V. Morgan collection).

**Right:** This view of the former South Wales Transport Company's garage at Copperworks Road, Llanelli, was taken in 2003, shortly before it was demolished. The Copperworks Social Club, is just visible on the extreme right - the white building with a blue canopy.

(V. Morgan).

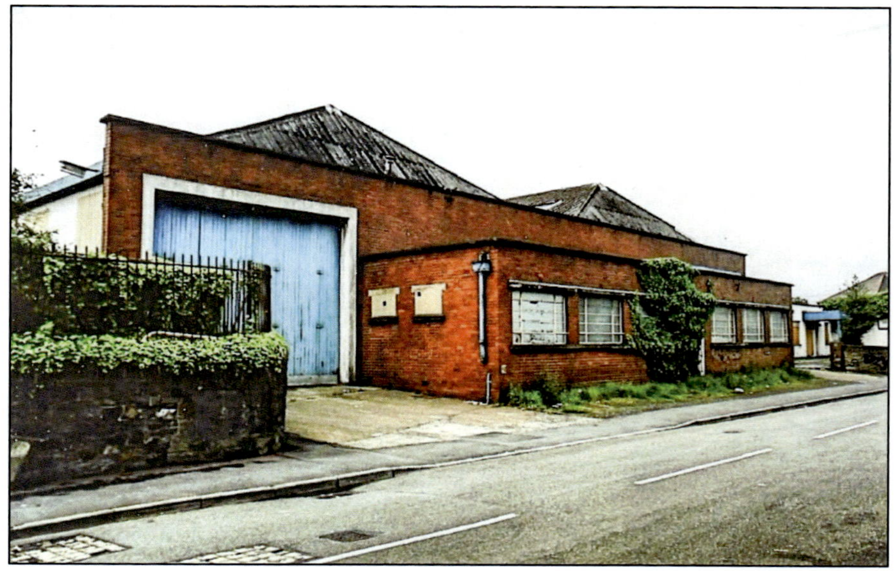

**Right:** The Llanelly & District Electric Supply Co. (LLAN-ES-CO) was a company that owned the Llanelli trolleybus system. They expanded their transport network by 40% in 1936 when they absorbed three local bus operators together with their twelve motor buses. The local services acquired were Furnace – Llanelli – Bwlch-y-gwynt; Penyfan – Llanelli – New Dock, by two different routes: Penyfan – Llanelli – Machynys; Dafen – Felinfoel – Llanelli; and excursions & Tours from the Town Hall. The companies absorbed were Gimblett Motors, Llanelli; R. A. Davies, Halfway; and H. G. Sage of Burry Port. The assortment of acquired vehicles was quickly replaced with new AEC saloons, as pictured here, standardising the motor-bus fleet. Being more versatile than trolleybuses the motor buses were regularly used for private hire duties, as seen below.

(V. Morgan collection).

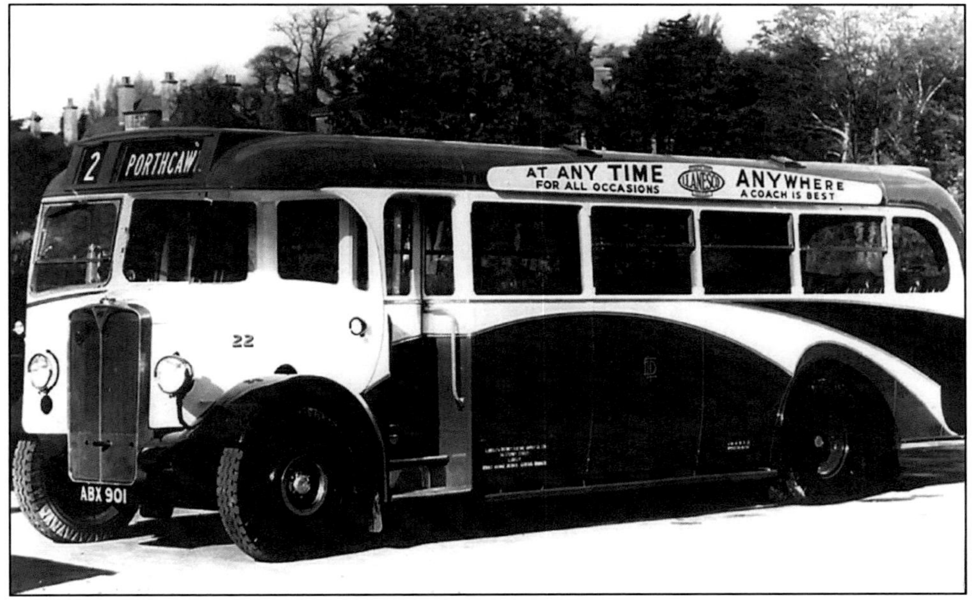


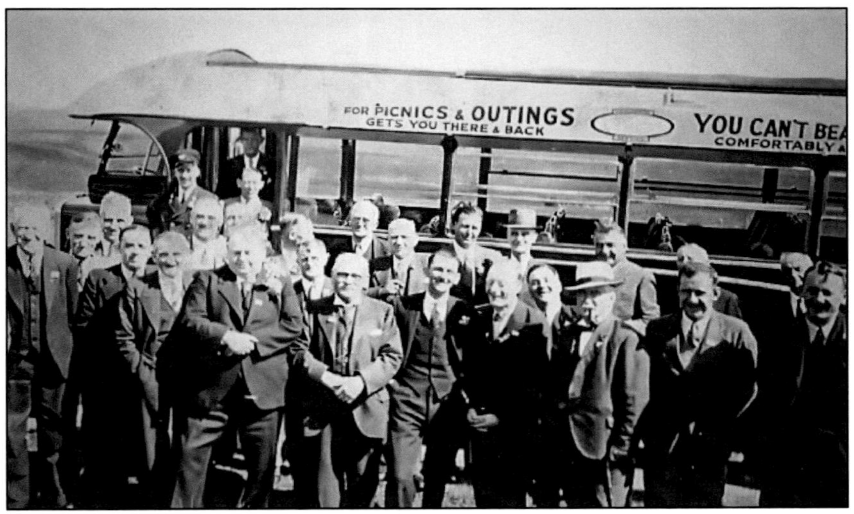


**Left:** This 'LLANESCO' bus is captured here during the 1940's carrying out a private hire job for a party of unknown men on their works outing.

(V. Morgan collection).

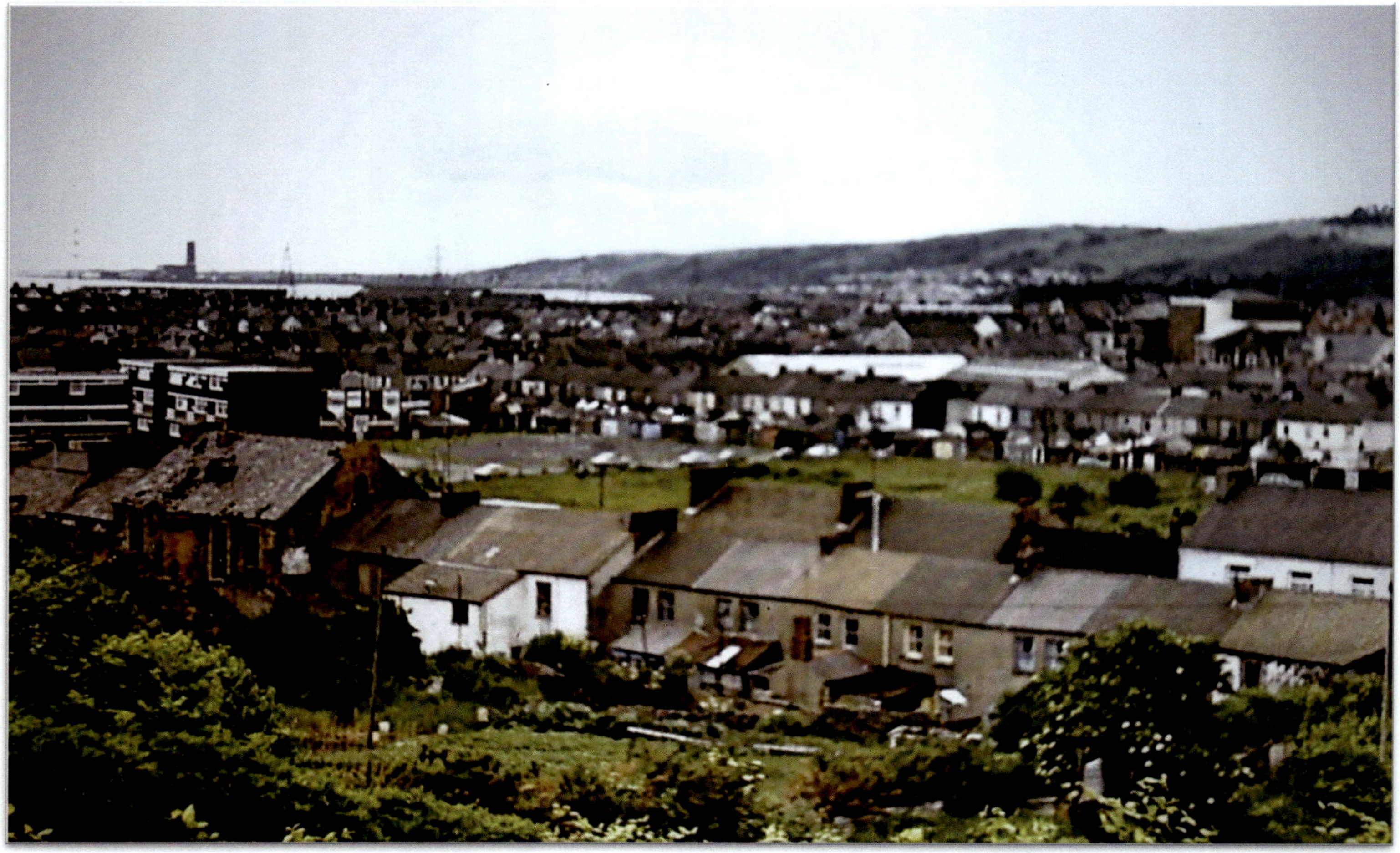

A view of Llanelli from Bigyn School, taken in June 1985, after all the properties in this part of Ann Street (foreground) had been vacated under a compulsory purchase agreement. The derelict building, on the left, had once been a workshop with William Davies & Co. furniture manufacturers of Station Road. In the background, behind the William Davies' building, were the flats of Old Lodge, since demolished and re-developed, along with all the area of lower Ann Street. Robinson Street is the nearest street in the background. Pwll village and Carmarthen Bay Power Station can be seen in the far distance.

Right: This is how Llanelli's 'Jubilee Pool' (swimming pool) looked when it first opened in 1962. It has altered somewhat since the photograph was taken, and it now forms part of Llanelli's leisure centre.
(V. Morgan collection).

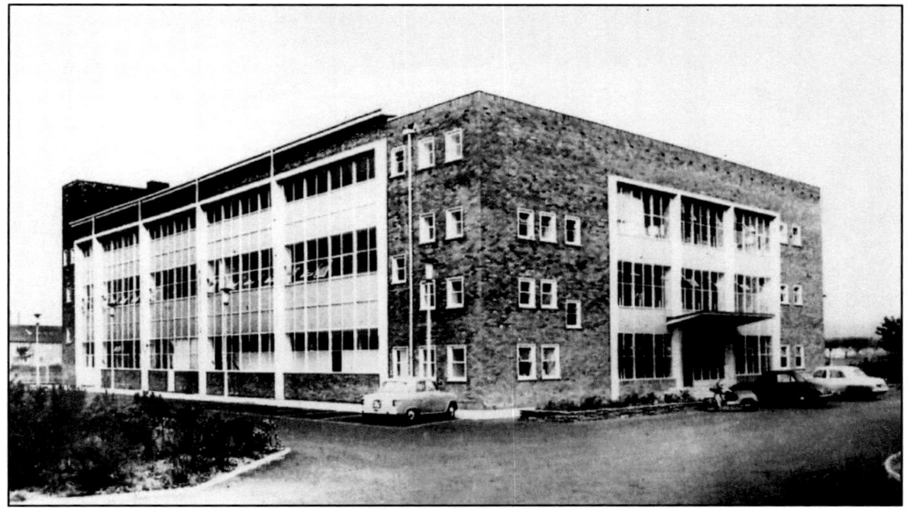

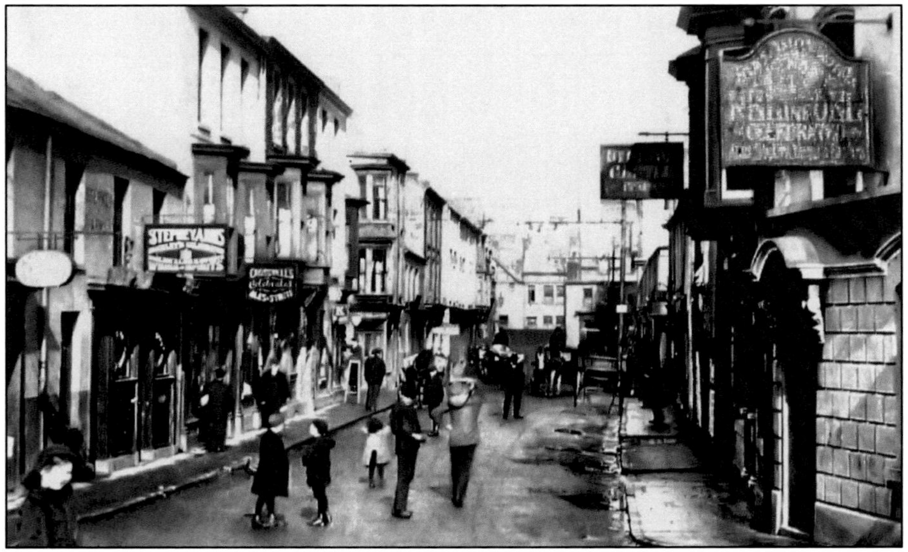

**Left:** Market Street was a very busy street in Llanelli's town centre during the last century. There were numerous shops, public houses, and two cinemas along the street. Five of the pubs are visible in this view dated 1914. They are: Stepney Arms; Cambrian Vaults; The Barley Mow (left hand side), with the Black Lion and Dynevor Castle (right hand side). On the furthest end of Market Street, stood the Bush Vaults, another public house. Most of this street has disappeared during the re-development of Llanelli.
(V. Morgan collection).

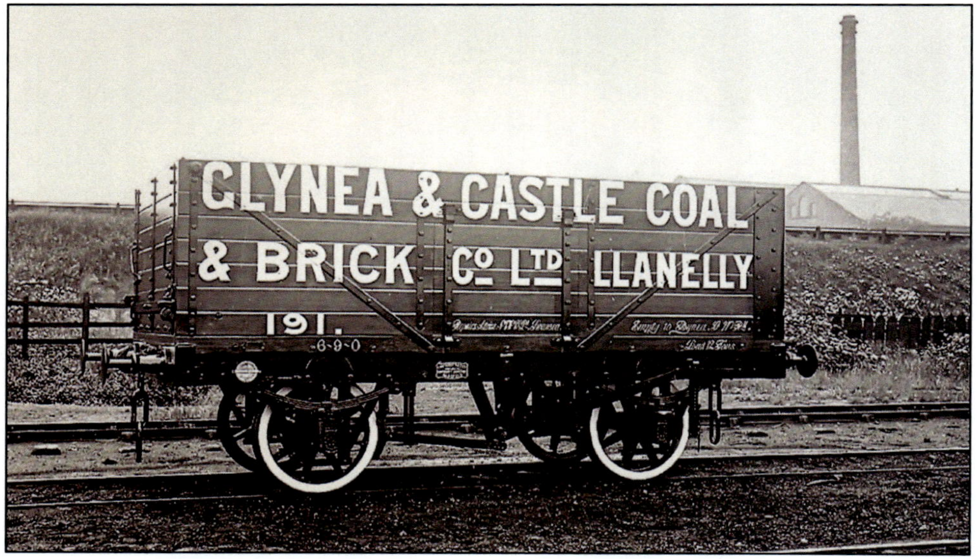


**Left:** Most collieries owned a fleet of railway wagons to transport their products to customers. Glynea Colliery (sunk in 1861) and brickworks was situated in Bynea, adjacent to the railway line, south of Bynea railway station. Remnants of the colliery are still visible today. The business was owned by Neville Druce & Co. of the Llanelli Copperworks, who abandoned the colliery 16th December 1926.

(T. S. Powell collection).

**Right:** Heol-y-bwlch, Bynea is the backdrop of this view taken in 1938. Bynea railway bridge can be seen in the far distance, with a trolleybus en-route for Loughor Bridge, terminus of the trolleybus service from Llanelli railway station.

(T. S. Powell collection).

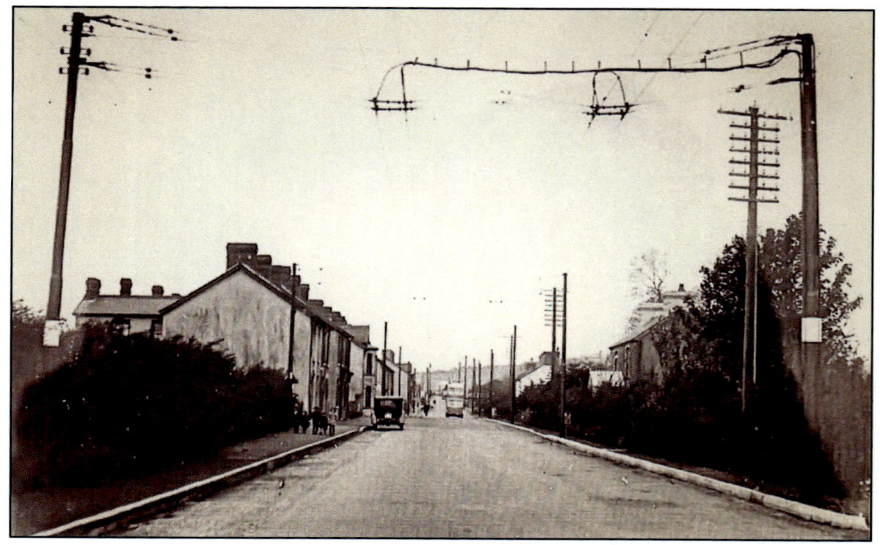

**Right:** The first crossing of the river Loughor at Bynea, was by means of a makeshift ferry, or by foot at low tide. The first road bridge pictured here, was a wooden structure, which had a speed limit of 12 mph imposed on it. This picture, date stamped 1904, is viewed from the Bynea side of the river, looking across to the village of Loughor. The second road bridge to cross the river was built in 1923, and was constructed from concrete. This developed structural defects after 60years, resulting in a weight restriction imposed until a third new road bridge with a steel span was erected and commissioned in 1988.

(V. Morgan collection).

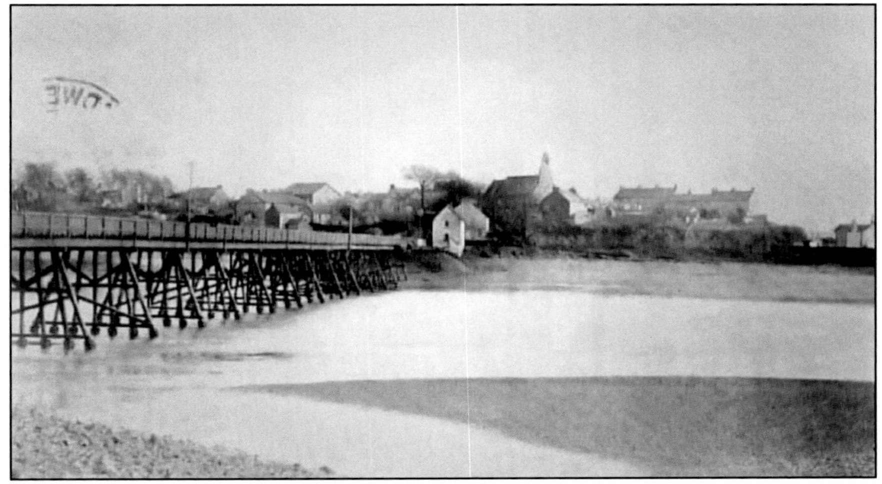

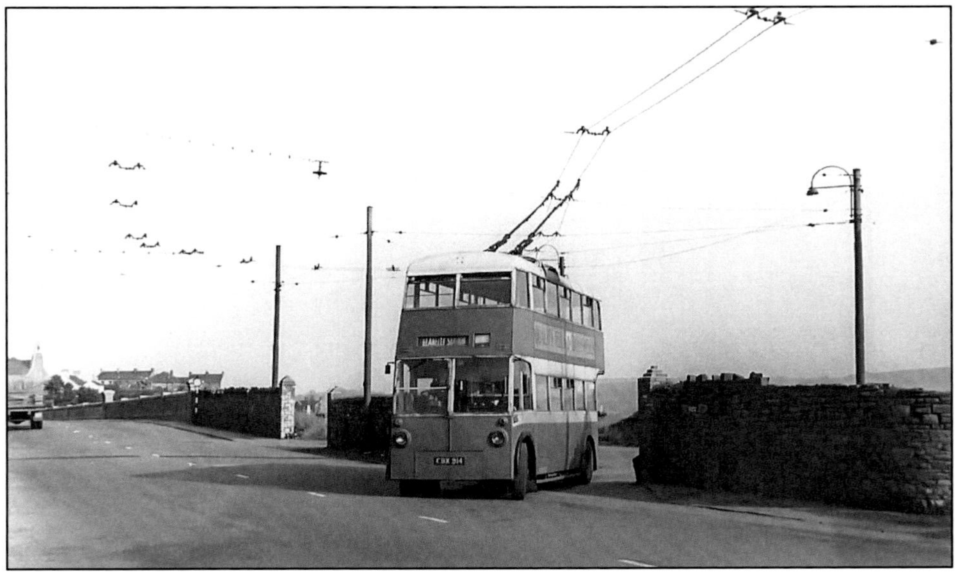

**Left:** The second 'Loughor Bridge' (built in 1923) is visible in this 1952 view of the trolleybus terminus at Yspitty Road, Bynea. Note the overhead wiring for the trolleybus turning circle at this location. For the record, the trolleybus was a 1946 Karrier W, with 85 horse power electric motor and 56 seat utility body, fitted with 'utility' type seats – wooden slats - just like park bench seats. It was new to the Llanelly & District Traction Co., but seen here operating with the South Wales Transport Co., after the L & D T Co. merger in March 1952.

(Chris Carter).

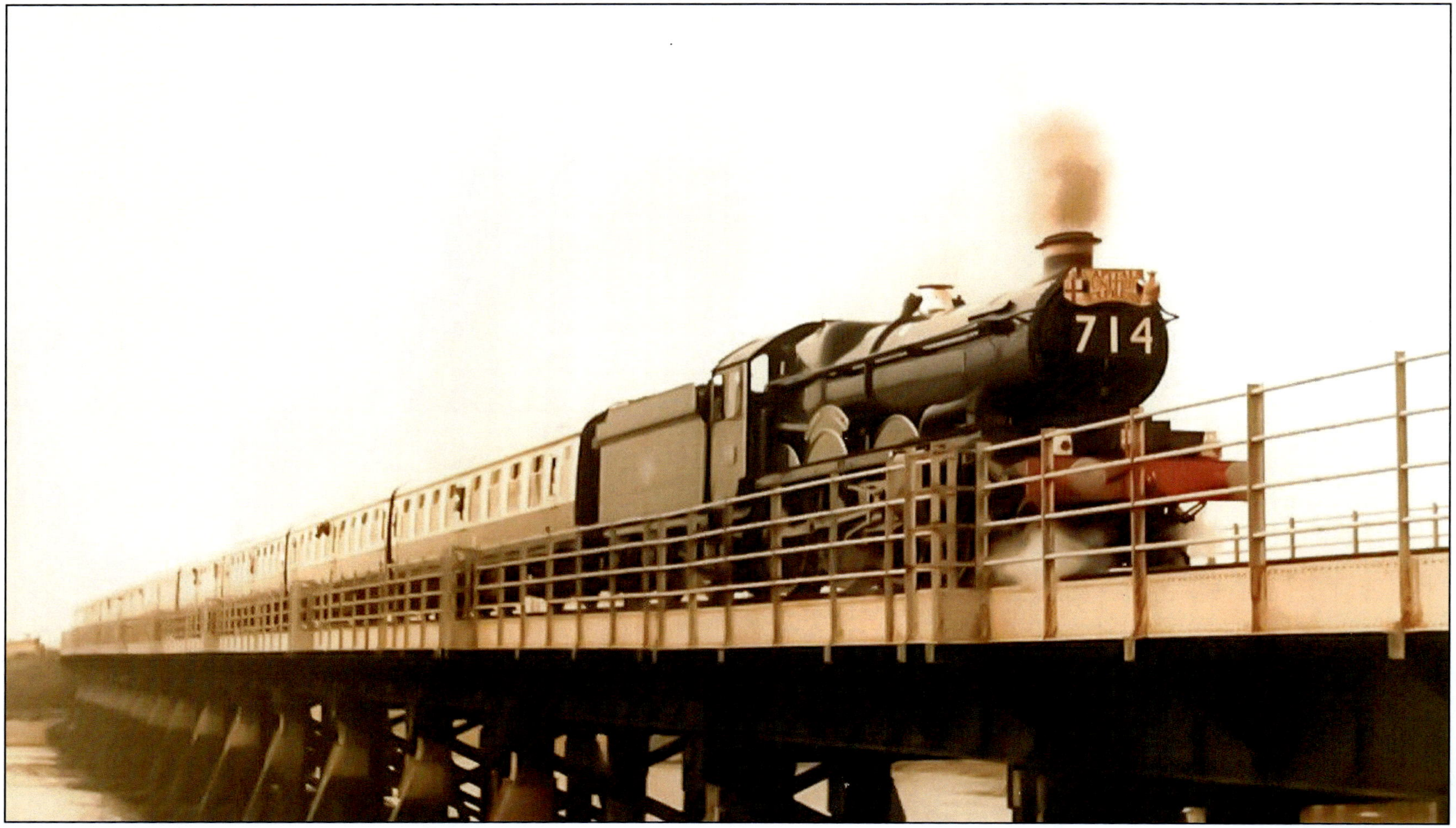


The original railway bridge spanning the river Loughor at Bynea, (seen here) had a much longer history than the three road bridges combined. It was designed by the brilliant engineer, Isambard Kingdom Brunel, and built entirely from timber in 1852, with a swing bridge section to allow ships through. The swing bridge was removed in the 1880's and the timber decking completely replaced with steel, but the timber supports of the structure, which were battered by the tides of the estuary twice daily were retained. These were still mostly original when the bridge was replaced by a new concrete and steel structure in 2013. For the record, the steam train crossing the 250 yard long bridge was a special excursion, returning from Carmarthen on 20th September, 1987, hauled by 7029 Clun Castle.

(V. Morgan).

**Right:** This 'man made' reservoir at Swiss Valley was constructed in 1874, to supply the needs of Llanelli and district. Known then as Cwm Lliedi Reservoir, the embankment was built to collect water from the Lliedi river flowing through the valley. The Upper Lliedi reservoir was constructed later, in 1900. These reservoirs today only provide industrial water. The household supplies to Llanelli come from a different source. Photo dated c.1960.

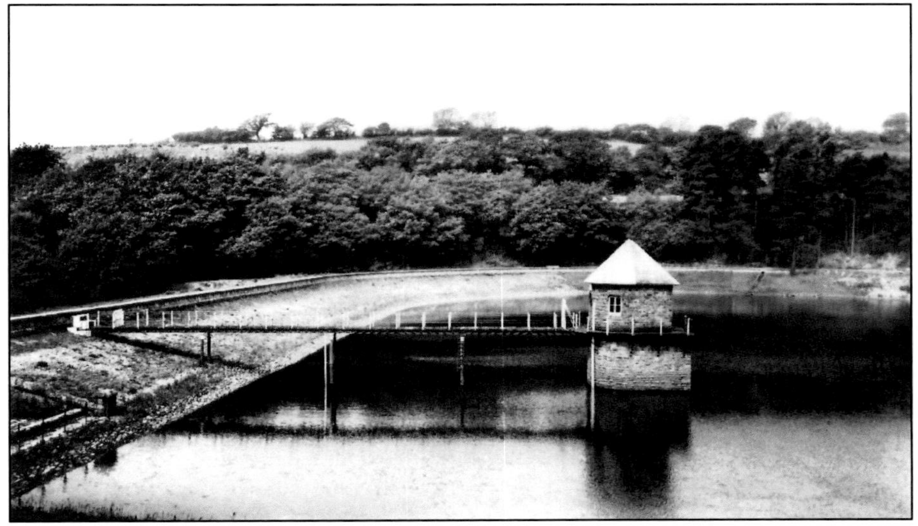

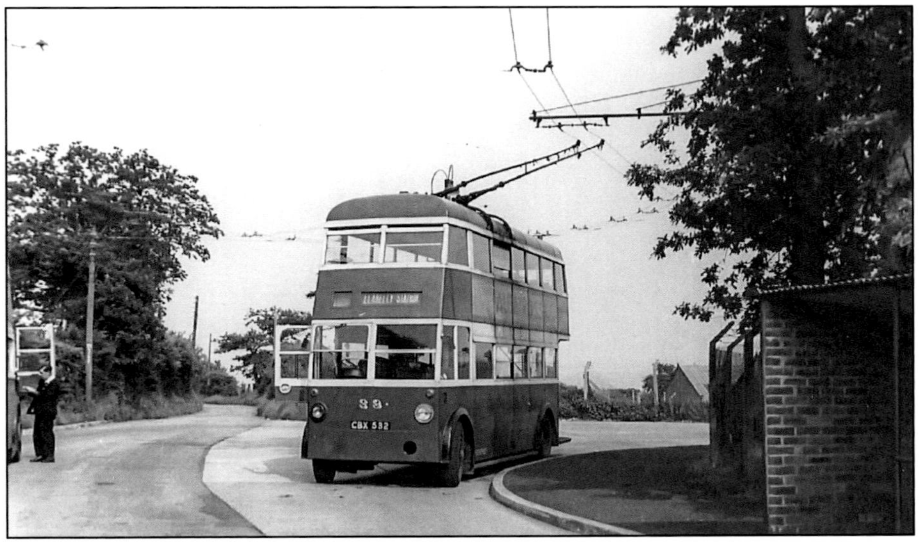

**Left:** Llethri Road, Felinfoel is the backdrop for this picture of the trolleybus turning circle outside the Morris Motors Factory (now Calsonic). This view was taken in 1952, long before the houses were built along Llethri Road, and the road widened. The turning circle has since disappeared. It forms part of the car park alongside Calsonic Social Club. The brick building on the right is a bus shelter.

(C. Carter).

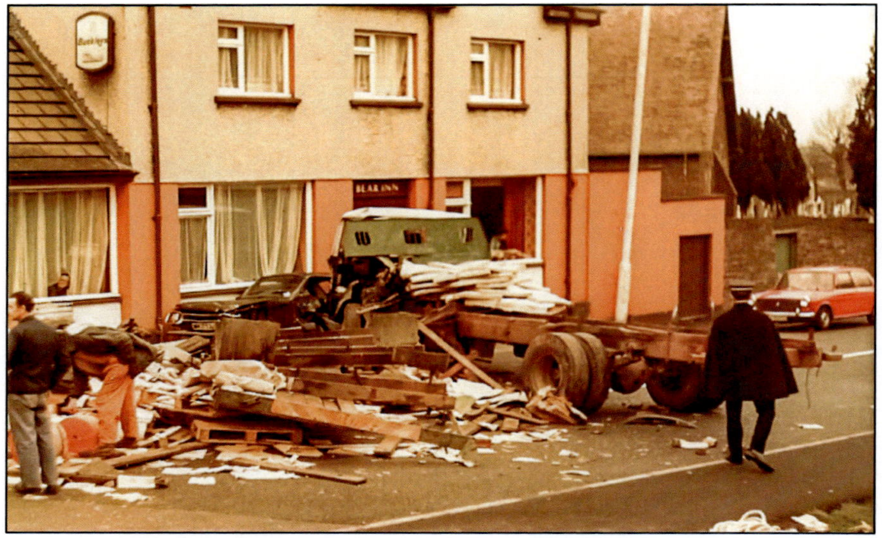

**Left:** 'Allo 'Allo, what's happened here, then?

This was the scene outside the 'Bear Inn', Felinfoel on 26th April, 1978, when a lorry suffered brake failure whilst travelling down Millfield Road (Swiss Valley hill). Note the Ford Escort crushed against the pub wall.

(V. Morgan).

**Right:** Viewed from a different angle, the Ford Escort is more visible in this view. The White Lion is also seen in this photograph, with damage visible to their boundary wall. Quite noticeable is that both pubs have received structural changes, and the Bear Inn is now renamed 'Harry Watkins'.

(V. Morgan).

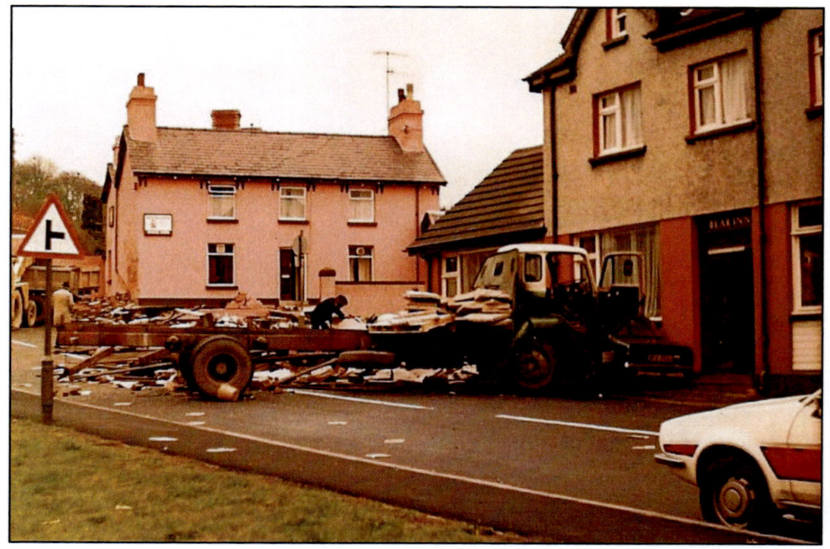

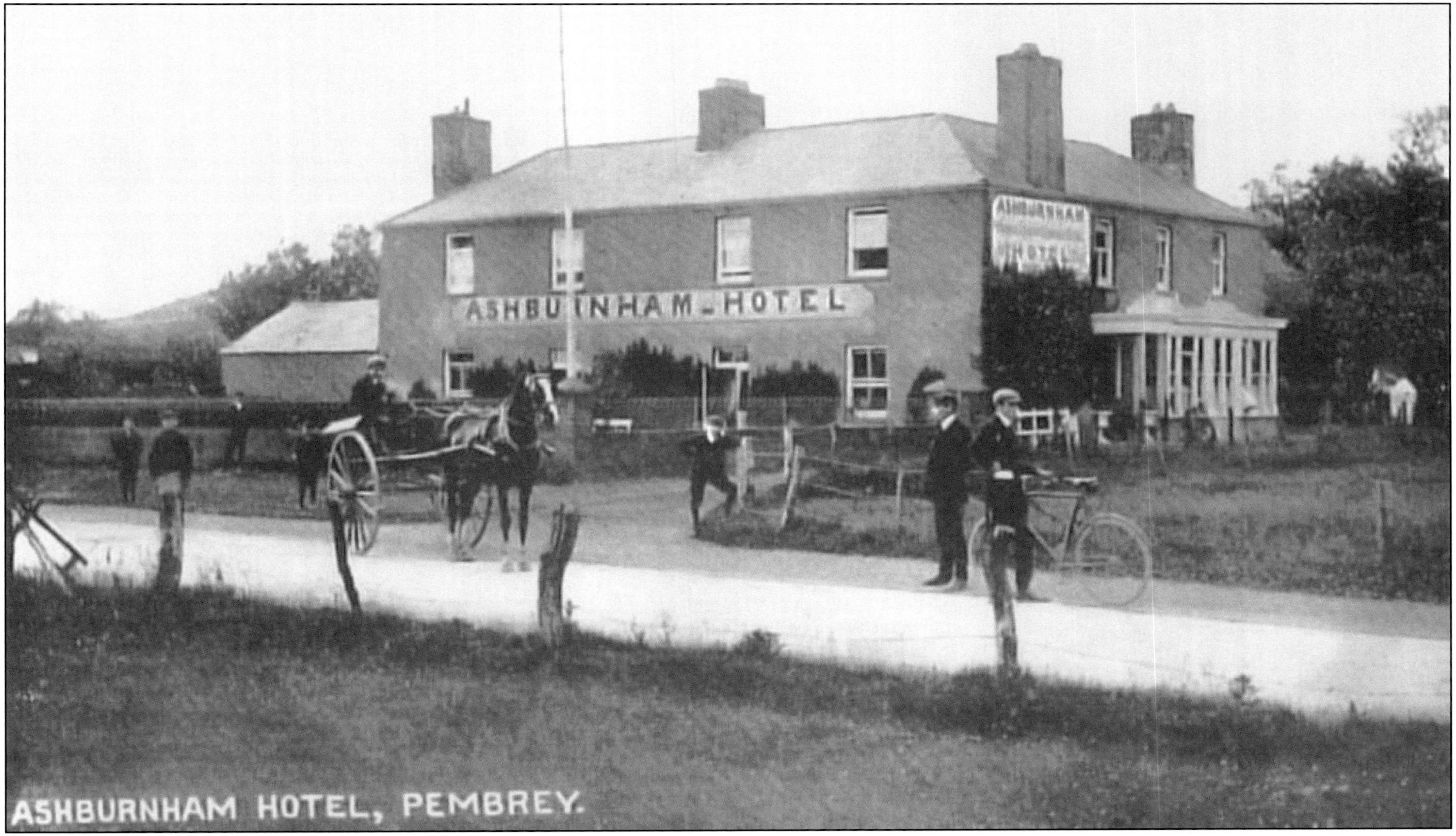


The Ashburnham Hotel, at Pembrey, was originally named 'Ashburnham Inn' when it was built in 1823 by the Pembrey Iron & Coal Company. Famous for its wedding receptions and other functions, its appearance has changed tremendously since this superb postcard view was taken around 1900, by C. Snook, the tobacconist, of Burry Port.

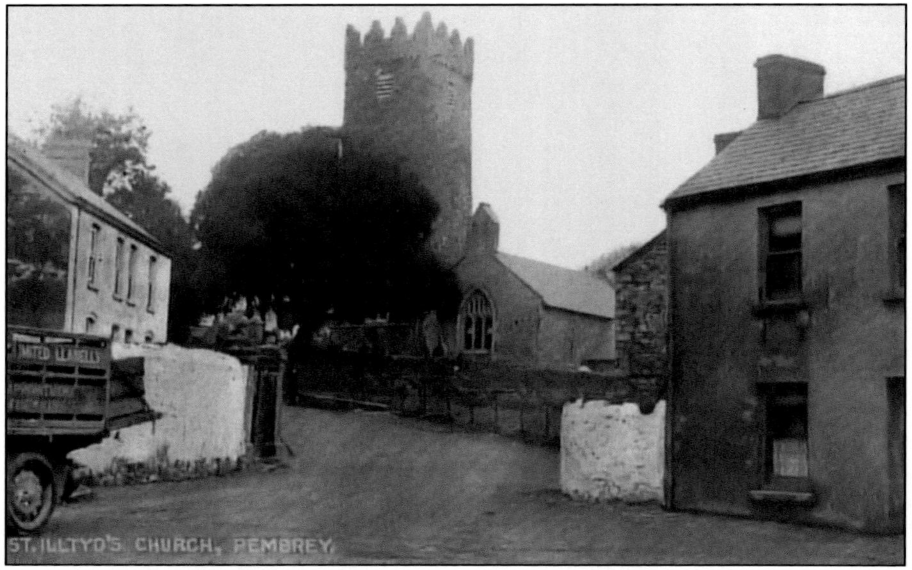


**Left:** 'St. Illtyd's Church or the Pembrey Parish Church dates back to the 1300s. This picture by C. Snook of Burry Port, dates from the 1920s and features a solid tyred lorry of Buckley's Brewery making a delivery to the Red Lion Inn, here at Randall Square, Pembrey. The roadway in the background was originally the main thoroughfare between Kidwelly and Llanelli, before Randall Square was by-passed to the north with a new section of Gwscwm Road, around 1930. The semi- detached house on the right hand side of the picture has since been absorbed into the Pembrey Inn next door (previously The Commercial Arms). Note the absence of clocks on the church tower. Three electric clocks were the gift of the late R .T. Hammond, which were later fitted to the 70 feet high tower in 1936.

(C. Snook. Burry Port).

**Right:** Another view of Randall Square, Pembrey, which was again taken by C. Snook around 1900. Randall Square was named after a well-known ship's captain, Francis Randall, who owned the Commercial Arms, pictured here on the left. The Commercial Arms is dated at 1830. Francis Randall had previously been proprietor of the Ashburnham Arms, pictured on page 93.

(Mrs. C. Ridgeway collection).

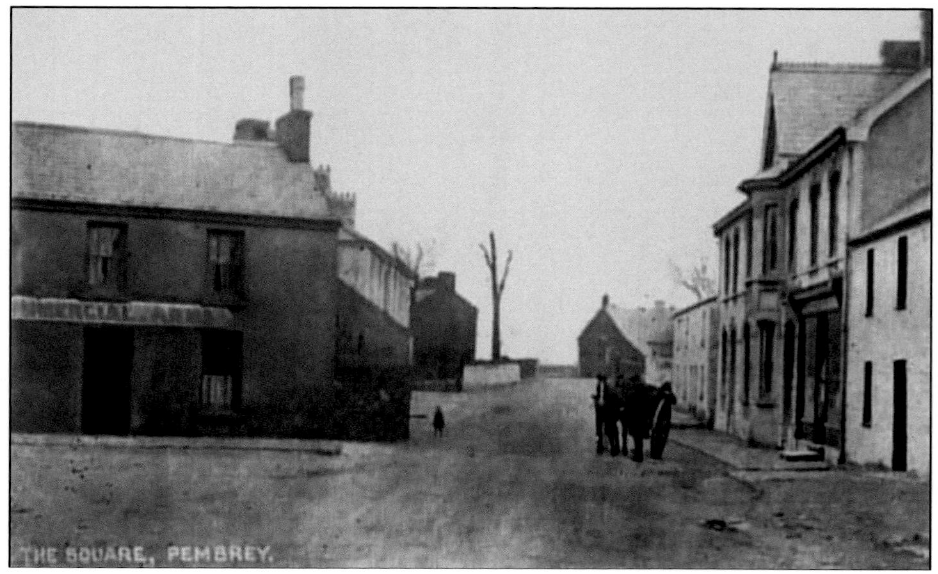

**Right:** Formerly an imposing Manor House, Court Farm, Mountain Road, Pembrey, was abandoned around 1948, and is now an overgrown ruin which is still capable of restoration.
This was another picture taken by C. Snook, circa 1900.

(Mrs. C. Ridgeway collection).

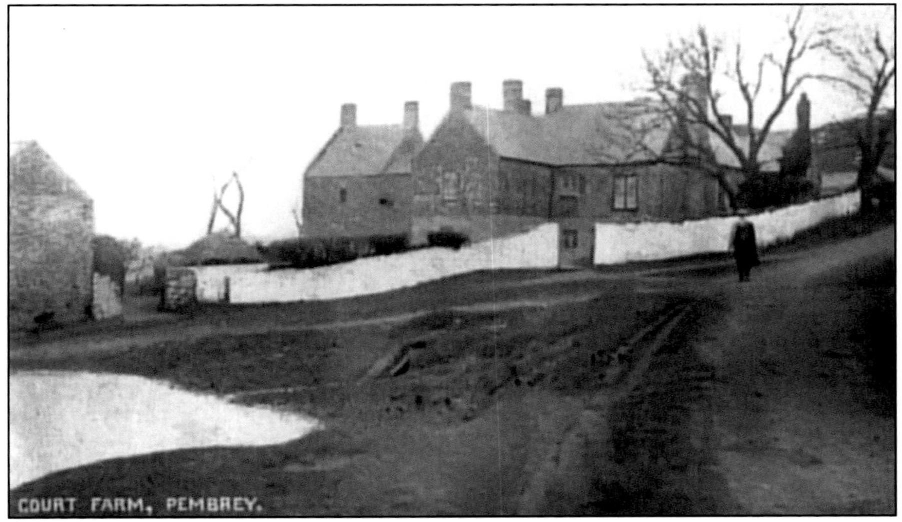


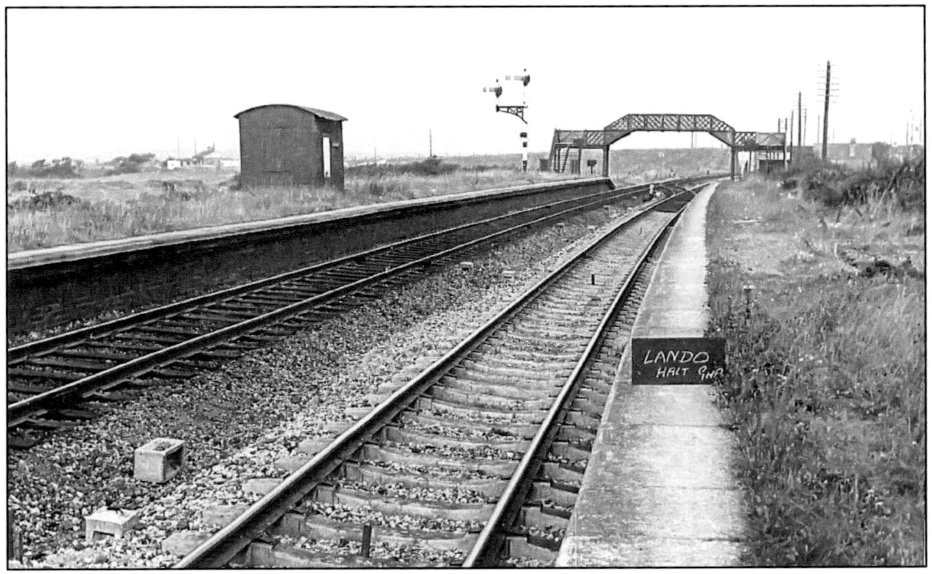


**Left:** 'Lando Halt' in Pembrey was built by the Great Western Railway Company in 1915, solely to serve the nearby Royal Ordnance Factory (a munitions factory). Situated on the main South Wales railway line, it was adjacent to Lando Road – hence the name – and did not serve the general public as a railway station. The road bridge to Factory Road is just visible behind the footbridge in this view looking westward, The platform closed in 1964 when the munitions factory closed, and was subsequently demolished.

(V. Morgan collection).

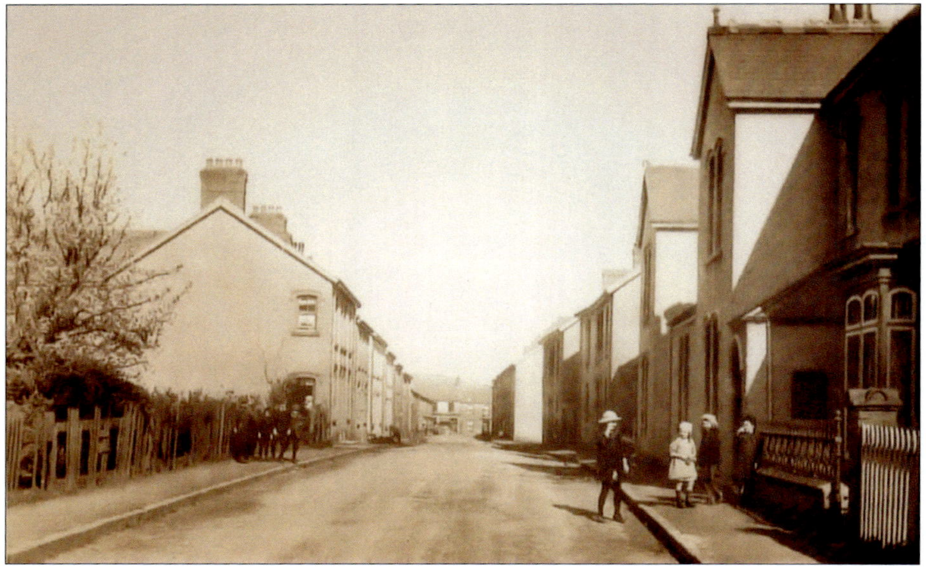

**Left:** This view of Mansell Street, Burry Port, looking eastward, was taken around 1910 by local photographer, W. T. Perrott (Stationer), 22 Station Road, Burry Port. It was one of a set taken by Perrott in the early 1900s, long before several properties had been erected in the street. Also noticeable is the absence of motor cars. It's a very different scene today!

(Mrs. C. Ridgeway collection).

**Right:** Another view taken by W. T. Perrott, is this one of Elkington Road, Burry Port, which was probably taken at the same time as Mansell Street, above. This view was taken looking southward down Elkington Road, at a point close to the junction of Mansell Street (seen on the left), with the Baptist Church visible left of centre.

(Mrs. C. Ridgeway collection).

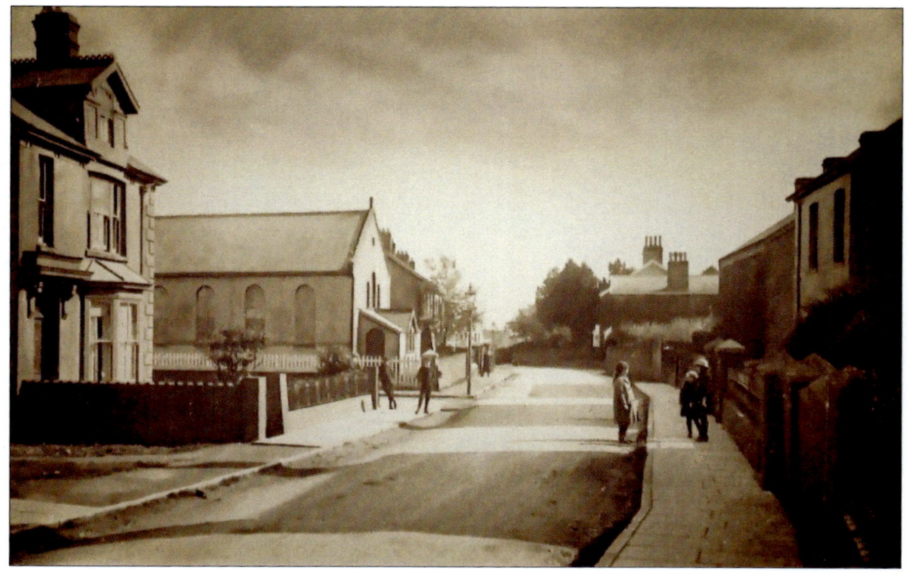

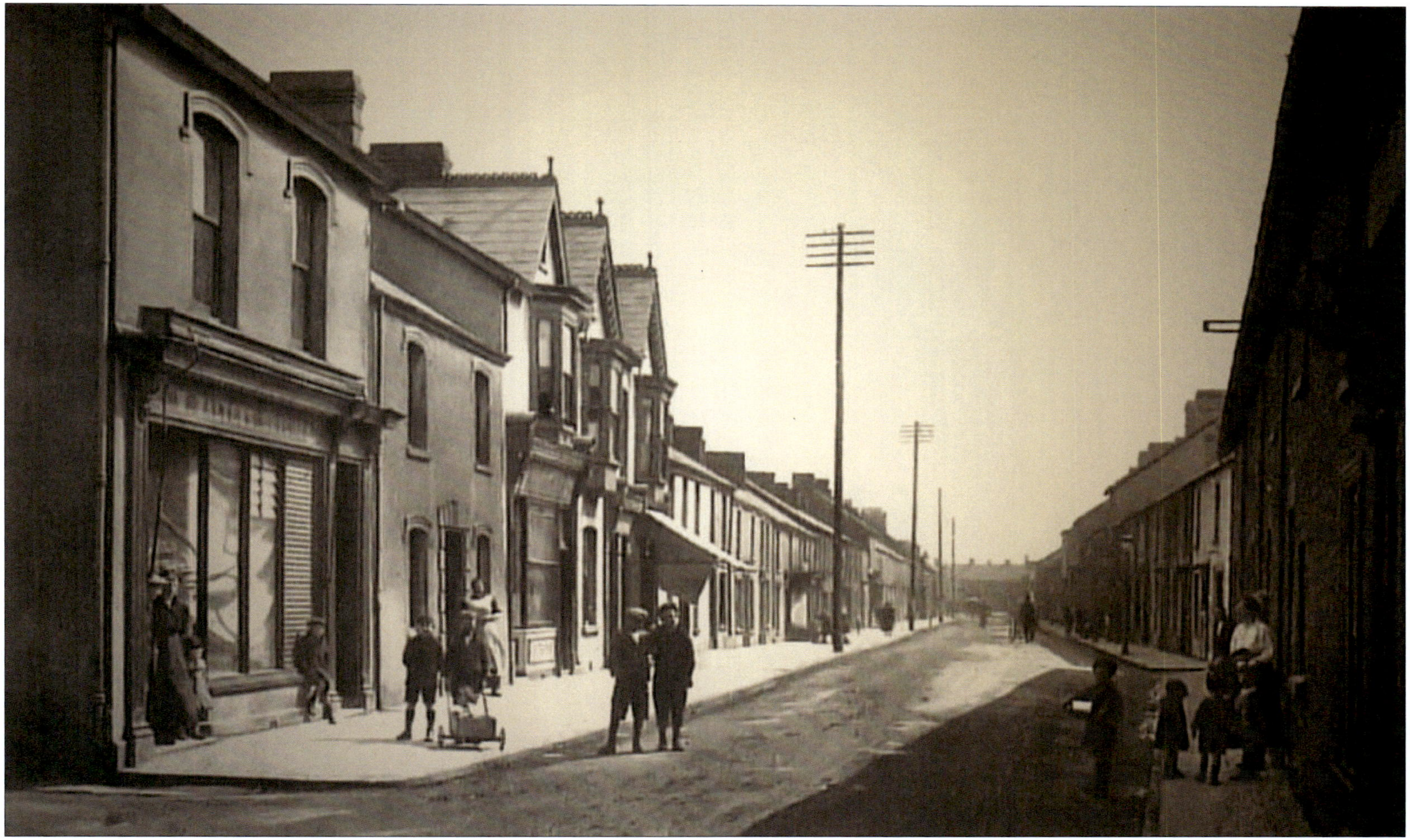

Devoid of any vehicular traffic is New Street, Burry Port, pictured here around 1910. It's a different scene today with all the heavy traffic. The road surface is now tarmac, and all the shops have disappeared, including W. Walters butchers shop, on the left. The Butchers Arms public house, which was further down the street (on the left), has also gone. (Mrs. C. Ridgeway collection).

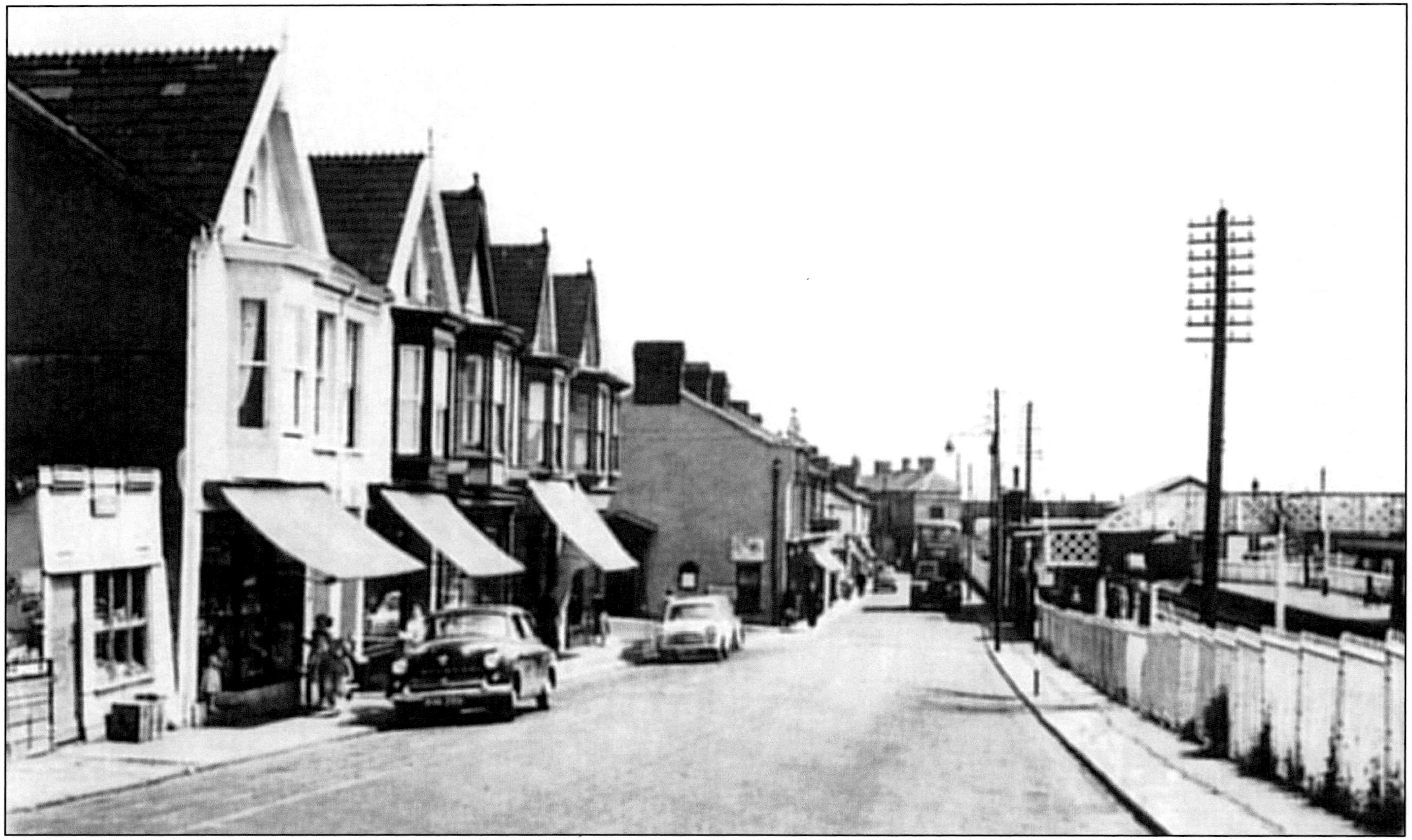

Not much has changed here in Station Road, Burry Port, since this view was taken in 1957. The noticeable differences are that the Station Hotel, pictured on the junction with Stepney Road (centre), has gone, and the small 'timber constructed' shop (left) has been replaced by a new permanent structure. The foot bridge on the railway station has been renovated.
(Mrs. C. Ridgeway collection).

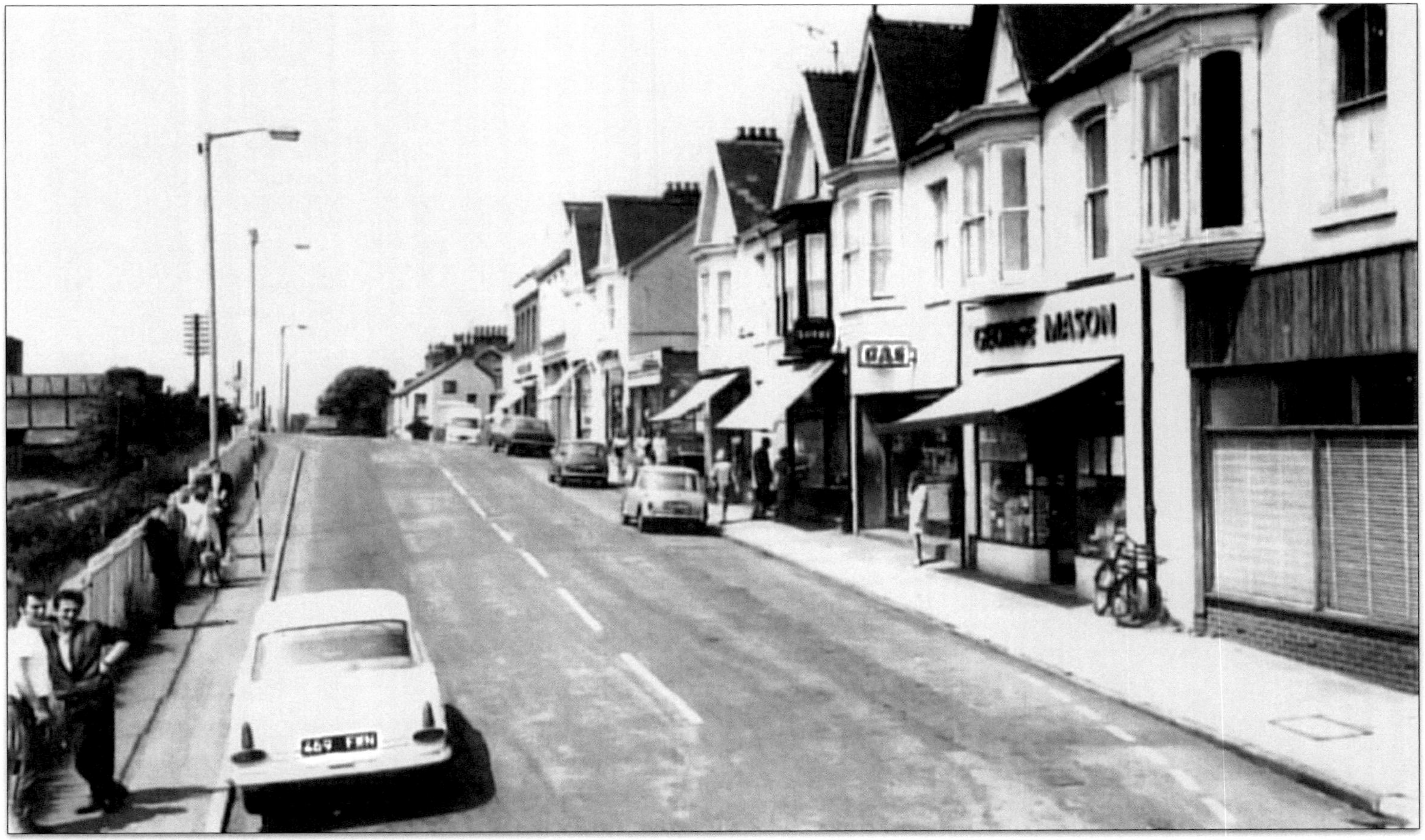


This view of Station Road, Burry Port, is taken at the same location as the opposite page, but is viewed in the opposite direction, ten years later. Most of these shops appear to have changed hands now, but the Co-operative Store (visible on the brow) is still there, along with the Cornish Arms visible furthest away from the camera, at the bottom of Elkington Road.

(Mrs. C. Ridgeway collection).

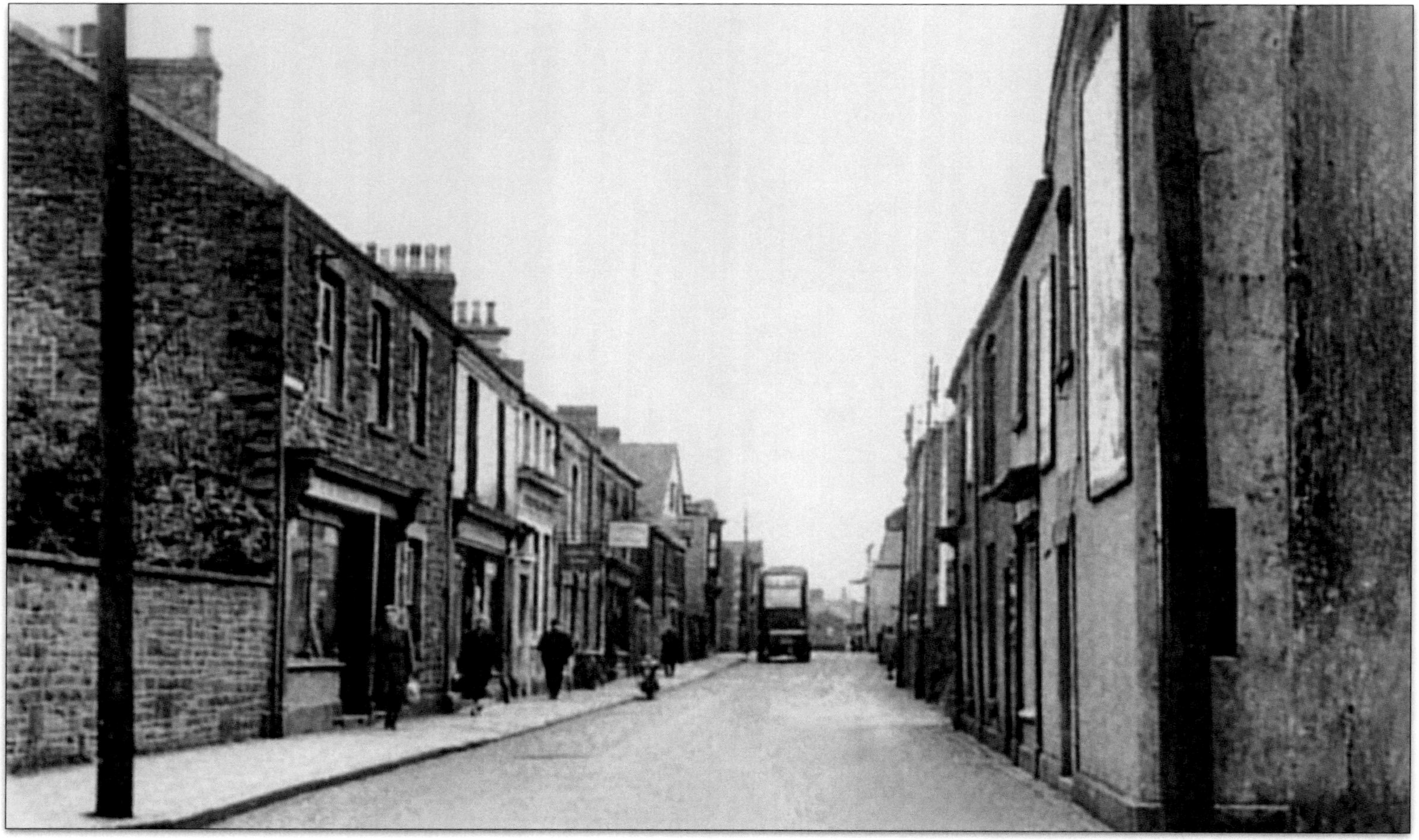

This is the eastern end of Station Road, Burry Port, looking westward towards the railway station. This view was taken in 1957, and captures the buildings on the right hand side which were demolished around 1960 for a road improvement. One of the buildings on the right had been occupied by a motor cycle dealer selling 'Raleigh Mopeds'.

(Mrs. C. Ridgeway collection).

**Right:** This privately owned railway station, at Burry Port, was built in 1909 by the Burry Port & Gwendraeth Valley Railway Co., after receiving a light railway order to legally carry passengers on what had previously been a mineral line. As the company's financial situation was poor, second-hand carriages were purchased from LSWR and the Metropolitan Railway, London, as pictured here in 1910. This station was located 30 yards to the south of Burry Port (GWR) main line station, close to the Neptune Hotel, pictured here, in the centre of the view.

(W.T. Perrott. Burry Port).

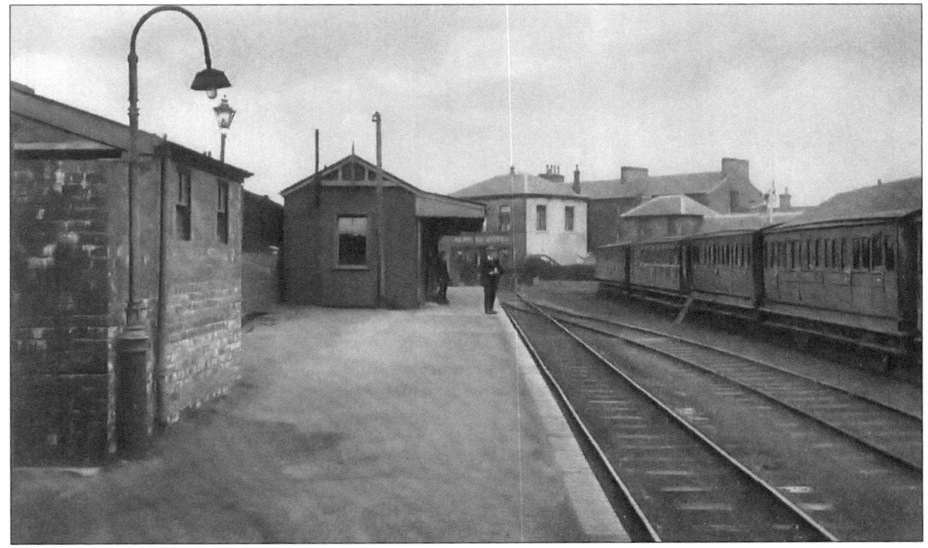

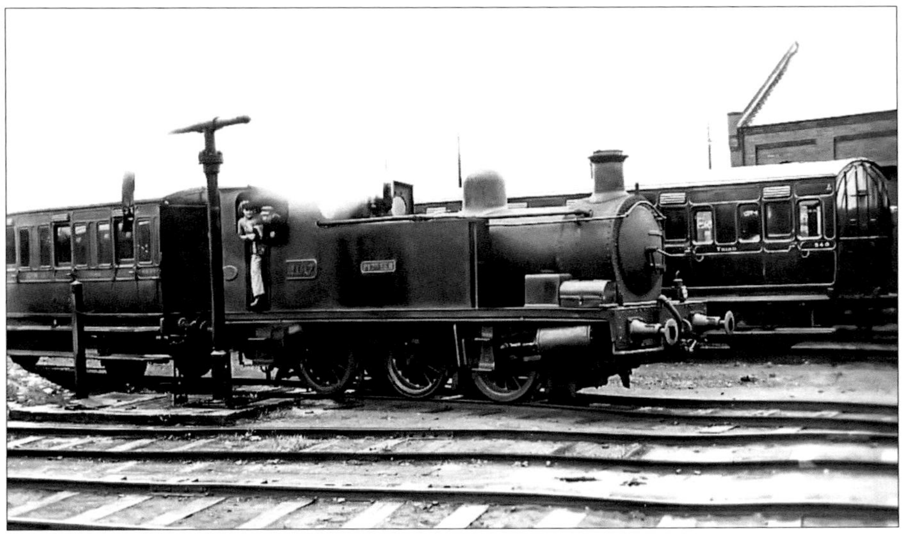

**Left:** Another view of the Burry Port & Gwendraeth Valley Railway's rolling stock is captured here. The locomotive, 'Pioneer', was No. 8 in a fleet of fifteen, operated by the BP&GVR, and was built in 1909 by Hudswell Clarke of Leeds. 'Pioneer' ran the first official passenger train on 2nd August 1909. However, after continued financial problems, the BP&GVR was absorbed by the Great Western Railway in 1923, where 'Pioneer' was numbered 2197. Here, it is pictured during GWR ownership, handling a passenger train of 3rd class carriages in Burry Port, working the BP&GVR line. Note the subsidence under the railway lines.

(V. Morgan collection).

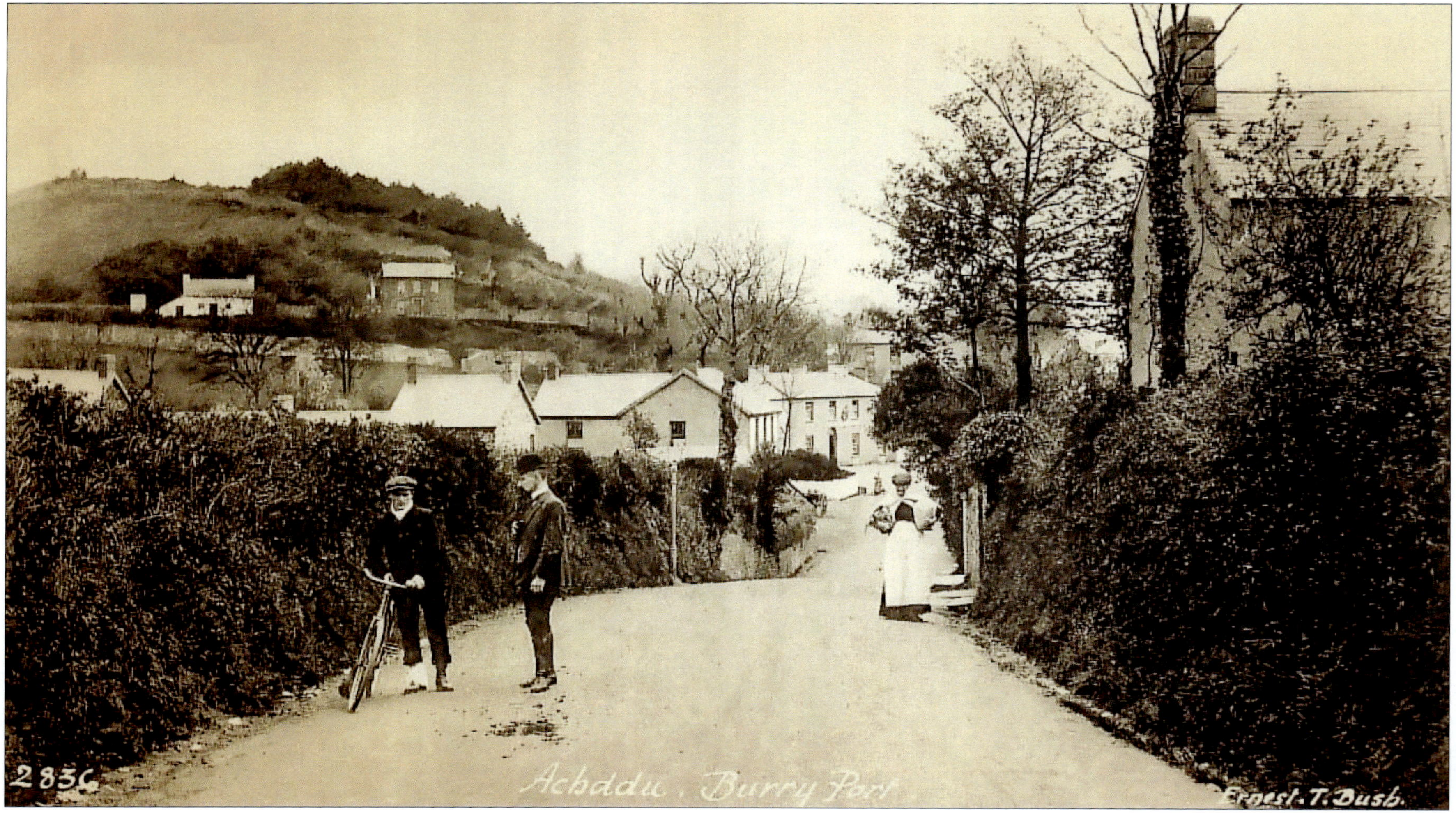


This is a splendid view of Achddu, in Burry Port, looking eastward down the hill known as Colby Road, circa 1900. The junction of Dandorlan Road is just visible to the left, at the foot of the hill, and the Pemberton Arms, a famous watering hole is also in view at the bottom of the hill. The house on the right is built on the junction of Pencoed Road.

(Mrs. C. Ridgeway collection).

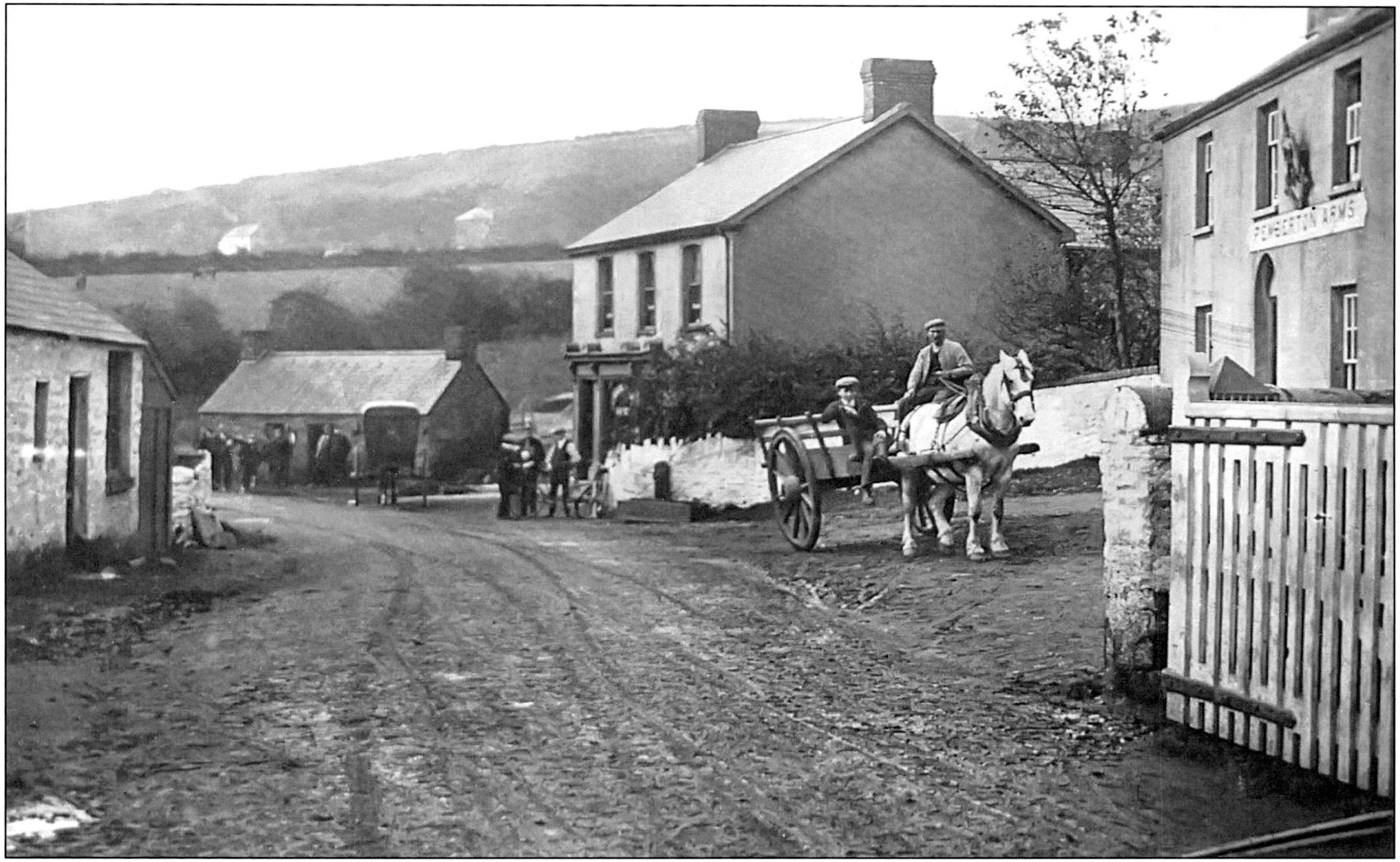


This is a very early view of Colby Road, Burry Port, on the main A484 trunk road between Llanelli and Kidwelly. Visible on the extreme right hand side of the picture is the very popular public house, known as the Pemberton Arms. The gate on the right hand side was a railway crossing known as Pemberton crossing, a branch line of the Burry Port & Gwendraeth Valley Railway, running from East Quay at Burry Port docks to Cwm Capel Colliery (Graig). It had been converted from a narrow gauge tramway to a standard gauge in 1876, and closed in 1931. The track was lifted in July, 1940.

(Mrs. C. Ridgeway collection).

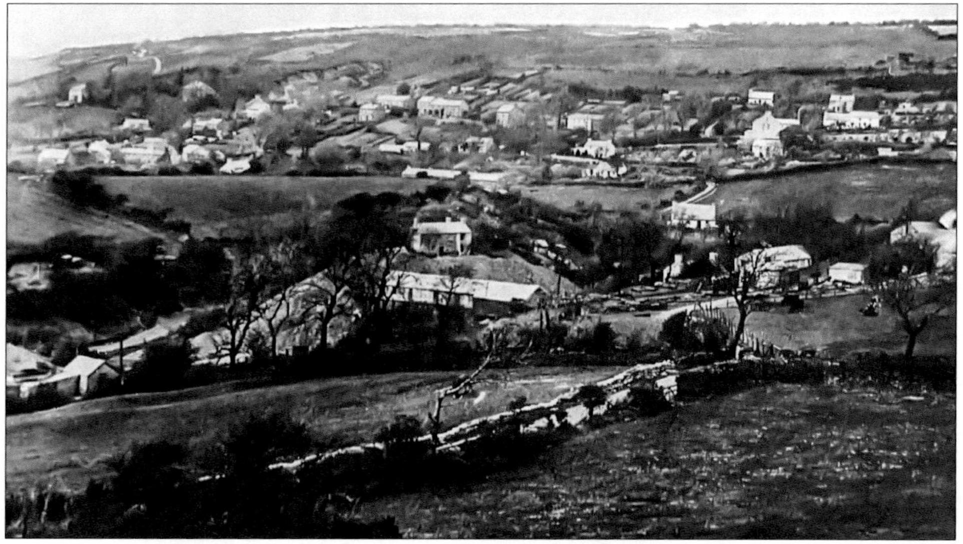

**Left:** A splendid view of The Graig at Burry Port, with Cwm Capel Colliery visible in the centre of the picture.

(Mrs. C. Ridgeway collection).

**Right:** This view of Stepney Road, Burry Port, was taken in the early 1950s. The shop visible in the right hand background, at the entrance to Pencoed Road was demolished in the 1960s. The Monument in the foreground was erected to commemorate Amelia Mary Earhart's success, the first woman to successfully fly the Atlantic Ocean, on 18th June, 1928. Amelia, from Boston, Massachusetts, had taken off from Trepassey, Newfoundland, on a journey which took her 20 hours 49 minutes, in a seaplane named 'Friendship'. The entrance to Snowdon Road is just visible in the centre of this view.

(Mrs. C. Ridgeway collection).

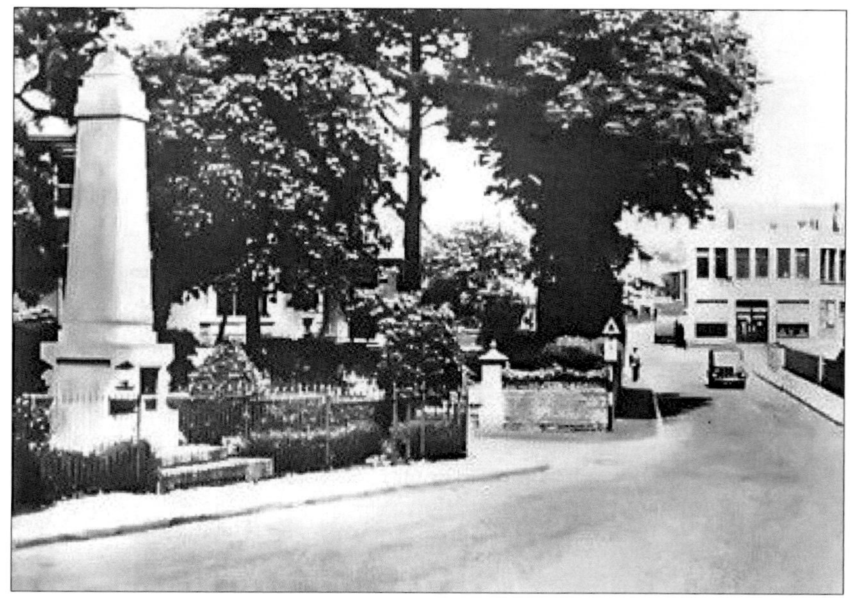

**Right:** This view of Burry Port engine sheds was taken in the early 1960s. Built by the Burry Port & Gwendraeth Valley Railway Co., in 1868, it was the company's only maintenance depot, and passed into GWR ownership in 1923, and to British Railways upon nationalisation in January 1948. The loco shed, situated 100 yards north of Burry Port's East Dock, closed in February 1962, and was demolished in 1990. The East Dock is just behind the diesel locomotive shunting in the background.

(V. Morgan collection).

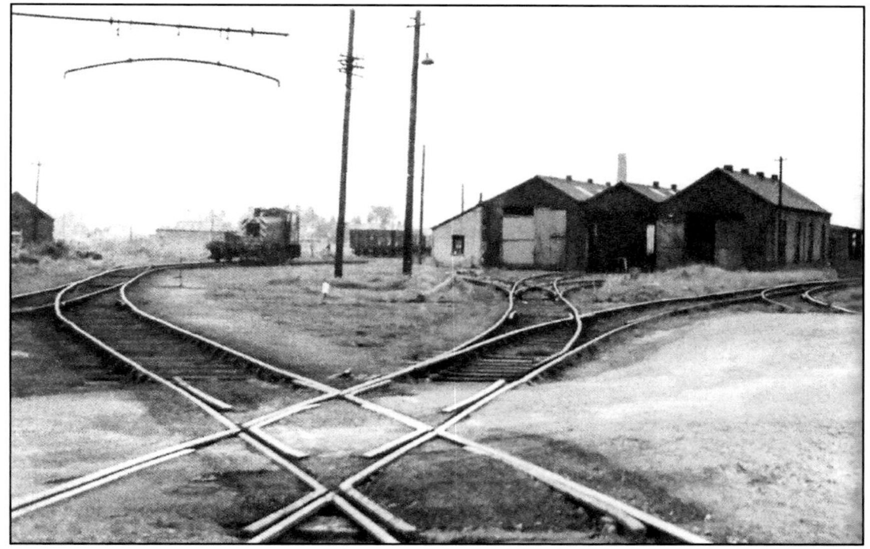

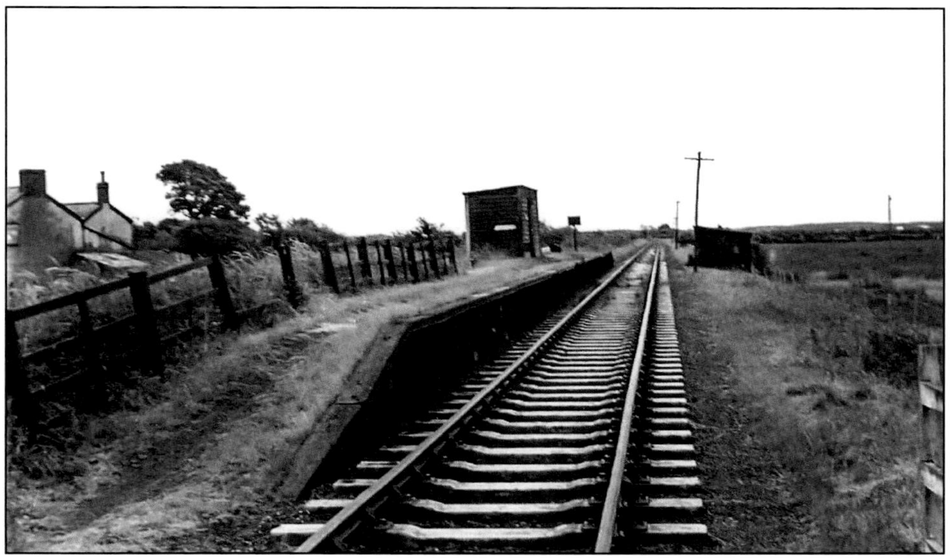

**Left:** The tiny hamlet of Pinged (near Kidwelly), was once served by a passenger train on the Burry Port & Gwendraeth Valley Railway, between Burry Port and Cwm-mawr. This single track railway was closed to passenger traffic on 21st September, 1953, but remained open for freight. This view of Pinged Halt (or station), looking southward, was taken in the mid 1950's, long after the last passenger train had operated the line.

(V. Morgan collection).

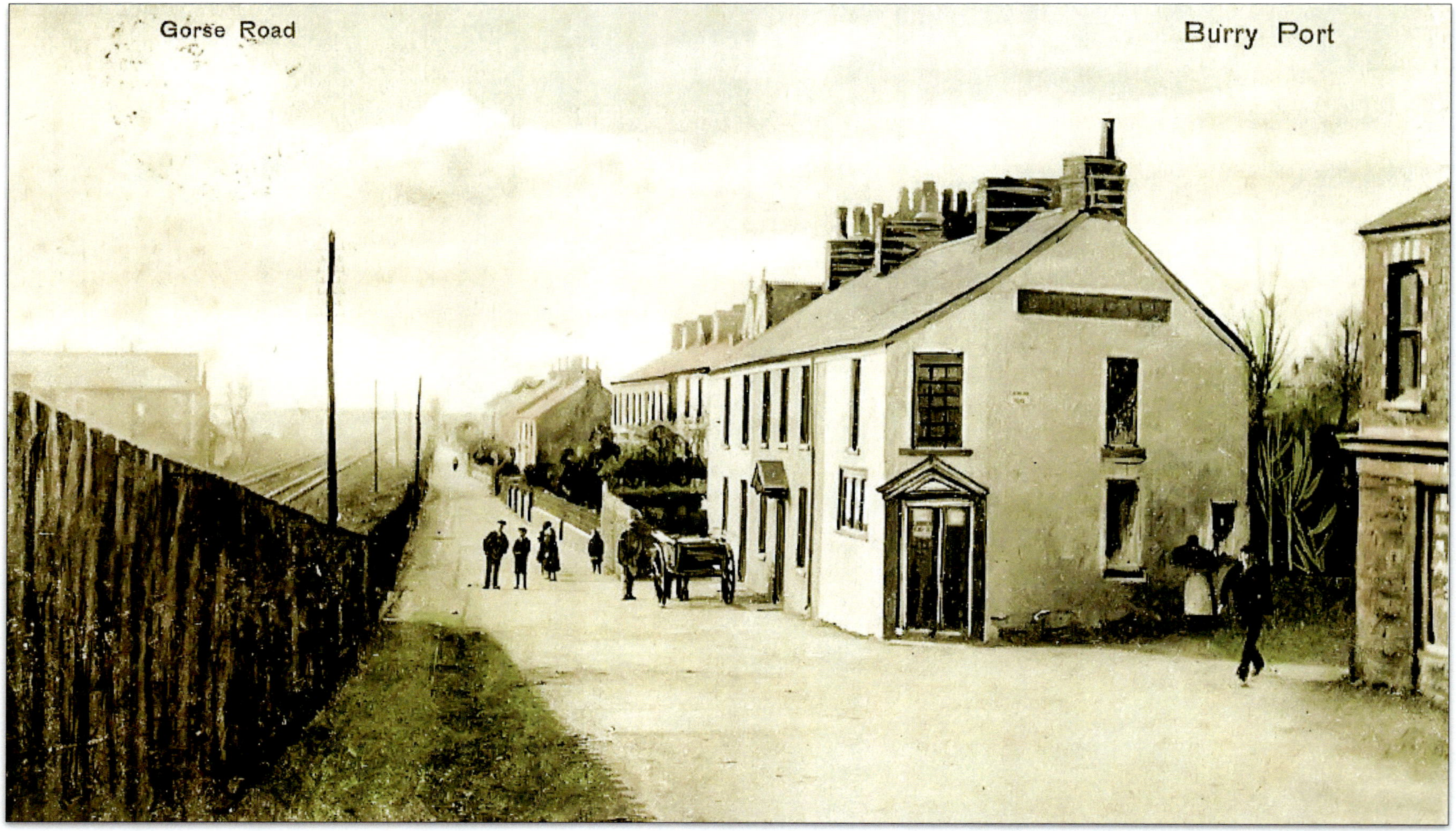


This view of Gorse Road, Burry Port, is postmarked July 1904, and captures the Adelphi Cinema (extreme left), and Gorse Road (centre). The Cornish Arms is in the foreground, and the entrance to Elkington Road to the right of it. The South Wales Railway (London - Fishguard railway) can be seen on the left hand side of the view, running parallel with Gorse Road.

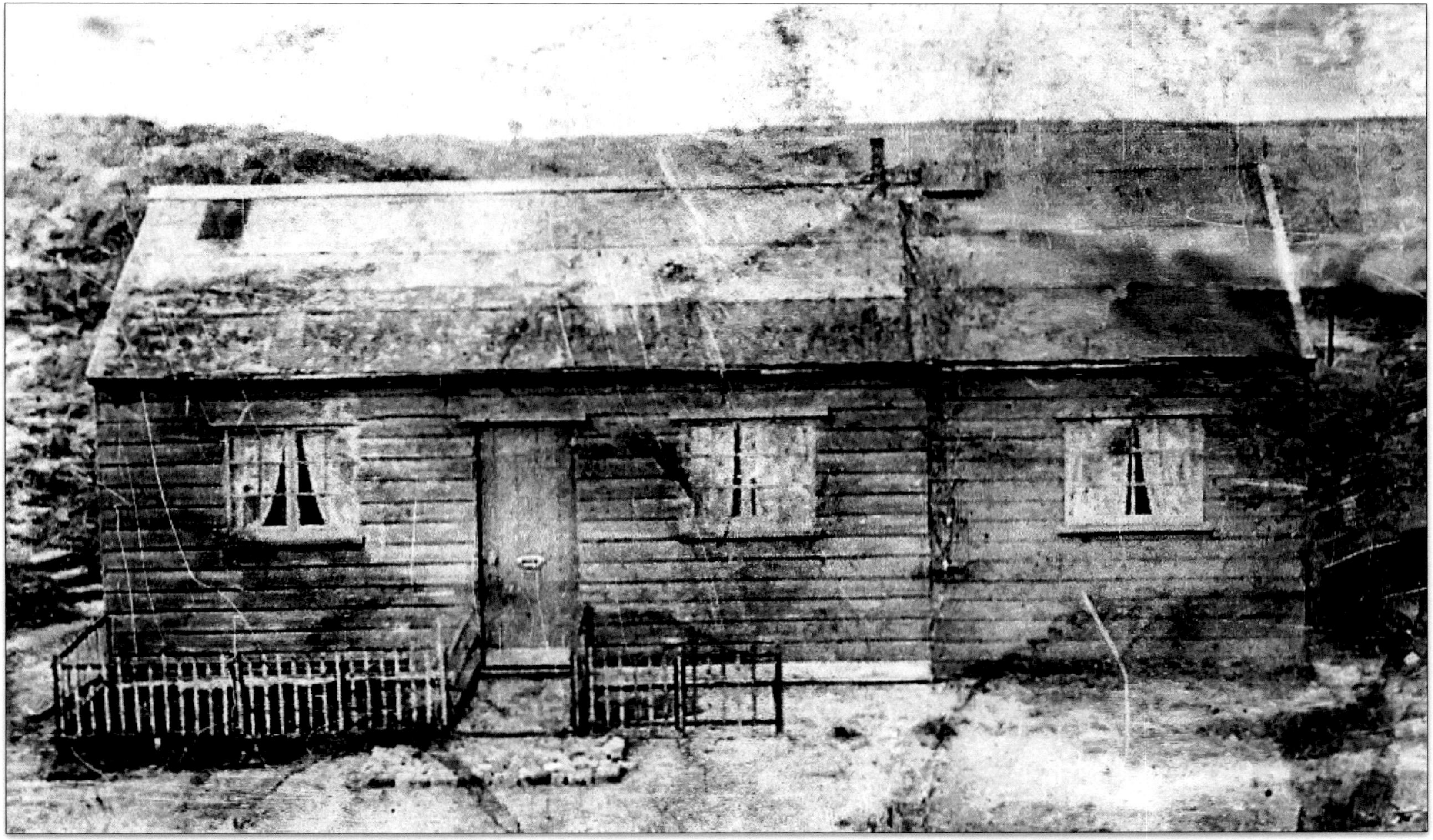

This cottage, named 'Milton Cottage', was located at 'Derwydd' Burry Port, close to Pembrey harbour. The photograph is dated 1917.
If anyone has any information regarding this cottage, the publisher would be glad to hear from them.

(Mrs. C. Ridgeway collection).

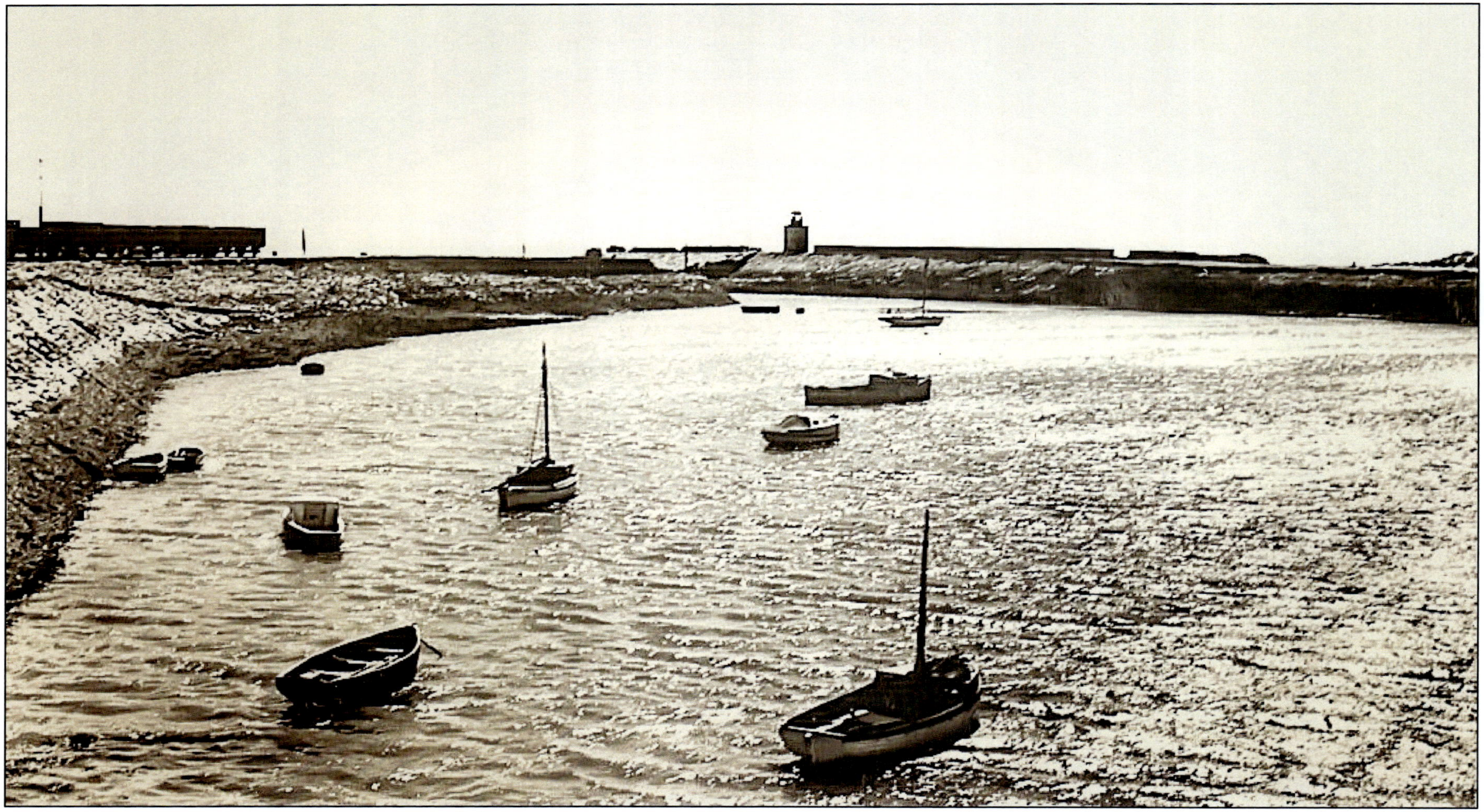

This view of Burry Port harbour was taken around 1958, and shows railway wagons awaiting repair at the Marcroft Wagon Repair Shop, located to the left hand side of this view.

(Mrs. C. Ridgeway collection).

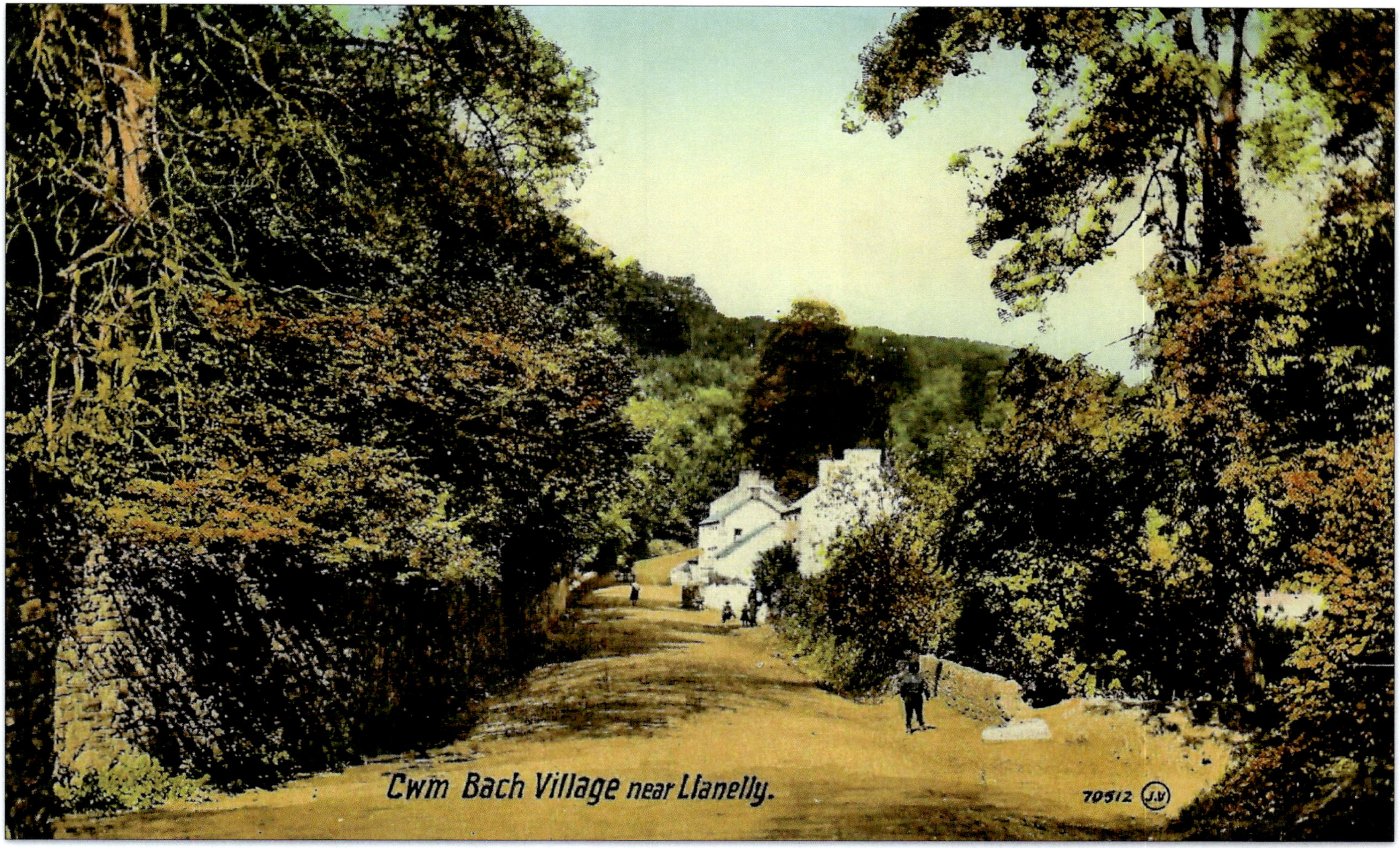


This postcard view of Cwmbach village is postmarked February 1916.
The village, situated two miles north-west of Llanelli, on the B4308 road between Llanelli and Trimsaran, has not altered much in the last 100 years.

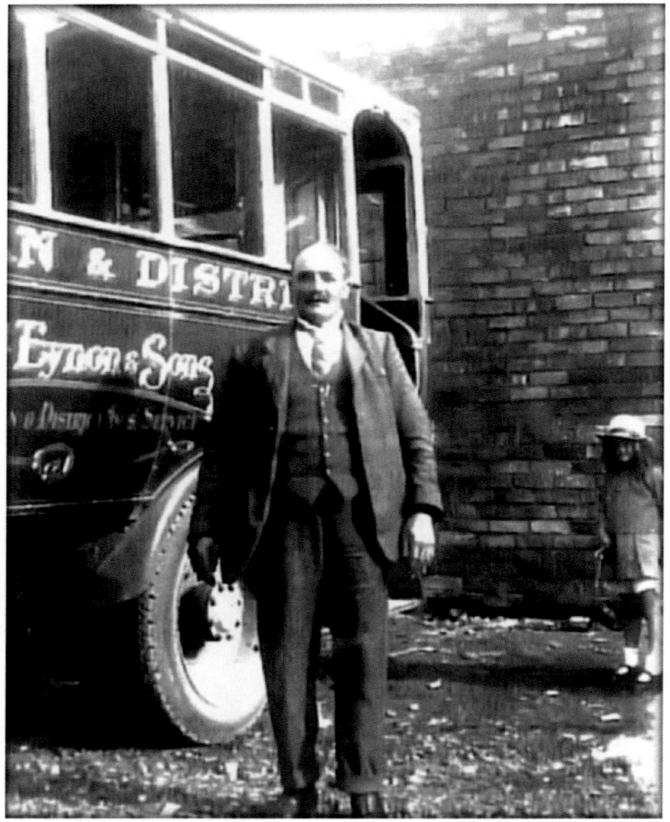


**Above:** Pictured here, alongside one of his early Leyland buses in the mid 1930s, is Samuel Eynon, the pioneer of public transport in the village of Trimsaran. He first began operating a service from Trimsaran to Llanelli in 1917, with a motor-cycle and sidecar, and later enhanced the service with a Studebaker motor car. The first charabanc arrived in 1919, from whence the business expanded. However, he had fierce competition from the beginning, but the determined family partnership fought off all their rivals, absorbing their last competitors: James Hughes & Son, Trimsaran, and John Davies, Carway in 1935/6 respectively.

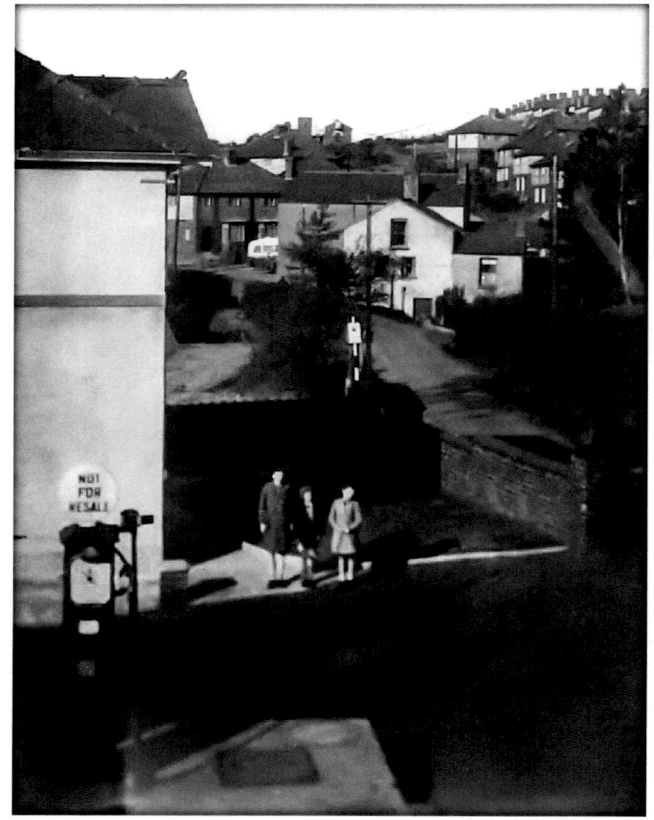

**Above:** A view from Samuel Eynon's bedroom window at 'Bryn-villa' in Trimsaran, takes in the petrol pump standing on the garage forecourt, and the roadway Heol Waunyclun in its original form. The back end of the 'Star Inn' and Garden Suburbs, are visible in the background. The land to the left of the road traffic sign, was acquired by Samuel Eynon in 1947, to construct a new garage suitable for double-deckers. This photograph, dated mid-1930s shows three of Samuel Eynon's grand-children on the original garage forecourt (Bryn-villa Garage).

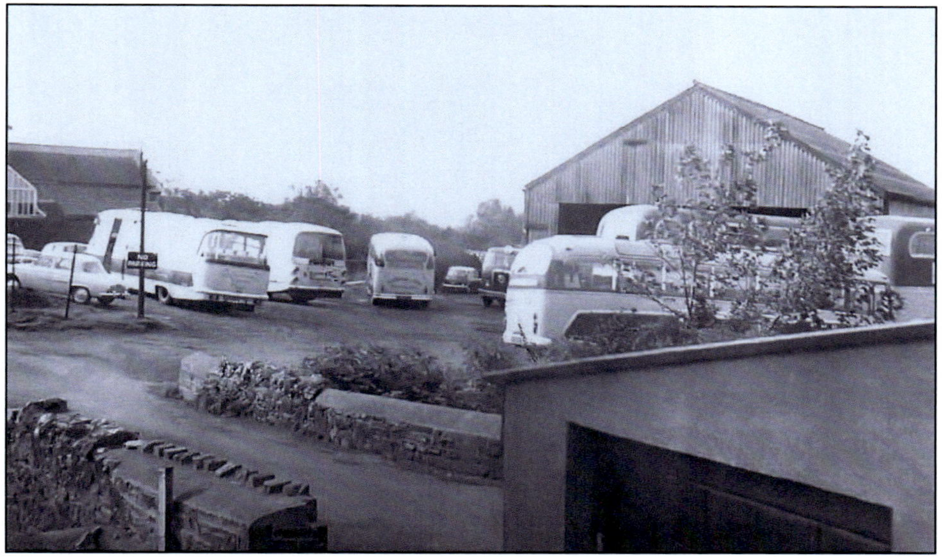

**Left:** This view of Eynons' 'new' garage was taken in 1967, with AEC, Leyland, and Bedford coaches prominent on the yard. Heol Waun-y-clun, and the river bridge in the foreground, were the subject of a road improvement scheme in 1977, resulting in the loss of half of Eynons' yard. Parking facilities for their 36 vehicle fleet was then re-located to a new yard behind the garage, after purchasing a neighbouring field.

(V. Morgan collection).

**Right**: The Star Inn, Trimsaran, is the backdrop for this picture of an Eynons' Leyland RTL double-decker, making a left turn into Heol Waun-y-clun, in 1967. Felinfoel Brewery sold the Star Inn to Trimsaran R.F.C., sometime later, for continued use as a club-house. The building has seen several changes with its new owners over the years, and is still serving a good pint of 'Felinfoel'.

(V. Morgan collection).

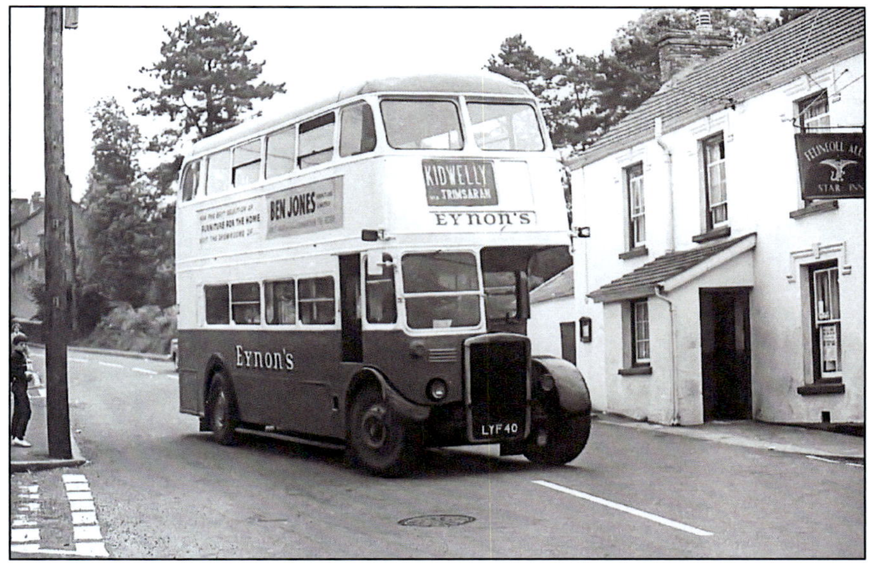

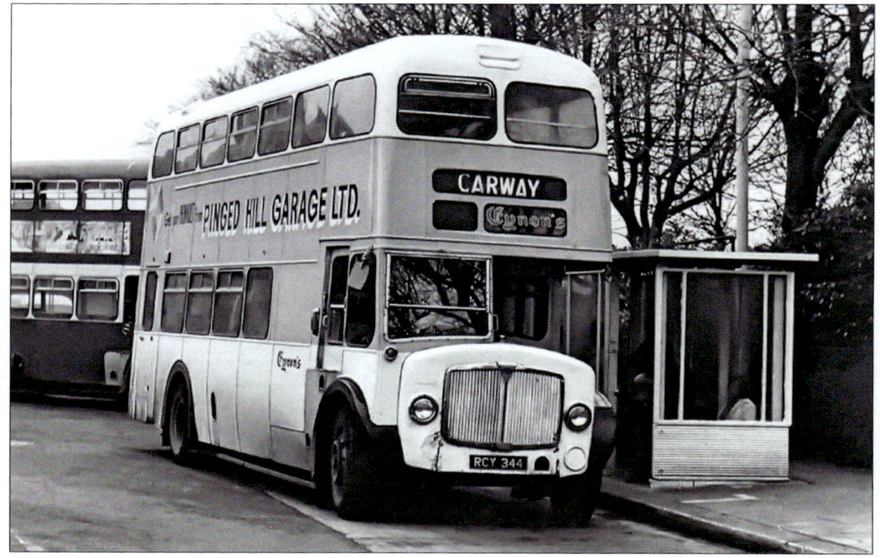


**Right:** There was a close association between Eynons and Pinged Hill Garage, Kidwelly, which prompted the re-painting of this AEC Regent double-decker into an all over advertisement for Pinged Hill Garage. The livery was yellow between decks, with white roof and bottom deck.

(V. Morgan collection).

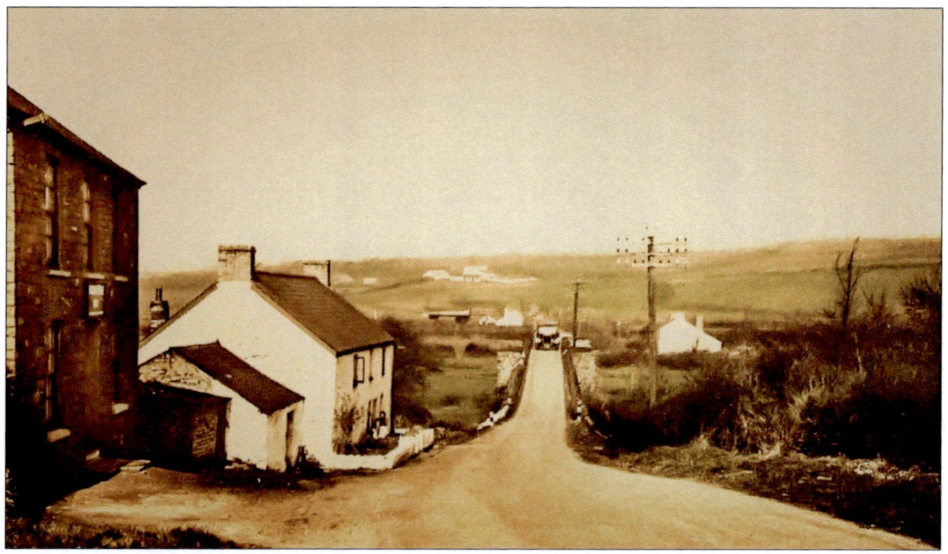

**Left:** The Roman bridge, known as 'Spudders Bridge', on the B4308 road between Trimsaran and Kidwelly, is pictured here during the 1930s. Although still in existence, the bridge is no longer in use. Now recorded as an ancient monument by 'Cadw', Spudders Bridge was by-passed with a modern bridge in 1972, built in the vicinity of the white house, on the right hand side of this view. Known as Laburnham Cottage, it was demolished to make way for the new bridge. The public house (on the left hand side of the road), called the Spudders Arms, closed around 1960, and was converted into a private residence. The cottage next door (now demolished) was previously 'The Bridgend Inn', but had been converted into a cottage before this view was taken.

(V. Morgan collection).

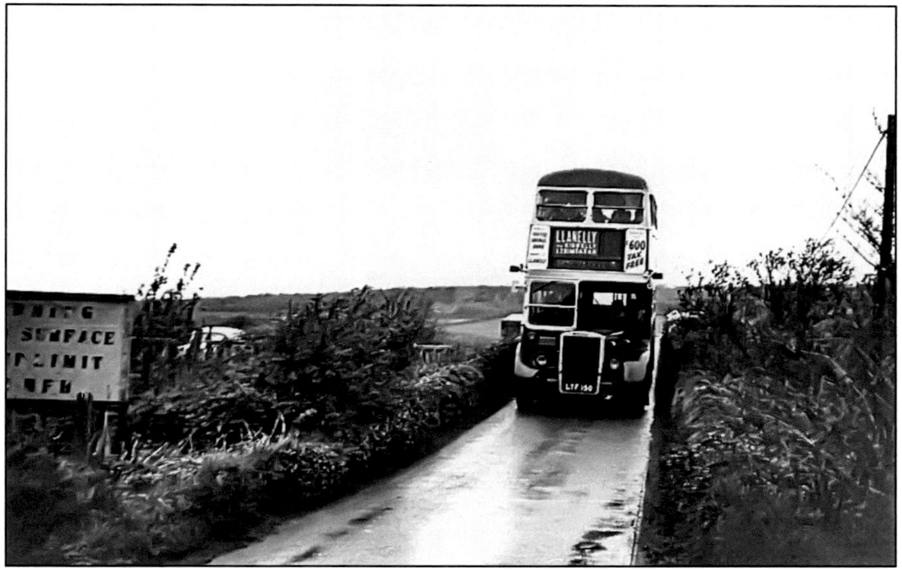


**Left**: A closer view of Spudders Bridge, in 1964, reveals the amount of clearance. Taking into consideration that these Ex. London Transport Leyland with Eynon's were only 7 feet 6 inches wide, other double-deckers were 8 feet wide, and coaches at 8 feet 2 ½ inches, so there was no room for error. The bridge was barely 9 feet wide. Just visible on the left hand side of this view is a Hillman Minx, crossing a temporary bailey bridge that had been erected by Sir John Jackson Ltd, to carry their heavy coal lorries from Carway open cast site, to the Coed Bach coal washery plant near Kidwelly. Normal traffic was also permitted to use the bailey bridge, with a 'Keep Left' one-way system in operation. Nevertheless, Jackson's lorries were so large and heavy, they were eventually banned from using the Roman bridge, travelling in both directions across the bailey bridge controlled by traffic lights.

(M. J. Haywood).

**Right:** The bailey bridge, mentioned above, constructed by Sir John Jackson Ltd, is seen here in 1964 with a Llansaint bound Eynon's bus crossing the steel structure. The decking of the bridge had a timber surface which was quite slippery when wet. Eynon's were very fond of these Ex. London buses, acquiring no less than 14 between 1958 and 1970.

(M. J. Haywood).

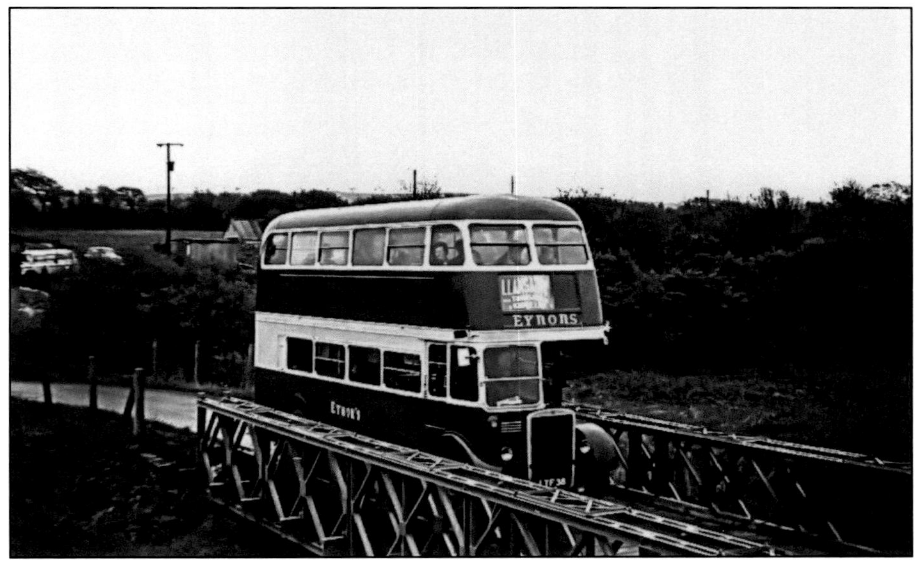

SERVING THE COMMUNITY FOR 70 YEARS

# EYNONS

**Your Independent Local Company**

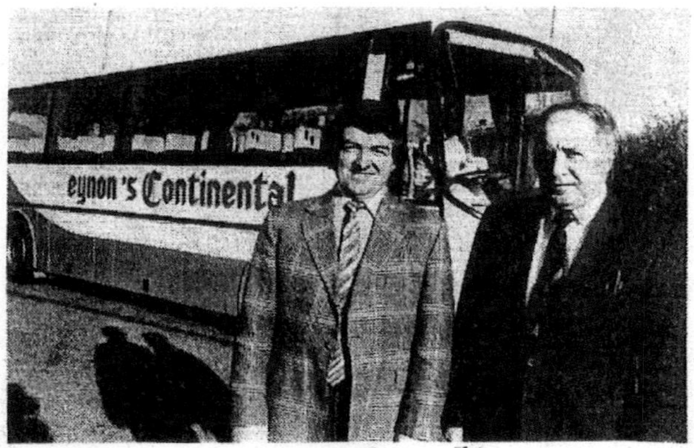


**DAVID EYNON & THOMAS JOHN EYNON**

*Join us on our regular local services between Carmarthen and Llanelli including*

*BURRY PORT, KIDWELLY, LLANSAINT, TRIMSARAN, FIVE ROADS, PONTYBEREM, etc.*

**PLUS Weekly Trips to LONDON & CARDIFF**

***PLUS, PLUS, PLUS***
**PRIVATE HIRE for those Special Functions**

We would like to thank the Members of the Public and Traders for their continued support over the past 70 years, and look forward to being of service to old and new customers in the future

**Our long term plans are for Continental and British Holidays**

***TRAVEL*** *with*
***YOU*** *in mind*

**S. EYNONS & SONS**

Bryn Villa Garage, Trimsaran
☎ 810385

This advertisement was published in the Llanelli Star in December 1987, just six months before the business passed to Davies Bros. (Pencader) Ltd.

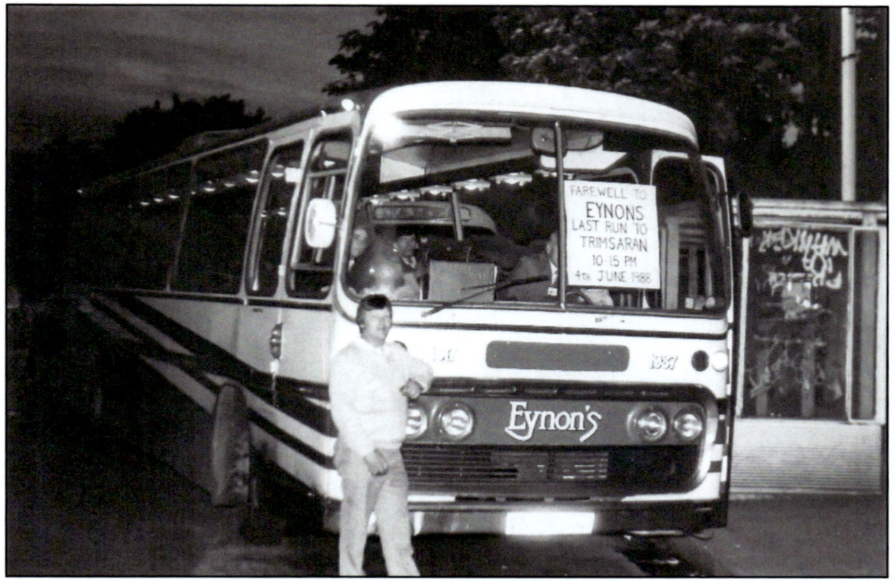


**Left:** Every picture tells a story – Farewell to Eynon's. The very last Eynon's bus to leave Llanelli Town Hall bus station for Trimsaran and Kidwelly, on Saturday 4th June, 1988. Davies Brothers of Pencader took over Eynon's 71-year-old business, on 5th June, 1988. A sad end to a much loved and reliable family business. The coach was driven on this historic trip by my colleague, David Thomas (Dai Bach), posing for the camera in front of the 20 year old Leyland Leopard, VNY468G.

(V. Morgan).

**Right:** A selection of bus tickets used by Samuel Eynon & Sons, on their Llanelli to Carmarthen service, throughout their seventy-one year existence.

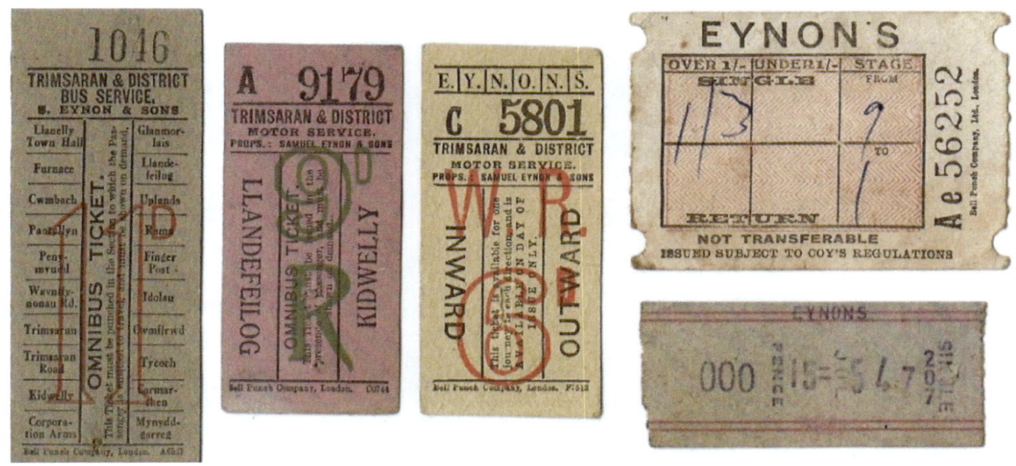

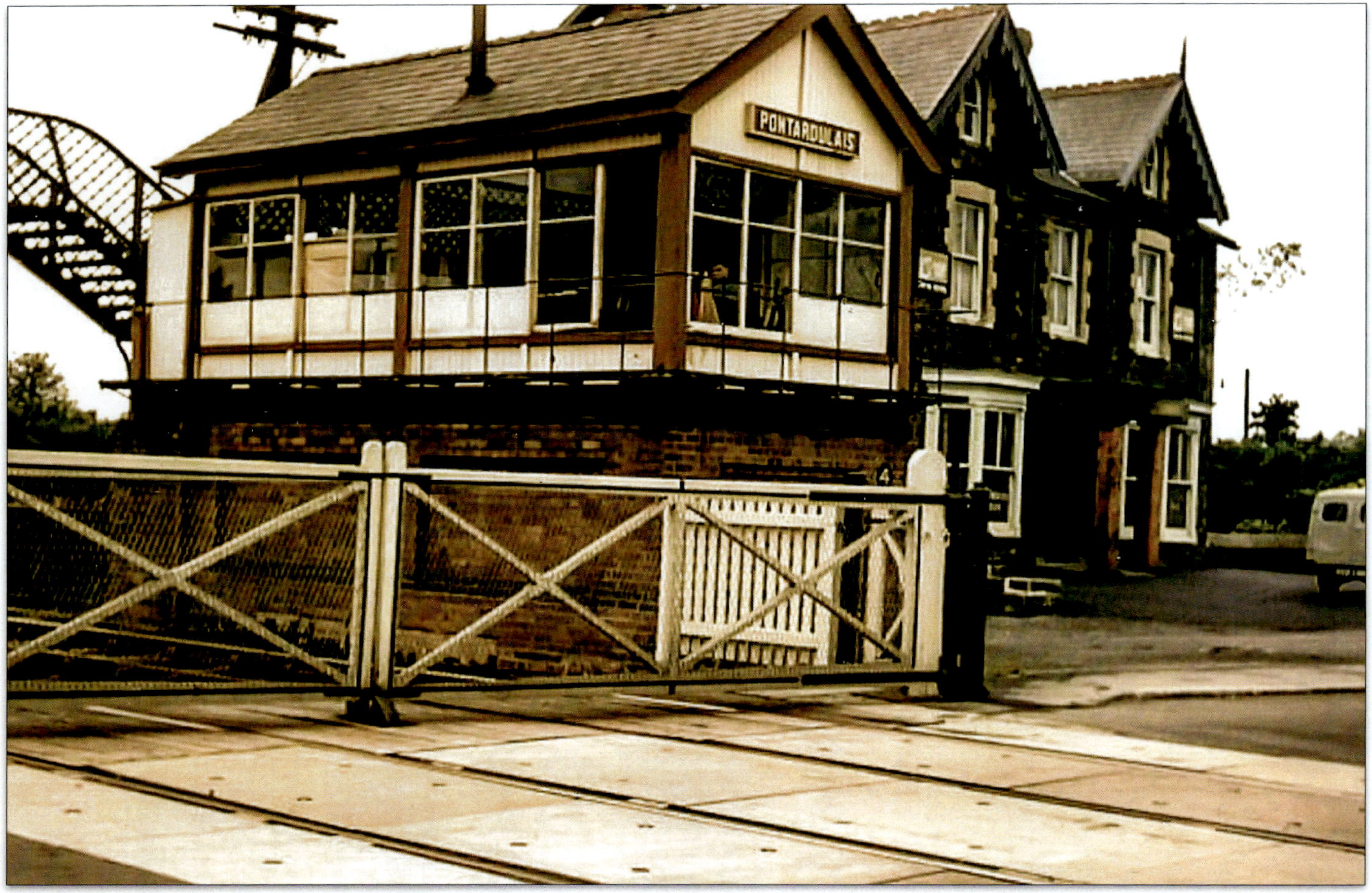


An interesting view of Pontardulais signal box on the LNWR railway-line in 1963, shortly before its closure. The Gwyn Hotel is just visible in the background, with the level crossing of St. Teilo Street, visible in the foreground. A roadway has recently been built on this former track-bed, to serve a new 'Tesco' supermarket in the town.

(T. S. Powell collection).

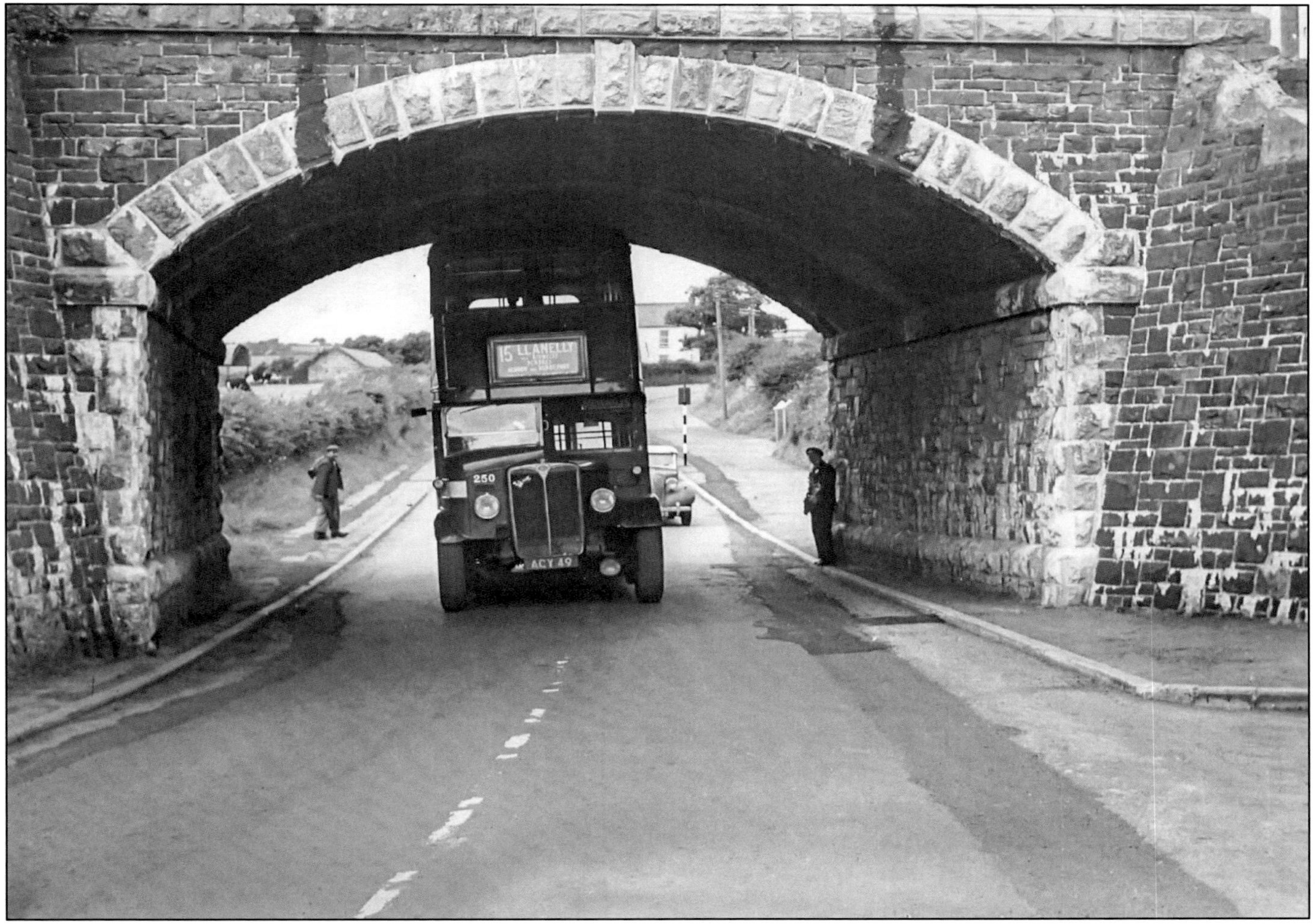


This arched bridge at Heol Pen-bre, Kidwelly, was built by the Gwendraeth Valley Railway (GVR), who were also shareholders of the Kidwelly Tinplate Works. The railway opened in 1871 to serve the Tinplate Works, Smart's Dinas Silica Brickworks, and the Mynydd-y-garreg quarry and lime-works. Connected to the South Wales Railway at Kidwelly, and to the B. P. & G. V. Railway at Ty-coch, it passed into GWR ownership in January, 1923, and to British Railways in January, 1948. Rail traffic ceased altogether in February, 1959, and was officially closed 29$^{th}$ August, 1960. Demolition of the bridge was carried out mid 1960s. Due to the bridge's awkward shape, high vehicles like this SWT double-decker, had to travel in the centre of the road to avoid a bridge strike. One bus driver's misfortunes led to dismissal, and a one week strike by his colleagues.

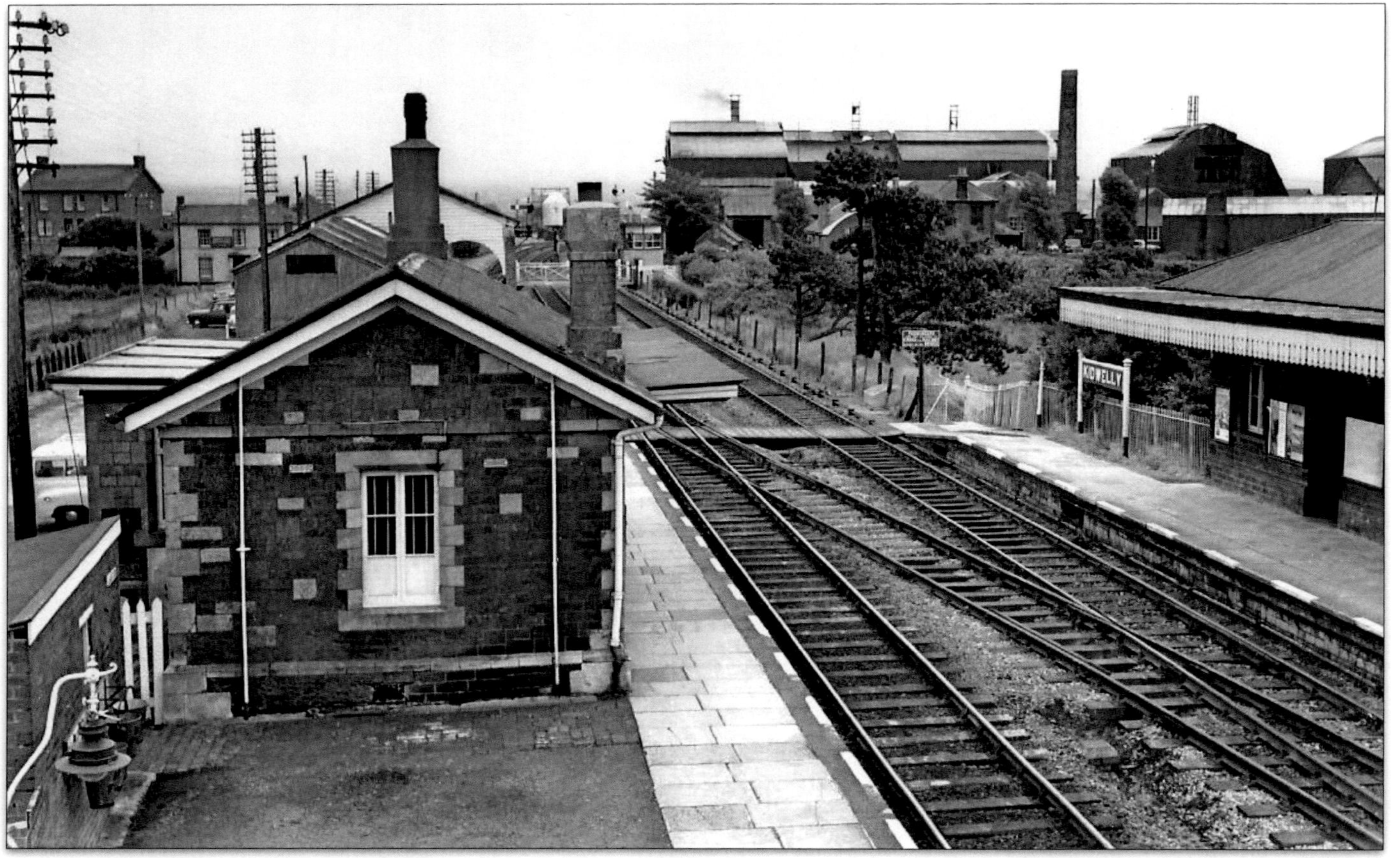


Kidwelly railway station was built in 1852, by the South Wales Railway Co. This view of the station, looking southward (or up-line towards Llanelli and London) was taken in 1958, and shows the Dinas Silica Brickworks in the right of the background. The level crossing gates of the roadway to Kidwelly Quay, are just visible in the centre background, along with Anthony's Hotel, to the left of the level crossing. The station's goods shed, is just visible behind the waiting room on the left. It is a much different scene today, all of these station buildings have disappeared, along with the Brickworks.

(V. Morgan collection).

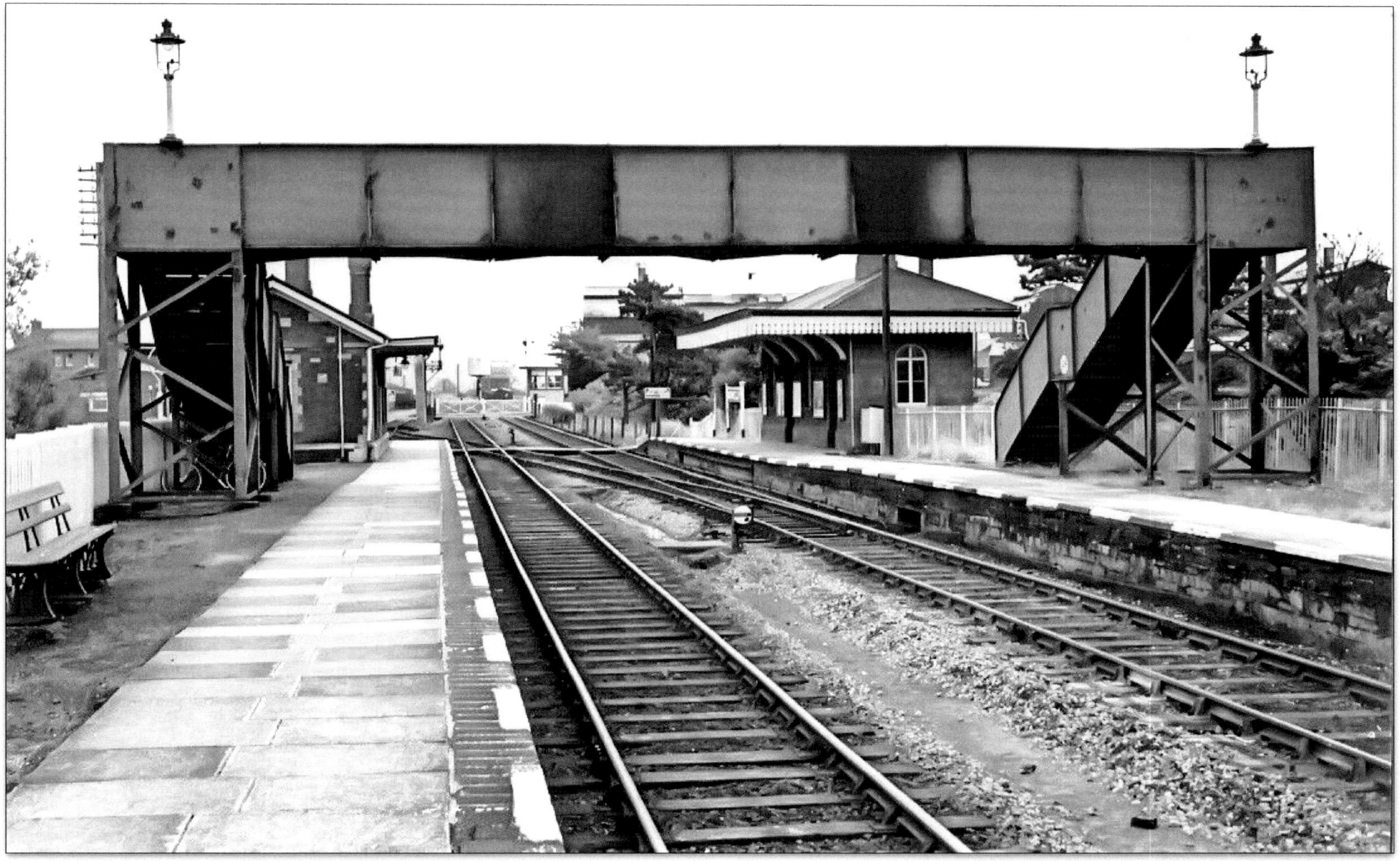

Another view of Kidwelly railway station, again viewed from the 'up' platform, on the same day in 1958. The view on the opposite page was taken from the footbridge seen in the foreground. All the station buildings have since gone, including the footbridge, with each platform now housing a bus shelter to protect intending passengers from the elements.

(V. Morgan collection).

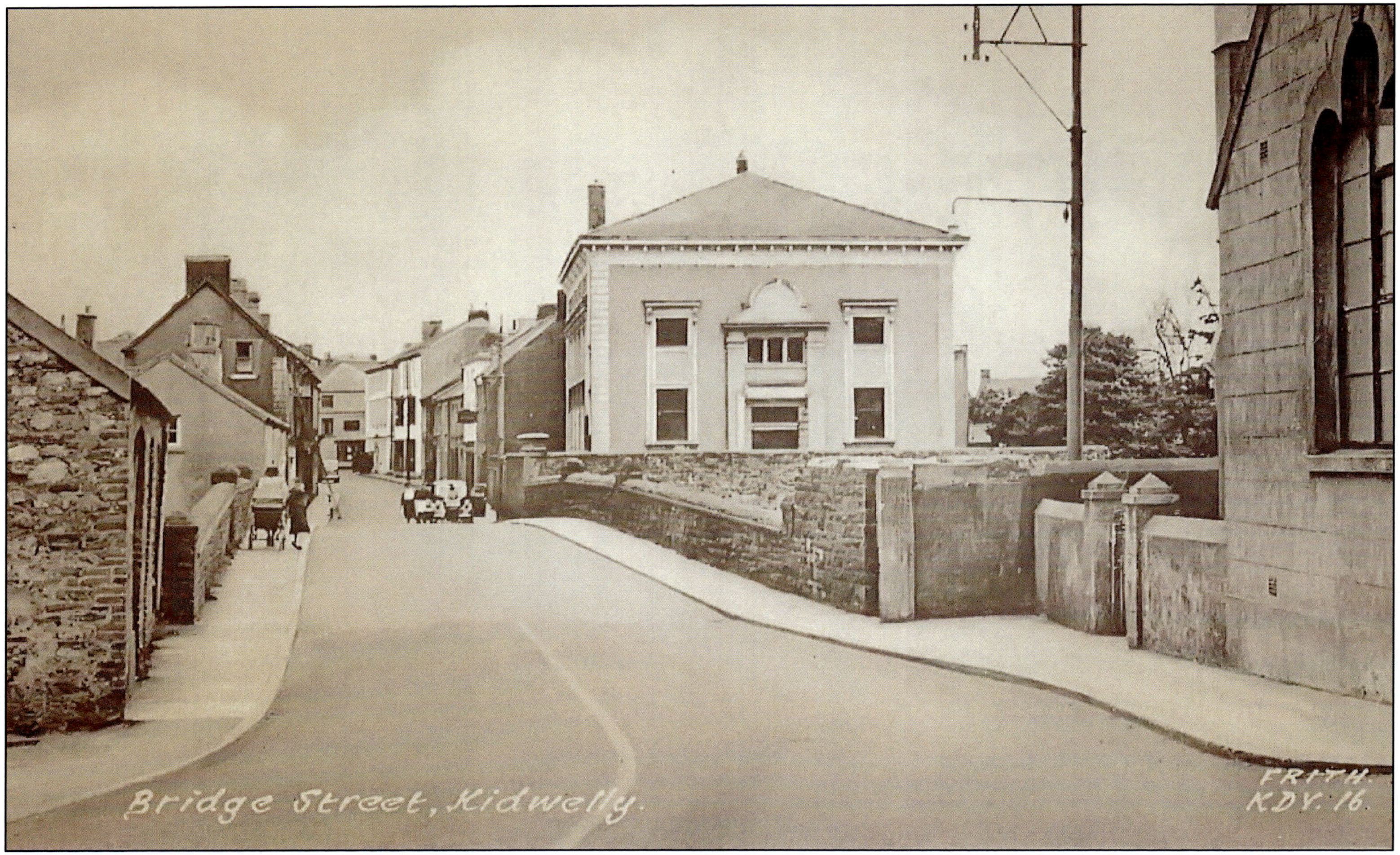


Bridge Street, Kidwelly, was previously the main thoroughfare through the town, until a long awaited relief road or by-pass opened in 1995. The name Bridge Street, emanated from the bridge which crosses the Gwendraeth Fach river at this point. Since this view was taken c.1948, the small building on the left, nearest the camera, has gone. All the others remain intact including the Trinity Church (right hand side), which has since received a face lift. 'Capel Sul' is the building prominent across the bridge on the right hand side.

**Right:** Causeway Street in Kidwelly has again hardly changed since this view was taken in c.1948. The only noticeable change is the bus stop area; the pull-in on the right where two small cottages have disappeared. They can be better seen in the next view.

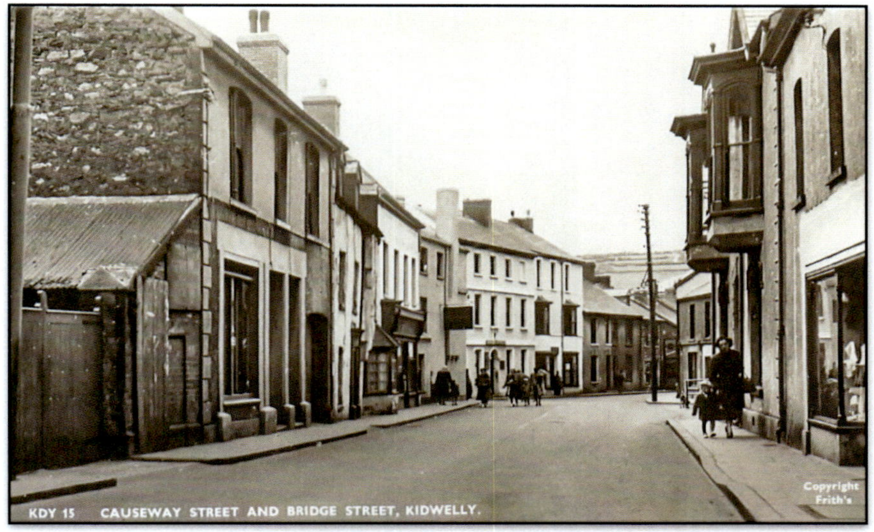


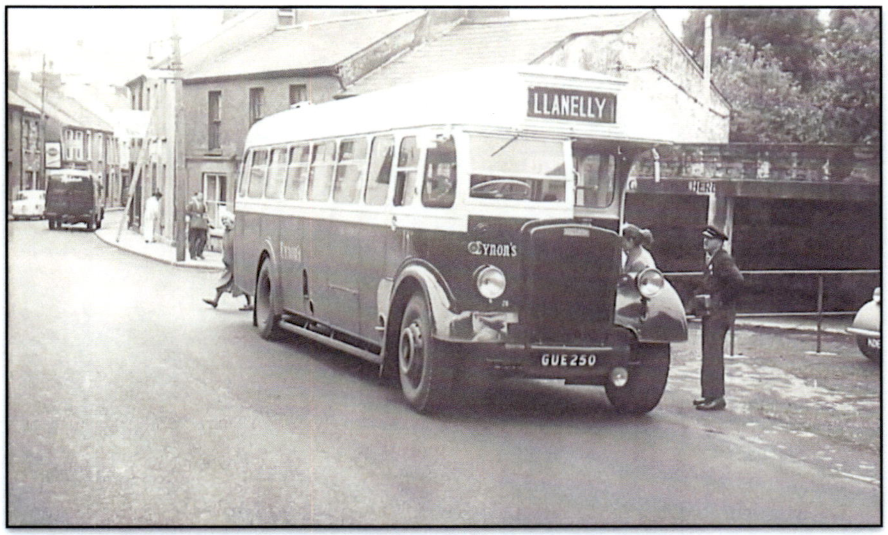


**Left:** In this view of Causeway Street / Bridge Street, taken in July, 1959, the two cottages mentioned in the preceding photograph, which were removed to provide better access to the bus stop, can be seen with the Fisherman's Arms on the right hand side of Bridge Street.

Incidentally, Eynons' buses provided an efficient and reliable service to the residents of Kidwelly, and competed well against their rivals, The South Wales Transport Co. The conductor, 'Jack Flash', complete with his Bell Punch ticket machine, stands outside the bus, awaiting its departure time for Llanelli - in those days, spelt 'Llanelly'.

(V. Morgan collection).

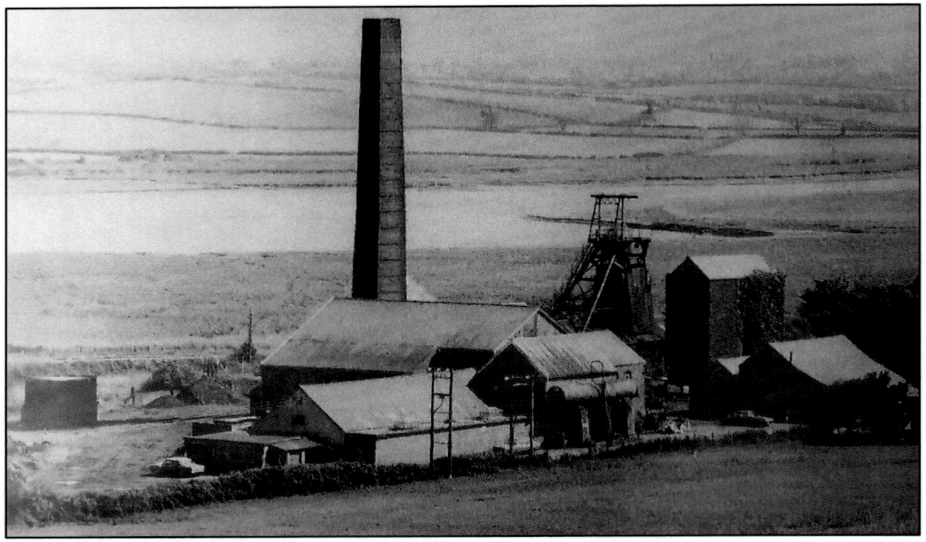

**Left:** Morlais Colliery, Llangennech.

The shaft of Morlais Colliery was operational in 1894, replacing a drift mine or 'slant' on the same site. In 1976, Morlais was connected underground with Brynlliw Colliery at Grovesend, by tunnelling a roadway under the Loughor Estuary. This inevitably led to Morlais' early closure on 8th May, 1981, resulting in the coal being worked from neighbouring Brynlliw, instead. Morlais' shaft and winding gear, nevertheless, remained operational for safety reasons, and for the pumping out of floodwater. The pumping continued until Brynlliw's inevitable closure in October, 1983. Morlais Colliery was finally demolished in 1985, and the shaft filled in – but flood-water kept rising from the abandoned shaft. The floodwater came not only from the Morlais workings, but from the many other abandoned workings linked to Morlais underground, i.e., Graig Merthyr; Clydach Merthyr; Brynlliw; Garngoch, and Cae Duke – all of which were at higher levels. This contaminated water is now filtered in purpose built lagoons on the site before being released into the Loughor Estuary. The headgear (winding gear) from this colliery was donated to the Kidwelly Hertitage Centre & Museum Trust. Brynlliw Colliery was situated across the estuary, visible in the background of this view.

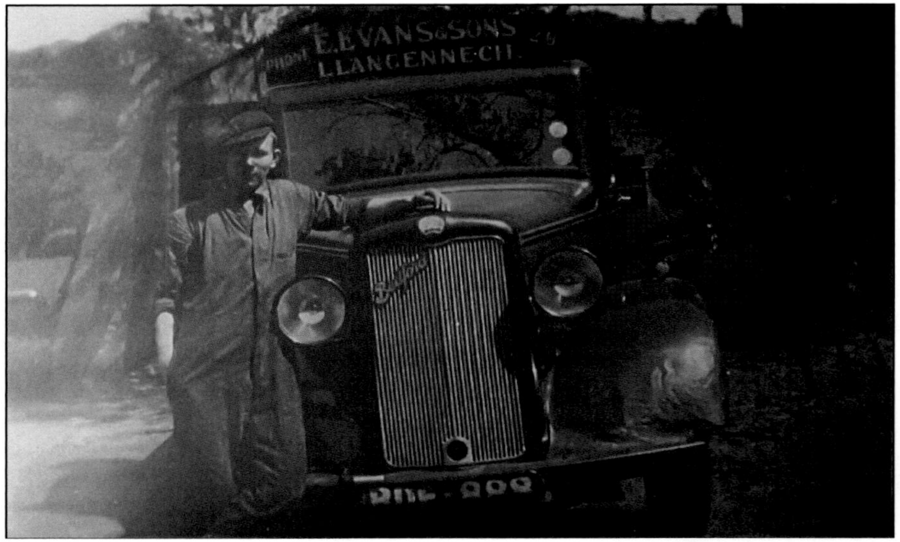


**Right:** Ebenezer Lewis Evans of Ty-fry Farm, Llangennech, first began a twice-daily market day passenger service into Llanelli with a horse drawn wagonette, around 1912, and also dabbled in road haulage. Changing to the mechanical mode of transport, in 1920, with a Vulcan 20-seater, his first Hackney Licence was issued by Llanelly Borough Council in January, 1922, for the market day service. After fierce competition from other competitors, the *service* was abandoned, but the transport business continued with a Citroën lorry, which had a detachable 14-seat body. As the transport business flourished, the fleet of lorries and coaches expanded, and Ebenezer's sons, Tom and Will joined the business. Seen here, is W. H. Evans (Will) standing alongside one of their early Bedford trucks, dating from 1938. Another feature of the business was their fleet of cattle lorries, and also the articulated lorries, hauling steel from Llanelli steelworks.

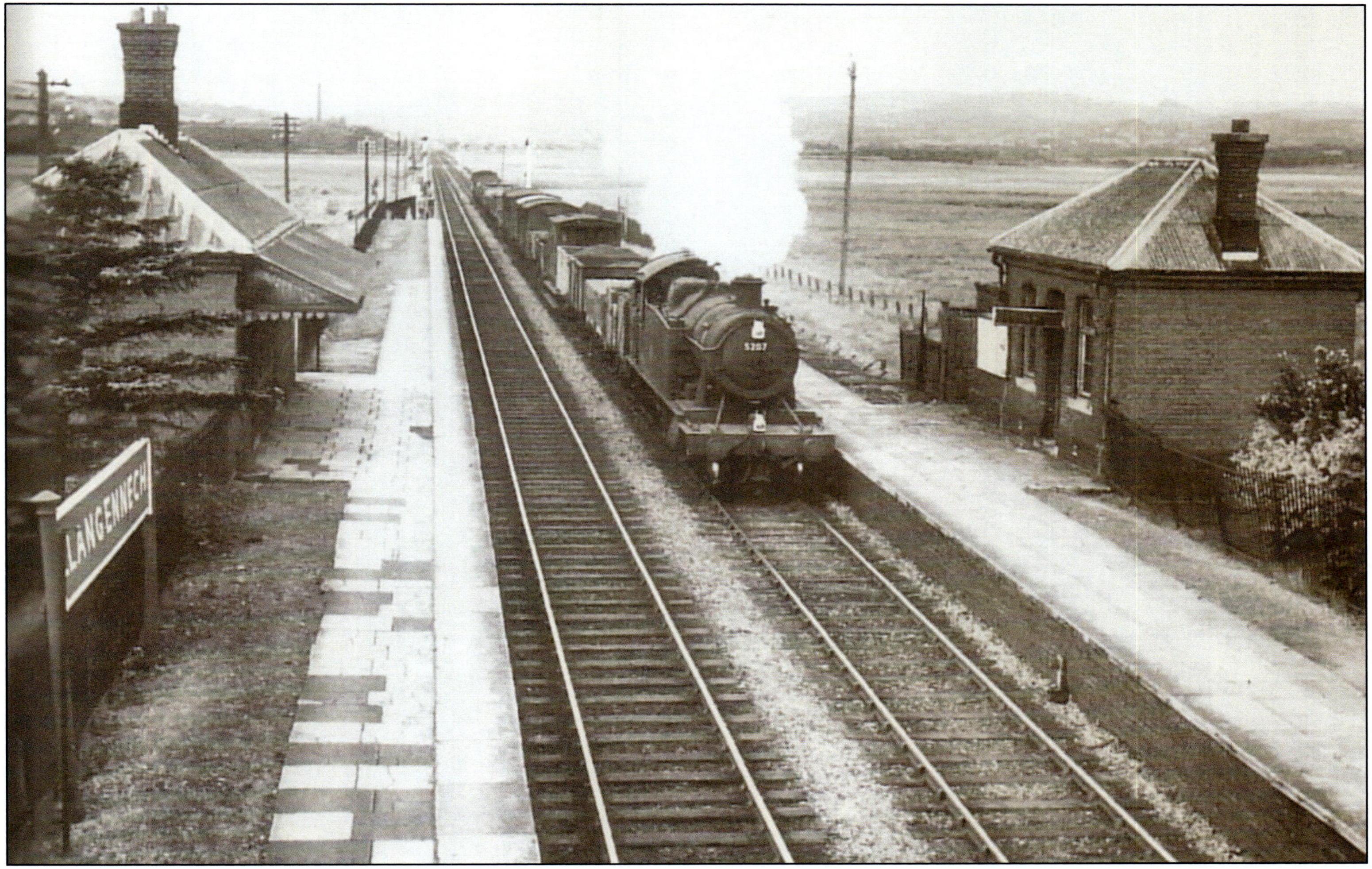


Llangennech Railway Station in its heyday, with a mixed-freight train heading south-west to Llanelli, circa 1955. All of these station buildings have since disappeared. Just visible in the left hand background, is the chimney stack of Morlais colliery, Llangennech, which can be seen on page 122.

(T. S. Powell collection).

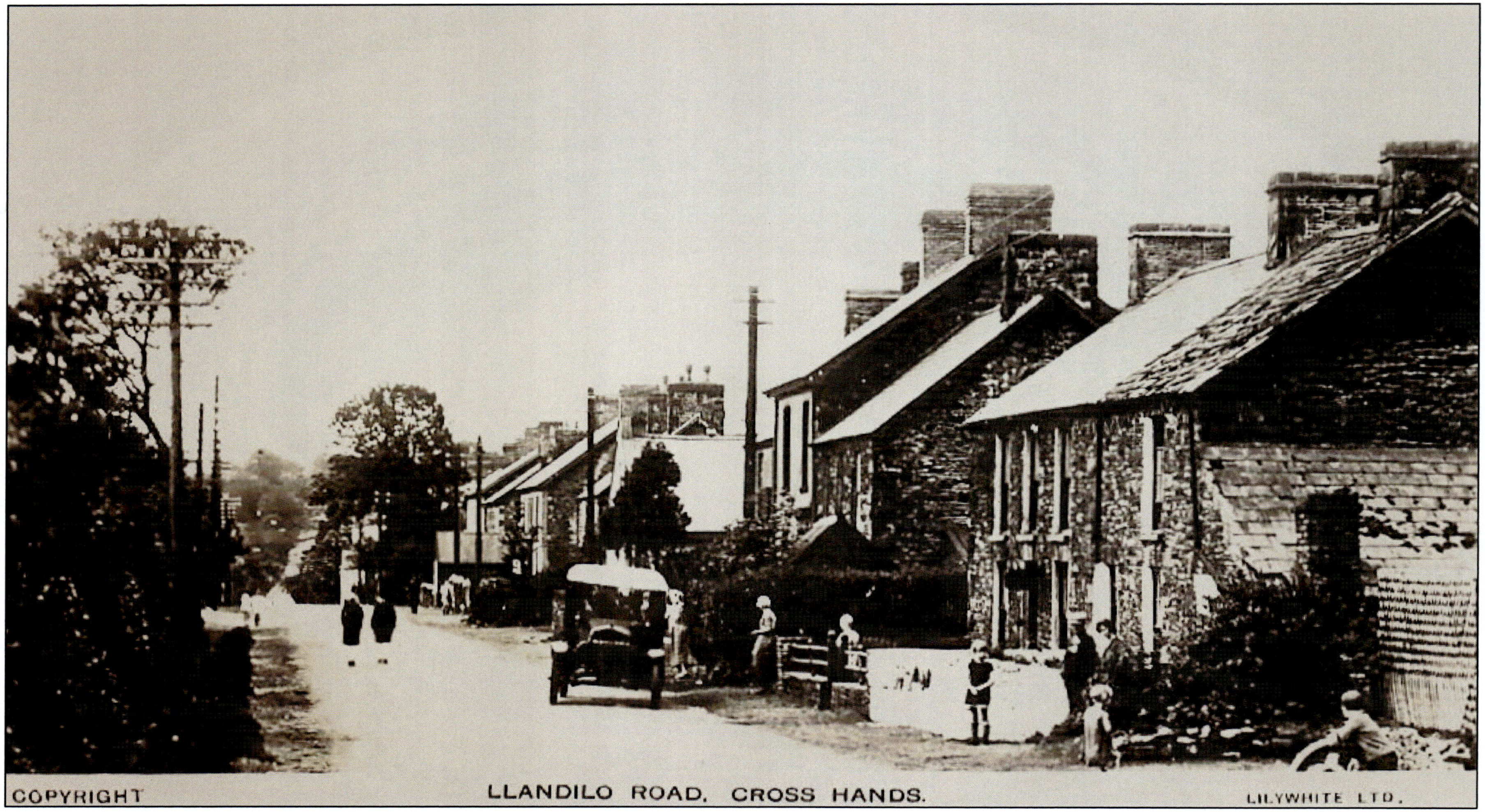


Although postmarked 1936, this postcard view of Llandeilo Road, Cross Hands, was probably taken in the 1920 era. This area of Cross Hands has changed tremendously since the picture was taken, the road is now a lot wider, and most of these buildings have been demolished, and the whole area redeveloped. Cross Hands Square, and Llanelli Road, can just be seen in the background.

(V. Morgan collection).

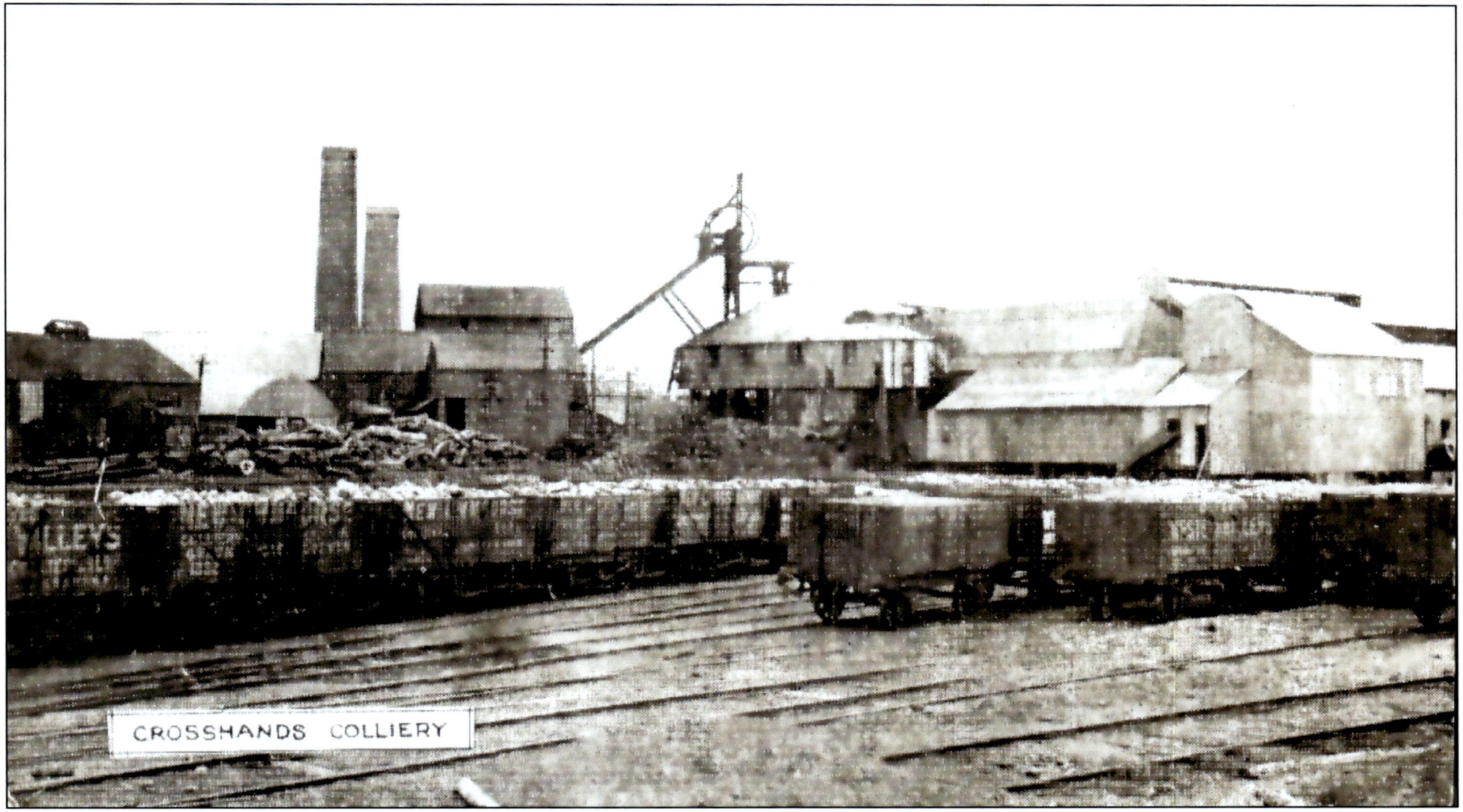


The 'new' Cross Hands Colliery opened in March, 1893, on the north side of Llandeilo Road, replacing the 'old' Cross Hands Colliery, which had been on the south side of Llandeilo Road. This postcard view, taken by J. James of Cross Hands, is postmarked August, 1930. It shows the colliery winding gear (centre), colliery buildings, together with railway wagons laden with coal, ready for shipment via the Llanelly & Mynydd Mawr Railway to its final destination, probably Llanelli Docks. This colliery closed in May 1962, superseded by Cwmgwili drift mine (see next page).

(Albie Smosarski collection).

**Right**: This was the entrance to Cwmgwili drift mine at the village of Cwmgwili, near Cross Hands. It opened in 1962 to work the vast reserves of coal in the 'Big Vein' seam. Despite severe geological problems, it produced an extremely high tonnage of top quality anthracite coal, with a workforce of 380 miners. British Coal sold the almost worked out mine to a private owner in 1989, and it was closed in 1995.

The colliery site now houses a 'transport training company', and a coach operator's operating centre with garage repair facilities.

(V. Morgan collection).

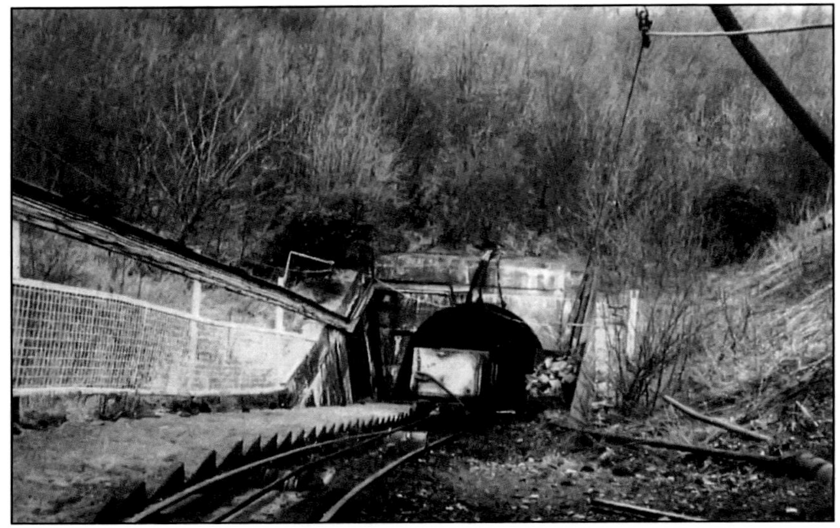

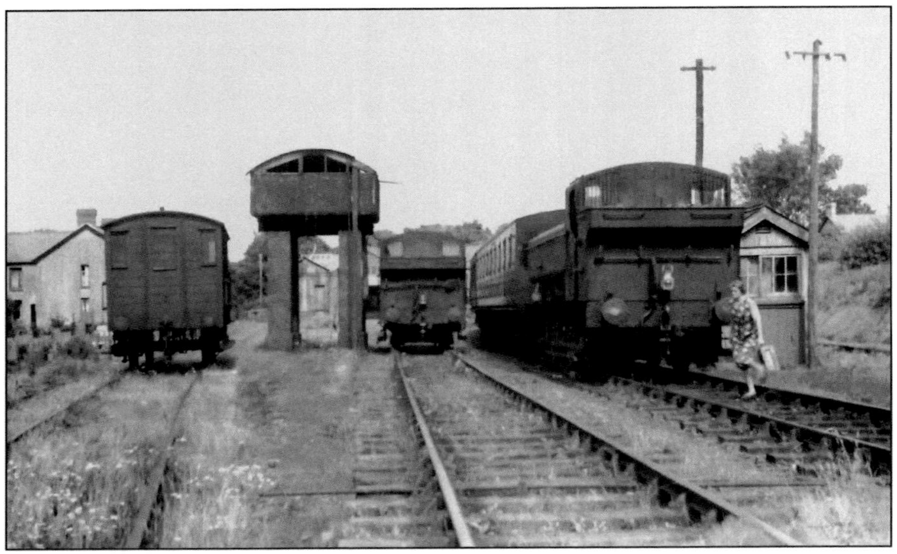

**Left:** Formerly part of the Burry Port & Gwendraeth Valley Railway, Cwm-mawr Railway Station is the backdrop for this view of a passenger train, loading up for its return journey to Burry Port, in 1950. Cwmmawr station was built in 1913, and was the northern terminus of the B. P. & G. V. Railway. It closed to passenger traffic in 1953, remaining open for freight traffic only, until June, 1965. The railway line to the nearby Cwm-mawr Opencast Disposal Point, remained open for a further thirty-one years, closing in March 1996.

(V. Morgan collection).

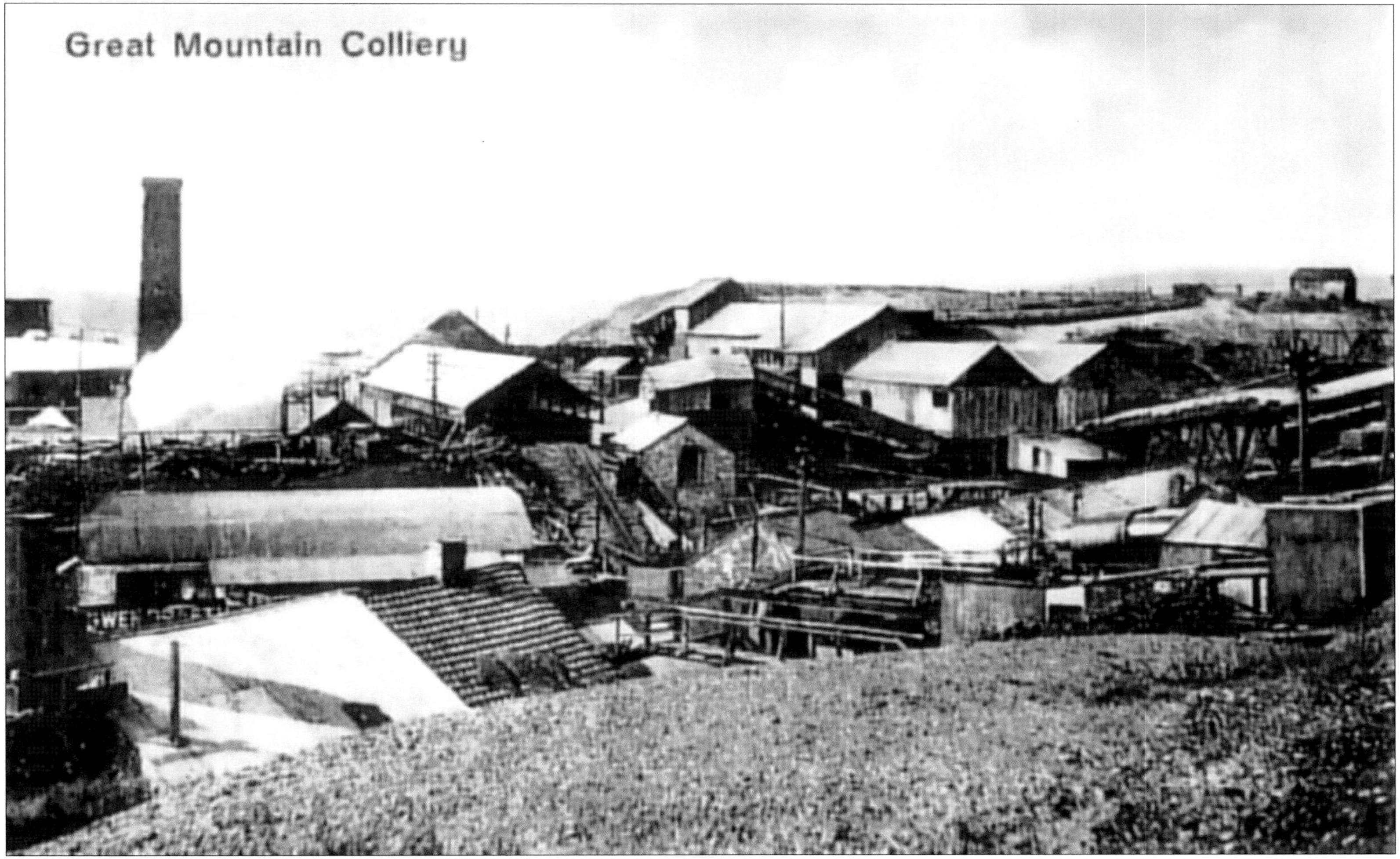


The Great Mountain Colliery, at Tumble, near Llanelli, opened in 1887, producing some of the finest quality Anthracite coal in the world. By 1892, the colliery employed 600 men, and the village of Tumble grew around the colliery, with numerous extra homes built to house the colliers. Great Mountain Colliery was linked to the Llanelli Docks by means of the elaborate Llanelly & Mynydd Mawr Railway. This colliery closed on 5th May, 1962, transferring the employees to the newly opened Cynheidre and Cwmgwili pits.

(V. Morgan collection).

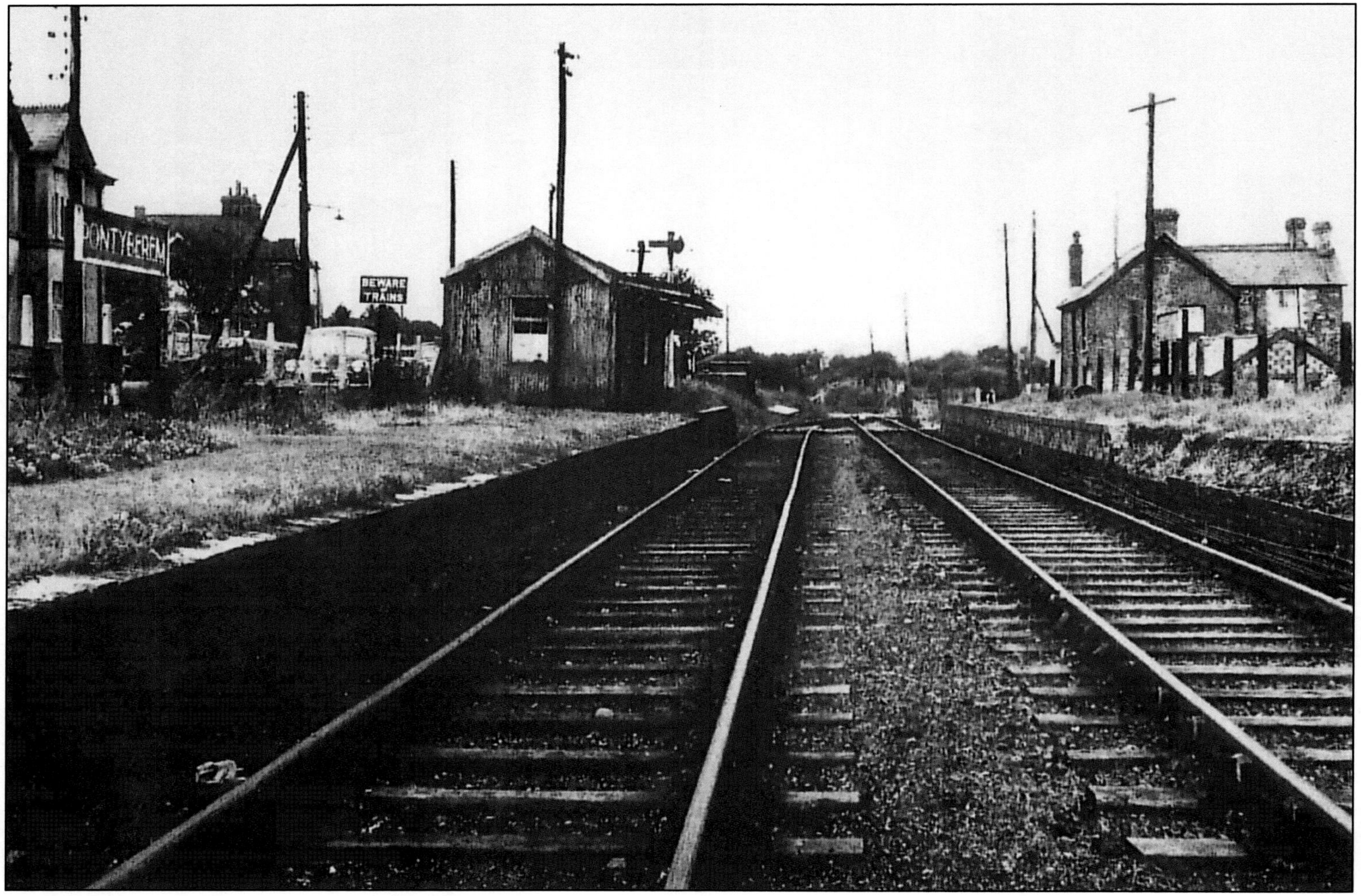


Pictured sometime after its closure in 1953, is Pontyberem Railway Station. The railway was built in 1869, by the Burry Port & Gwendraeth Valley Railway Co., along the route of a former canal, and used to transport coal to Burry Port harbour. The passenger service commenced on this line in 1909, and ceased in 1953, hence the derelict condition of the platforms. The line continued with goods traffic, and eventually coal traffic, until its final closure in 1996.

(V. Morgan collection).

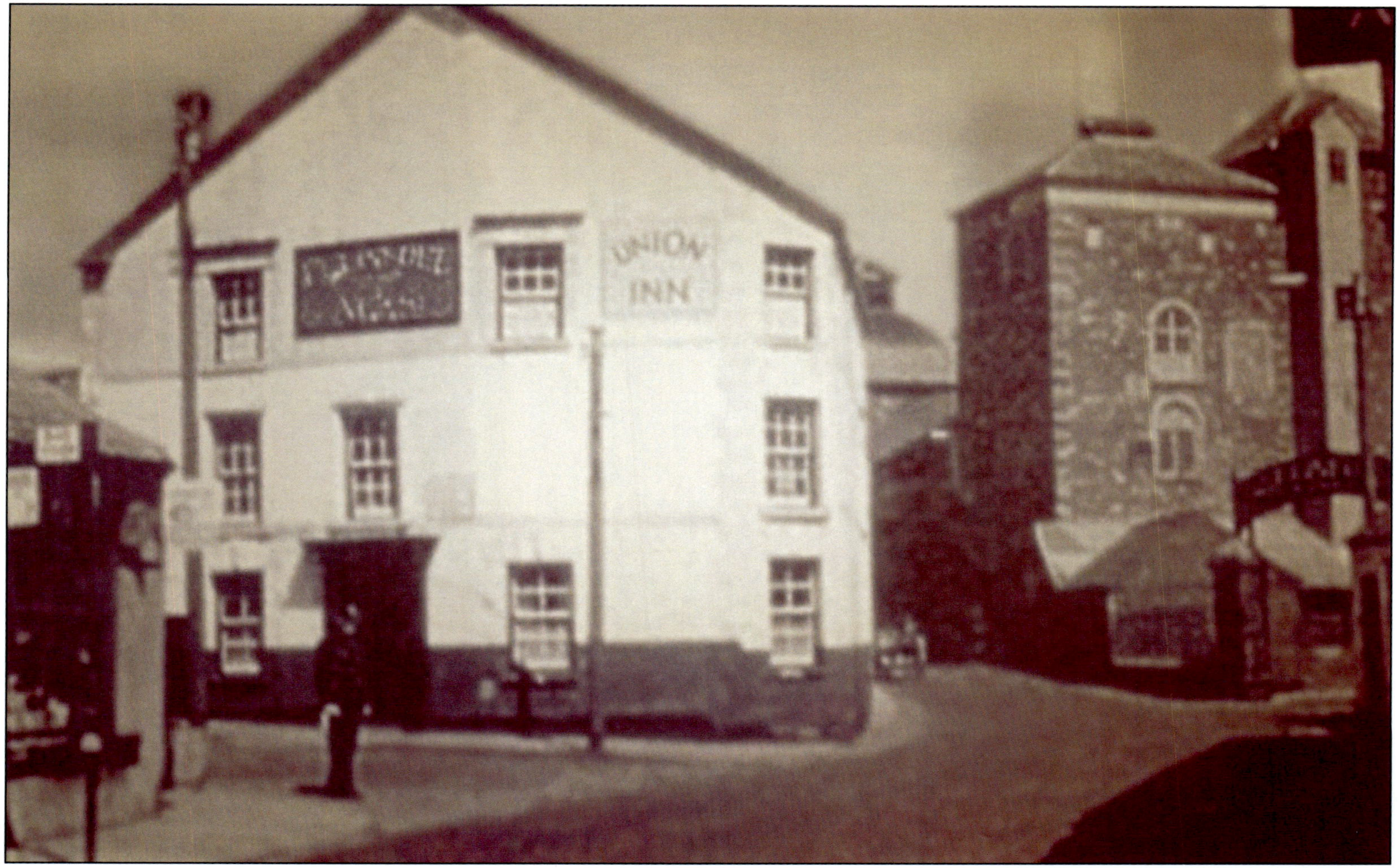


The Union Inn at Felinfoel, pictured here, was demolished in the mid-1960s to make way for improvement of the A476 road: the widening of Union Square (foreground) and Farmers Row (right). As can be seen, Farmers Row, passing between the Union Inn and Felinfoel Brewery was very narrow, with pedestrians having to walk along this roadway without a pavement.

(V. Morgan collection).

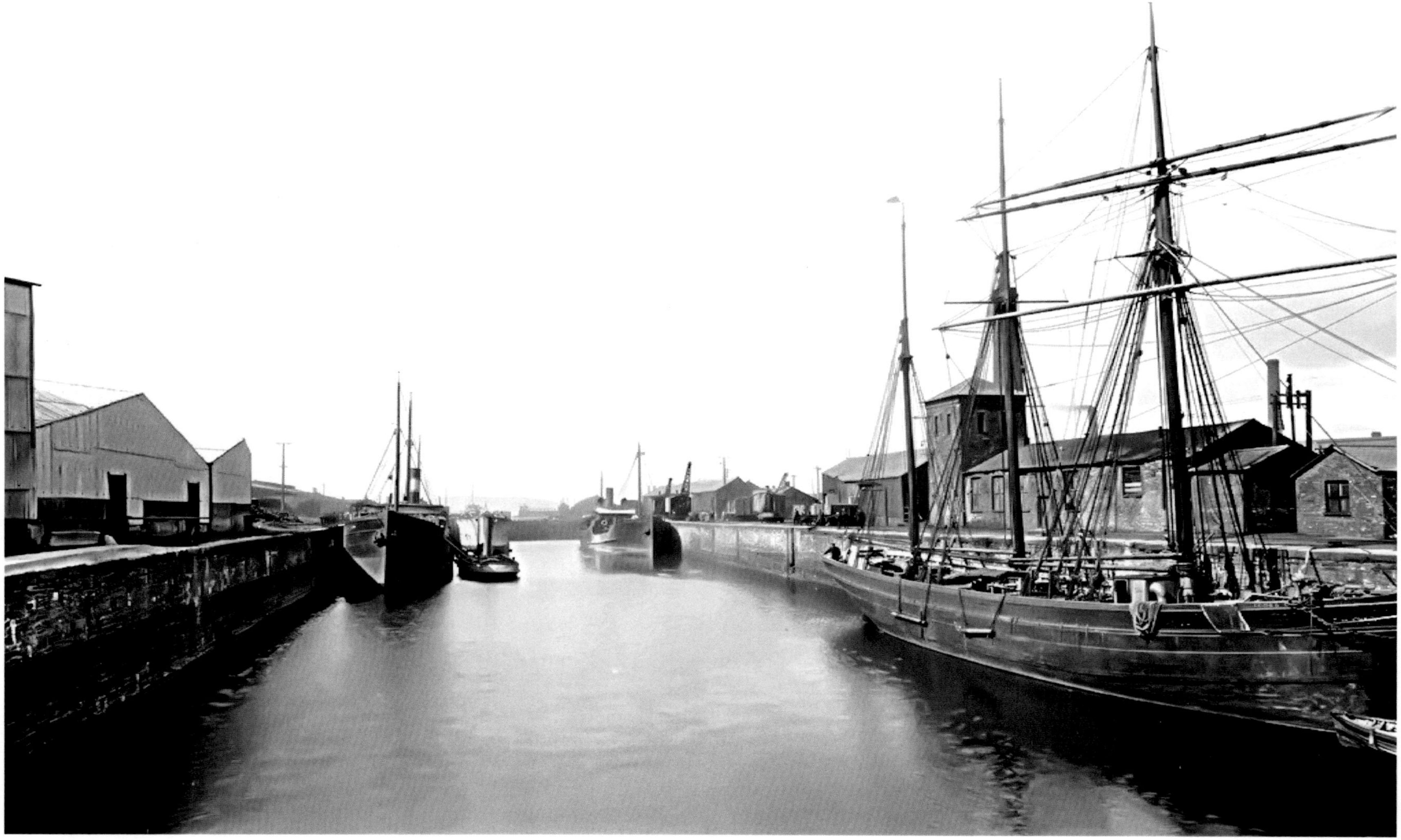

A superb view of the Copperworks Dock at Seaside, Llanelli, taken circa 1910. This Dock has since been filled in, and nowadays, the new Llanelli link road, B4304, crosses this area.

(V. Morgan collection).